WOMEN JEWELLERY DESIGNERS

WOMEN JEWELLERY DESIGNERS

Juliet Weir-de La Rochefoucauld

ACC ART BOOKS

Dedication:

To those close to me – My parents, Brenda and Donald Weir;
Guy-Olivier and his patience ... and my sons Melchior, Josselin and Rollo.

Front cover: Olga Tritt: Aquamarine and diamond necklace – aquamarine, diamond, platinum
IMAGE COURTESY OF WARTSKI, LONDON.

Back cover: Cindy Chao: Black Label Masterpiece XV, Bowtie brooch, c.2016 – ruby, 76.91ct old mine-cut diamond, black gold
(Provenance: Biennale des Antiquaires, Paris 2016.) IMAGE COURTESY OF CINDY CHAO

Half title page: Michelle Ong for Carnet: Wondorous Diamond Woodrose brooch – white rose-cut diamond, pale brown and brown rose-cut diamond, platinum, rose gold
(Provenance: Masterpiece, London, 2015.) IMAGE COURTESY OF CARNET, HONG KONG

Frontispiece: Alexandra Mor: Stack of rings, (showing Mor's signature DNA), 2016 – diamond, platinum, yellow gold
IMAGE COURTESY OF ALEXANDRA MOR

Title page: Luz Camino: Butterfly brooch, 2008 – moss agate, diamond, yellow gold
PHOTOGRAPH BY FERNANDO RAMAJO; IMAGE COURTESY OF LUZ CAMINO

Opposite page: Victoire de Castellane for Dior Fine Jewellery: Belladone Island Collection: Reina Magnifica Sangria necklace, 2007 – Paraiba tourmaline, ruby, demantoid garnet, lacquer, diamond, white gold
IMAGE COURTESY OF DIOR FINE JEWELRY

Overleaf: Cartier, Paris: Bird Nest brooch, 1948 – sapphire, emerald, natural pearl, diamond, platinum, yellow gold
IMAGE COURTESY OF VERONIQUE BAMPS GALLERY, MONACO

Printed in China
for ACC Art Books Ltd., Woodbridge, Suffolk, UK

FSC
www.fsc.org

MIX
Paper from
responsible sources
FSC® C104723

CONTENTS

Introduction   9

Arts and Crafts   12

PART I — Between the Wars: The Awakening

Setting the Scene   18
Alma Pihl   24
Coco Chanel   28
Suzanne Belperron   36
Juliette Moutard   50
Olga Tritt   62
Elisabeth Treskow   66
Margaret de Patta   72
Jeanne Toussaint   74

PART II — Post-war to 1980s: Full Steam Ahead – The Search for the Perfect Design

Setting the Scene   86
Line Vautrin   92
Margret Craver   98
Vivianna Torun Bülow-Hübe   100
Nanna Ditzel   108
Marianne Ostier   116
Barbara Anton   122
Gerda Flöckinger   124
Astrid Fog   126
Cornelia Roethel   128
Catherine Noll   130
Angela Cummings   134
Elsa Peretti   140
Wendy Ramshaw   148
Marina B   156
Marie-Caroline de Brosses   164
Marilyn Cooperman   172
Paloma Picasso   178

PART III — What is Happening Now in the Field of Jewellery Design

Setting the Scene	182
Colour and Light	186
Victoire de Castellane	190
Alexandra Mor	198
Ornella Iannuzzi	204
Neha Dani	210
Paula Crevoshay	216
Designing for the Brands	222
Nathalie Castro	226
Claire Choisne	230
A Sense of Place	236
Bina Goenka	238
Carla Amorim	244
Monique Péan	250
Michelle Ong – Carnet	256
Stories to Tell	262
Kara Ross	264
Lydia Courteille	270
Suzanne Syz	276
Sylvie Corbelin	282
The Natural World	288
Kaoru Kay Akihara – Gimel	290
Katey Brunini	296
Luz Camino	302
Cindy Chao	310
Aida Bergsen	316
Anna Hu	322
The Past is the Future	328
Barbara Heinrich	330
Jacqueline Cullen	336
Cynthia Bach	342

Appendix 1: The Designers – extra information   348

Appendix 2: Toussaint   354

Appendix 3: L'Affaire Chanel   356

It has always surprised me that throughout history the world of jewellery making has been dominated by men, even though it is women who on the whole wear their creations. Certainly there have been periods in the past when men have been equally adorned but these have only been fleeting moments in the time-scale of history.

My reason for writing this book has been to look at what women have been able to do since they gained emancipation through the suffragette movements towards the end of the 19th century and the beginning of the 20th century, and afterwards the change in society's attitudes to the role of women by the end of the WWI.

I have deliberately kept the Arts and Crafts movement to a brief essay; to try and cover the women jewellery designers who created the unusual and extraordinary creations of this period would be a tome in itself.

I have divided the book into three parts:

Part One addresses the extraordinary effervescence of talent between the two World Wars. Some are well-known designers and others less well known. I investigate Gabrielle 'Coco' Chanel's role as someone of huge influence in the fashion world and beyond. It seems evident that the International Diamond Corporation (part of De Beers) had hopes of kick starting a new fashion for diamonds in their choice of Coco Chanel, to whom they had supplied a huge collection of diamonds during the depression years at the start of the 1930s; the result was her 1932 Exhibition. You will see that by kind permission of the department for patrimony and archives at Boucheron, Paris, I have been able to include a document on the 'Chanel Affair', which erupted after the Diamond Corporation's choice of designer. (See Appendix 3, page 356). This is an historical document which under no circumstances reflects the attitudes of the Jewellery Houses today. In fact, through the Comité de Colbert there is collaboration between the Houses as they work to help support each other and to promote the extraordinary savoir-faire and knowledge of the Place Vendôme to other parts of the world.

Also included is the incredible story of Jeanne Toussaint for Cartier, the daughter of lace-making parents who left her home in Belgium as a young girl to be swept off her feet in the demi-monde of Paris before the First World War and where she met Louis Cartier.

Alma Pihl was an exciting personal discovery for me, even though she is well known to many Fabergé enthusiasts. Pihl was responsible for Fabergé's wonderful ice jewel collection. Olga Tritt was another, a Russian émigré who ended up in The States, via Brazil, and lived the American dream; starting from nothing, she became the quintessential New York jeweller.

On a special note, I was fortunate enough to be afforded in-depth interviews with experts on the work of Suzanne Belperron and Juliette Moutard for the famous jewellery house, René Boivin. It has not been easy to thread all the stories together and to find out who did what, as the archives for Boivin seem to have been spread to many different places. Olivier Baroin; Marie-Caroline de Brosses; Françoise Cailles; Ward and Nico Landrigan; Sam Loxton; Claudine Seroussi Bretagne; have all been extraordinary in their generosity, giving me the keys to their world of knowledge.

RIGHT, FROM TOP TO BOTTOM:
Line Vautrin's hands, 1944
Vautrin putting the finishing touches to the moulding for a brooch. In the foreground are three finished brooches.
IMAGE COURTESY OF MARIE-LAURE BONNAUD

Gabrielle (Coco) Chanel's hands, 1938
PHOTOGRAPH BY ANDRÉ KERTÉSZ; IMAGE COURTESY OF RMN-GRAND PALAIS © MINISTÈRE DE LA CULTURE

Margaret de Patta's hands, 1941
Margaret de Patta working on a brooch in her San Francisco studio.
PHOTOGRAPH BY ROMEO ROLETTE; IMAGE COURTESY OF THE MARGARET DE PATTA ARCHIVES, BIELAWSKI TRUST

OPPOSITE PAGE: Neha Dani: Amarante bracelet, 2015 – pink and deep purple-pink fancy coloured diamonds, rose gold

Part Two takes us from the end of the WWII up until the end of the 1980s. I had thought that this would be a small section. However, as I started to research this period, many jewellery designers appeared and I realised that I would have to make a selection. It was a privilege to be able to talk with many of the designers in this section, namely Elsa Peretti, Angela Cummings and Marina B. I have chosen jewellery artists with very different styles from Vivianna Torun Bülow-Hübe and Nanna Ditzel for Georg Jensen, each with their own interpretation of simple lines, to the intellectually charged jewels of Wendy Ramshaw and the poetic, pictorial creations of Line Vautrin. I have tried to include women who have left an indelible mark on jewellery design, those who have contributed to the history of jewellery design throughout the 20th century, even when their work has not been made using noble materials.

Marianne Ostier was an Austrian refugee who fled to the United States with her husband just before the outbreak of WWII. Ostier was to introduce many European ideas to American jewellery design in the 1950s, her influence cannot be underestimated. Others to join the family are Gerda Flöckinger, Margret Craver and Barbara Anton, each with a very distinctive style. The glitz of the 1980s is represented by the heavy beautifully crafted gold jewellery of Marina B. and the simple but voluminous offerings of Paloma Picasso for Tiffany's.

Part Three deals with the coming of age of women in jewellery design and fabrication. Jewellery is no longer the male dominated domain of yesteryear, women are to be found in every aspect of jewellery design and manufacture. (Some of the designers – Kaoru Kay Akihara, Luz Camino, Lydia Courteille, Anna Hu, Michelle Ong and Suzanne Syz – have been mentioned in my previous book, *21st Century Jewellery Designers – An Inspired Style*, published by ACC Art Books. As a result I have made the decision not to dwell on their work to perhaps the same extent as others in this section.)

This section is about what is happening now in the world of jewellery design and within these pages you will see very diverse sets of ideas. Some use gemstones in their crystalline state and frame nature's offerings preferring to enhance and accentuate; others are figurative and tell a story or let the wearer define what their jewel means to them. Some represent an interpretation of nature or an idea, a concept. The use of simple fluid lines that flatter the body's silhouette – as well as the skin, hair and eye colour – is another popular stance, all the while drawing attention to the image the wearer wishes to project. For other designers, the journey starts with the gemstone, where it comes from, the cultures of that country, its colour and shape.

There are so many starting points and it must be for this reason that jewellery holds such fascination for each and every one of us: it is personal, intimate, secret. And yet, it can be ebullient in its 'look I am here' and 'this is how I feel' statements – it reflects an infinity of themes and palettes of colour and emotion.

This book could never have happened without the help of so many generous people, galleries and collectors who have taken the time to find and give me permission to use their photographs. Many photographs that were given to me for use in this book have not been used due to layout and space restrictions, they are no less important for that and have helped me to gain a better global appreciation of each designer's work. All the photographs were kindly provided by each individual jewellery designer or jewellery house, unless otherwise stated.

I would like to highlight some points which may help the reader: all the jewellery mentioned is in 18ct yellow gold unless otherwise stated. The gems used have all been chosen for their quality, individuality or the story that they help to tell.

Jeanne Toussaint's hands
Toussaint wearing her signature ring and bracelet. Note the lack of beads at the clasp for comfort.
(Provenance: 'Les mains – Personnalités des métiers de la mode' (Personalities in the fashion industry) by Kollar François (1904-1979).)
© RMN - Photograph by François Kollar. Image courtesy of RMN-Grand Palais © Ministère de la Culture

ARTS & CRAFTS

"It was as if one had little fragments of the sunset, bits of landscape, or drops of the ocean, solidified in this or that chromatic variation, to be combined into jewels that should have a charm akin to that of nature as it is seen and perpetuated by the painter. Unity, in short, is the same quality whether it describes the work of a Sargent, a Whistler, or a Benvenuto Cellini. And in the fabrication of such jewels each detail must be of equal importance: the colour of the metal must harmonize with that of the gems; the decoration of the metal must produce a design by which the gems are not merely exhibited but of which they are actually an important detail… Such a conception of jewel-making takes its place immediately in the scheme of individual craftsmanship that has made the Arts and Crafts movement another "renaissance" after the "dark ages" in which for a while machinery so widely eliminated individuality from the decorative side of life."

Ralph Bergengren, 'Some Jewels and a Landscape' in *The House Beautiful*, 1915

TOP LEFT: Amy Sandheim (worked c.1915 - c.1939):
Pendant and chain, c.1935 – amethyst, chalcedony,
chrysoprase, emerald, pearl, sapphire
*Commissioned by Caleb Williams Elijah Saleeby and presented
as a gift to his second wife, Muriel Gordon, whom he married
in 1929. Saleeby was a pioneer of eugenics, he founded The
Sunlight League and fought passionately for clean air, improved
diet and healthy exercise warning against the evils of tobacco
and alcohol.*
IMAGE COURTESY OF THE TADEMA GALLERY, LONDON

BOTTOM LEFT: Dorrie Nossiter: Crescent 'Garden of Gems'
brooch, c.1930 – chrysoberyl cat's eye, sapphire, ruby,
peridot, white sapphire, silver, yellow gold
*In the Arts & Crafts tradition; note the gold wire and leaves,
reminiscent of the Wiener Werkstätte.*
IMAGE COURTESY OF THE TADEMA GALLERY, LONDON

OPPOSITE PAGE: Sibyl Dunlop: Bracelet, c.1930 – synthetic
sapphire, chalcedony, ruby, silver
In the Arts & Crafts tradition.
IMAGE COURTESY OF THE TADEMA GALLERY, LONDON

PREVIOUS PAGE: Elizabeth Bonté: Dragonfly pendant, c.1900
– horn, paste drop
Dimensions: 8.6 x 11cm
IMAGE COURTESY OF THE TADEMA GALLERY, LONDON

Women jewellers burst onto the scene of jewellery design with the advent of the Arts & Crafts movement at the end of the 19th century. After almost a century of industrial revolution and change and the celebration of all things mechanical, some writers and artists had started to question the artistic contribution of these miraculous machine-made discoveries. The distinct lack of artisan-made works of art at the 1851 Great Exhibition in London started a debate about the place of the craftsman's creative imagination. Middle class women were at the forefront of this debate. The result was the Arts and Crafts movement.

Championed by art critic John Ruskin and designer William Morris, it advocated a revival of traditional crafts, integrity of design, use of high-quality materials and, above all, respect of the craftsman. This was social reform through design; a direct riposte to the effects of industrialisation on the workforce. In 1884, the Art Workers' Guild was formed and in 1888, the Arts and Crafts Exhibition Society, founded by Walter Crane, held its first exhibition. By the turn of the 20th century over a hundred Arts and Crafts associations and guilds had risen up.

The Movement encompassed all aspects of design and the decorative arts, from architecture to book binding and cabinet-making to stained glass, embroidery, jewellery, metalwork, enamelling and ceramics. Designs referenced medieval styles, a period believed by the proponents to represent the ideals of the Movement. Craft schools were set up to teach women and men (though few men attended them). Although not specifically anti-machine, the ideology promoted handicrafts and hand-made items, which translated well to jewellery design and making. Considered a genteel pastime, this created an artistic and commercial opportunity for women.

Emerging Talent
Husband and wife partnerships were the first to gain recognition, such as Georgina and Arthur Gaskin from the Birmingham Group of Artist-Craftsmen and Edith and Nelson Dawson. They were quickly followed by the great individual names synonymous with the period: Ella Naper and Charlotte Newman, who started out working with the jeweller John Brogden in London and continued the business after his death.

Sibyl Dunlop (1889-1968) used coloured fine gemstones and symmetrical, abstract designs. Known for her 'Carpet of Gems' (mosaic-like) in silver settings, she had the gemstones cut in Idar-Oberstein. She was born near London to Scottish parents. Trained as a jewellery designer in Brussels, she returned to England and set up shop at 69 Kensington Church Street, London W8. She closed her shop at the outbreak of the Second World War.

Dorrie Nossiter (1893-1977) trained at the Municipal Art School of Birmingham before moving to London. Her work is a wonderful juxtaposition of cabochon and faceted gemstones set in gold in natural flower-like and grape-like clusters. She had a passion for flowers and took her inspiration from her garden, which reflected that of her mother, full of hydrangeas, delphiniums, phlox, roses, lupins, dahlias and chrysanthemums. Her work is frequently confused with that of Sibyl Dunlop.

Other jewellery designers of note include: Annie McLeish (1877-1919), who was inspired by Art Nouveau; and Jessie Marion King (1875-1949) from Scotland, who used enamelwork on copper. Phoebe Anna Traquair (1852-1936) was Irish and studied at the Royal Dublin Society for three years before moving to Edinburgh on her marriage. She was a prolific artist working as a muralist, illustrator and embroiderer, as well as making highly colourful enamel jewellery for which she found much renown.

The World Stage
Having initially emerged in Britain, the philosophy and style gained ground nationally and internationally. Across the English Channel in continental Europe the movement followed

different directions depending on the country in which it took hold. In France, Art Nouveau was dominated by highly skilled men, with perhaps the exception of one woman: Elizabeth Bonté, a Parisian jeweller inspired by natural themes and who used horn as her principal material. Jugendstil in Germany and the Secessionist movement in Austria had very few women if any, taking part in their ranks as jewellery designers.

In the United States, schools such as the School of the Art Institute of Chicago had a huge influence on the movement. Boston was the first city to have an Arts and Crafts Society, founded in 1897, followed quickly by Chicago at Hull House that same year. Cooperative shops popped up to sell much of these new works of art, including the well known Kalo Shop, which was founded by six women designers in 1900.

Florence Cary Koehler had started out creating ceramics. She was one of the founding members of the Chicago Arts and Crafts Society. In 1898, after visiting London and studying enamelwork under Alexander Fisher, she started to make jewellery that had historic and Renaissance style references, such as pendants with delicate chains, similar to much of the jewellery being made at that time in Great Britain. She preferred cabochon gemstones and her 'leafy designs and informal groupings of gems' were internationally acclaimed.

A pupil of Koehler, Elinor Evans Klapp became another great figure in the Chicago movement; she was also the only American woman to be represented at the 1900 Universal Exhibition in Paris. She took pride in using gemstones that originated from America.

Mildred G. Watkins (1883-1968), known for her exquisite enamelwork, had studied enamelling under Laurin Hovey Martin in Boston, he in turn had trained under Alexander Fisher in Great Britain. She came from a family of Ohio-based artists and trained as a jeweller and silversmith at the Cleveland School of Art. Later Watkins was to continue her career teaching at the same Cleveland School of Art.

Josephine Hartwell Shaw (1865-1941) trained at the Massachusetts Normal Art School and at the Pratt Institute, one of the main art schools in the United States. She was a medallist at the Boston Society of Arts and Crafts and exhibited on numerous occasions at the Art Institute of Chicago, winning awards for her jewellery in 1911 and 1918. Shaw was well known for the attention she gave to the settings she used to enhance the inclusions and colour of her gemstones. Her work can be seen at the Museum of Fine Arts in Boston. The wife of a sculptor, Josephine Shaw had been first a teacher of art and then a goldsmith and jewel-maker, because she saw in gems the possibility of combining and setting them, not only for their intrinsic value as precious minerals, but for their essential beauty.

Marie Zimmermann (1879-1972) was another prolific jewellery designer and although she started designing during the Arts and Crafts movement she continued well afterwards, drawing her inspiration from the archaeological discoveries of the early 20th century including those of Egypt, China and ancient Italy. Of Swiss nationality, she grew up in Brooklyn and attended the Art Students League of New York and the Pratt Institute. She started in jewellery working with bronze, copper, gold, silver and iron, experimenting with as many methods to shape the metals as she could find. The result was some wonderful millegrain filigree work, which she used to highlight her use of large colourful gemstones, both cabochon and faceted. Enamelling was another area in which she excelled, using bold blocks of colour alongside their transparent and translucent counterparts. Her work is in many museum collections including the Metropolitan Museum, the Carnegie Museum of Art, the Museum of Fine Arts in Boston and the Art Institute of Chicago.

Tiffany's

In 1902, Louis Comfort Tiffany took over as artistic director at Tiffany's, succeeding his father on his death. He experimented in almost every decorative sphere and came to jewellery late, exhibiting his first collection of twenty-seven jewels in 1904 at the Louisiana Purchase Exhibition in Saint Louis. His experimentation gave two women enamellers – Patricia Gay and Julia Munson – the chance to shine. Julia Munson became the head of jewellery in 1902 and she played an important role in Tiffany's early forays into the Arts and Crafts movement for jewellery. Her designs were influenced by nature using filigree, enamel and *plique-à-jour* often around central coloured stones. She had trained at the New York School of Design and the New York Institute of Artist Artisans and had been employed in 1898 under Patricia Gay, who was already working in the glass department and had been a fellow student.

> "*Our idea was to take an inexpensive stone and bring out its natural beauty and lustre by echoing its feeling in its treatment.*"
> Julia Munson quoted in 'A Jewel in his Crown' by Himilce Novas, *The Connoisseur*, October 1983

On Julia Munson's marriage in 1914, she was forced by convention to leave her employment and her position was taken by Meta Overbeck, who had been working in the enamels department since 1902. She was to remain head of the jewellery department until it closed in 1933.

> "*A sketchbook by Overbeck filled with many of the designs produced under Tiffany's guidance reveals a shift to larger stones and cooler, brighter colours... Deep blue opals and lapis lazuli were perennial favorite stones that were adorned with enameled leaves or borders and the moonstone became a focus for many delicate necklaces accented with sapphires.*"
> Jeannine Falino, *Maker & Muse*; p.124.

Under Overbeck, new gemstones saw the light of day, such as yellow sapphires and yellow-green tourmaline. After the First World War, strong colours came back to the fore; blues were mixed with greens and reds, creating new intense colour combinations. During the 1920s, the new archaeological finds influenced Overbeck's designs.

Both Julia Munson and Meta Overbeck are not as well known as some of Tiffany's later jewellery designers would become. In his book, *Bejewelled by Tiffany, 1837-1987*, John Loring suggests that this is because Louis Comfort Tiffany wouldn't allow this line of 'art jewellery' to be photographed and published in magazines.

Alongside the United States, Great Britain stood out as a country where women took full advantage of the new artistic trend and with the relative political calm at the turn of the century, they also used their new awakening to express themselves both artistically as well as politically.

RIGHT: Meta Overbeck for Tiffany & Co.: Multi-gem necklace, c.1918 – emerald, ruby, blue sapphire, champlevé enamel, silk cord, yellow gold
See Tiffany & Co. Archives, Louis Comfort Tiffany Scrapbook, vol.1, labelled 'F3332' for a photograph of the necklace.
IMAGE COURTESY OF TIFFANY & CO, NEW YORK

PART ONE

Between the Wars: The Awakening

The industrialisation of the 19th century brought factory jobs for women and by the end of the century, women were beginning to reap the rewards of a more open society and were demanding more equality and education. The suffragette movement and the actions of a courageous few were also helping to change the perception of women in the workplace.

Ironically, the world of jewellery making has by tradition always been a very masculine industry even though the jewels are destined to be worn mainly by women. Why? In the male dominated world of the 19th century where social niceties required that women born into polite circles be virtuous, demure home makers it would have been very unusual for a woman of social standing to choose a different path. Those who did work, usually worked out of necessity and then, only under the orders of a man. In family firms and workshops, women would have worked anonymously with the final article being signed by the head of the workshop or firm. When a woman married, she took on the name of her husband, thus making it even more difficult to track down their work, as an individual.

Jewellers were also members of guilds, which had their origins in medieval times. The traditional path used to teach the next generation of jewellers was the apprentice system, handing down the skills learnt from a master's former master. Most apprentices started to learn their trade when they were around thirteen years old, so unless a girl was a family member, the more conventional route would have been domestic work or perhaps work in the textile industry as a weaver or seamstress. Women were banned as a matter of course from many guilds, thus reducing any opportunities further.

The turn of the century

Several artistic styles coexisted until the start of World War I. The Arts & Crafts movement, the Art Nouveau style and the Garland style of Edwardian jewellery in Great Britain and Belle Époque jewellery on the European continent. Fashion was an important catalyst to the jewellery designs that followed. The delicate silks and crinolines, in those first years, called for simple light 'white' jewellery (diamond and platinum). The discovery of an abundant supply of diamonds in South Africa and the use of platinum as a hard, strong, yet malleable 'white' metal to set off their lustre, coincided with the invention of the oxyacetylene torch in 1903. This was an important advance in jewellery workshops just as the laser would be in the 1990s, it allowed the bench jeweller to achieve the high temperatures needed to 'tame' the platinum and to transform it into the many intricate lace-like garlands and bows that were so popular.

Diaghilev's Ballets Russes

Few cultural events can claim to have had such an earth shattering effect on fashion as Diaghilev's Ballets Russes. It took Paris by storm in 1910 with costumes designed by Léon Bakst, whose notoriety was assured by using peacock feathers, embroidered costumes in scarlet reds and emerald greens for their performance of *Schéhérazade*. Paul Poiret, the uncontested leader of the French couturiers at that time, was entranced by all that he saw and was encouraged to create even more colourful and daring fashions. Lamé turbans, dresses encrusted with precious stones, and Oriental-style harem pants became all the rage.

The Belle Époque was a period of great wealth and a social whirl of dinners, balls and salons for the prosperous upper classes. There was peace and the industrial advances of the last century had created new fortunes and helped those already well off to become even more so. Two of the great women jewellery designers of the twentieth century were both making their way through the labyrinthine complexity of social etiquette and the Parisian demi-monde. Gabrielle (Coco) Chanel was making a name for herself as a talented milliner and seamstress whilst Jeanne Toussaint was creating stunning bags using her family background in lace-making. At more or less the same time, Paul Poiret's sister Jeanne married the jeweller René Boivin, bringing with her the same artistic talent as her brother. With her new ideas and her brother's connections, she transformed her husband's business.

Overnight, WWI brought to an end the expensive soirées and the great balls that had had such an influence on fashion. Its effect on women's fashion was a death knell to long gowns, hobble skirts and romantic delicate fabrics. The men went off to war; the women took up their vacated jobs in factories and on the land, or went to the Front as nurses. The consequence of these new roles for women, was a more practical way of dressing, looser fitting and more adapted to an active lifestyle. At the end of The War in 1918, everything had changed, women were now active members of society and having tasted freedom were not about to return to their demure rolls of the Belle Époque era.

Les Années Folles

Many women had seen the atrocities and the horrors of the War, as had those men lucky enough to return. The Spanish 'flu epidemic was taking its toll. Yet out of this grew the insouciance of a new age, the frenetically paced and artistically rich period of the 1920s, 'Les Années Folles'. Air travel had become possible, cars were the norm and trains were by now a very efficient mode of transport. People started to discover the far away cultures of places such as Egypt, popularised by Howard Carter and Lord Carnarvon's discovery of Tutankhamun's tomb in the Valley of the Kings in 1922. The great jewellery house, Cartier had travelled to India before the War and had popularised exotic Indian-inspired designs using magnificent gemstones, many of which had been entrusted to them by Indian Maharajahs to be reset in more contemporary designs. Women artists were to have a huge influence on this period between the two great Wars: Madeleine Vionnet popularised the bias cut; Elsa Schiaparelli ('Scap' to her friends) loved to play with unusual themes and create witty humorous statements; and Jeanne Lanvin was appreciated for her romantic fashions. Coco Chanel's no-nonsense attitude to fashion, and her beautifully made simple silhouettes found many wearers. Lesser known names, but just as important, at the time were Maggy Rouff, the Callot sisters and in London, Lucile (Lady Duff Gordon); these were women who designed for women, even the twenties iconic Cloche hat was designed by a woman, Caroline Reboux. Dress took in the new craze for sport and the new energetic dances, such as the foxtrot, tango and the Charleston. Plastics, such as bakelite were used to imitate hard stones such as agate and to replace enamel and ivory. New and exciting, they were adapted and used to inspire new designs in jewellery.

Paris was where it was all happening

Paris was abuzz with new ideas and styles: Art Deco, Bauhaus, Cubism, Dadaism, Fauvism, Modernism and Surrealism all coexisted. Women writers and artists, such as Tamara de Lempicka, Natalia Goncharova came into their own; exhibiting in the numerous small galleries that had popped up all over Paris, they were taken seriously, contributing in no small measure to the exchanges of the time. African themes, helped by Josephine Baker's highly successful Revue Nègre and the emphasis given to all things African at the 1925 'Exposition Internationale des Arts Decoratifs et Industriels Modernes', became fashionable. The Americas and the Pacific Islands were also 'au rendez-vous', it all served to create a rich and vibrant backdrop for Paris's artist population and its notoriety worldwide.

Jeanne Boivin with Suzanne Belperron, and later Juliet Moutard, held sway designing jewels that bridged two very definite styles that co-existed in the '20s and for the better part of the '30s. On the one hand, the established jewellery houses produced exquisite plaque bracelets, ear pendants and sautoirs to decorate a wearer's bare back in the evening, rarely straying from a pallette of exotic and expensive precious gemstones. on the other, the artist jewellers (regrouped into the UAM, Union des Artistes Modernes) used gemstones such as agate, coral and turquoise to create blocks of strong uniform colours within a structured framework of angular, geometric shapes. Black and red lacqueur was introduced to these colour schemes and by the 1925 Exposition International des Arts Decoratifs, colour abounded. Perhaps popularised by Coco Chanel in 1924 when she introduced couture jewellery to accessorize her clothing, colour was once again in vogue; though, by the end of the 1920s, white was again

ABOVE: Cartier: Rose Clip brooch, 1938 – diamond, red lacquer, black lacquer, silver, platinum, pink gold, yellow gold
IMAGE COURTESY OF CARTIER, PARIS

the order of the day for jewellery. Both Boivin and Belperron used diamonds and rock crystal in geometric forms that were to become more voluminous and curvilinear in form and silhouette, introducing exotic woods, pearls and cabochon gemstones to the mix.

Why did Paris have such an influence between 1918 and 1939?

Couture was of great importance to the French economy before the War; the 'Chambre Syndicale de la Couture parisienne' had at least 80 members at its foundation in 1910, employing thousands of specialised seamstresses and people in related professions. After the War was over, the French government invested heavily to help the textile and couture industries get back on their feet.

Paris became the world capital of artists. The 1924 Olympics were held in Paris, followed by the 1925 Exposition Internationale des Arts Décoratifs et Industriels Modernes (which gave its name to the Art Deco style), the Salon d'Automne in 1928, the exhibition 'Les Arts de la Bijouterie, Joaillerie et Orfèvrerie' at the musée Galliera in 1929, and the Exposition Coloniale in 1931. This quick succession of high profile arts events served to keep Paris at the forefront of people's minds.

One artist whose designs were an outstanding success at the 1925 exhibition was Madeleine Chazel, who designed a series of jewels for the jewellery house Dusausoy on boulevard des Capucines in Paris. Amongst her designs was a Stalactite diamond bracelet set with three cabochon emeralds, the 'stalactites' were composed of lapis lazuli and malachite; it was awarded with the grand prize. The chairman of the judging committee, Georges Fouquet (a well-known jeweller in his own right) said of this collection of jewellery that it was "one of the most interesting in the French section, showing beautiful stones in combinations of lines ingeniously arranged." Unfortunately, there is very little information about Madeleine Chazel, so we only have this glimpse of a person, who was evidently hugely talented.

Artists flocked to Paris from everywhere to be inspired and to live alongside other great artists. It was a time of exchange of ideas and everyone knew everyone. Jean Cocteau was a friend of Coco Chanel (they collaborated on the sets and costumes for the ballet, *Le Train Bleu* with Pablo Picasso), and of Jeanne Toussaint and Suzanne Belperron; Colette was also a friend of all three jewellery designers and they shared many of the same clients, including The Duke and Duchess of Windsor, Millicent Rogers, Barbara Hutton, Florence Gould and Daisy Fellowes, to name but a few. Salons and movements abounded, the School of Paris grouped many of the foreign artists working and living in Paris and, in particular, Montparnasse, the Parisian quarter on the Left Bank, where writers, artists and musicians rubbed shoulders with each other, exchanged ideas and caroused through night time.

Fashion photographs took over from illustrations and were circulated worldwide in new magazines, such as *Vogue*, *L'Officiel* and *Harper's Bazaar*. Just as these magazines helped spread the news about Parisian fashions, so too films and the new phenomenon of Hollywood helped to publicise the new styles by reaching a wider, international audience. Jewellery went hand-in-hand with couture; costume (popularised by Coco Chanel) and authentic jewellery became a vital part of an ensemble, helping jewellery designers and jewellery houses to become household names. The great photographers of the time – Horst P. Horst, George Hoyningen-Huene and then Cecil Beaton and Man Ray – popularised this new mode of communication, often photographing for the fashion magazines. Chanel dresses and Schiaparelli's creations would be matched with the great jewels of the time from big Belperron bangles and brooches to Boivin classics, and Cartier and Van Cleef & Arpels masterpieces.

Even when recession hit after the Wall Street crash in 1929 and the subsequent recession in Europe at the beginning of the 1930s, Paris remained a magnet for fashion and the artistic scene, so much so that the international guild of Diamond Merchants asked Coco Chanel to create a collection of diamond jewellery in an attempt to pump new vitality into the diamond industry.

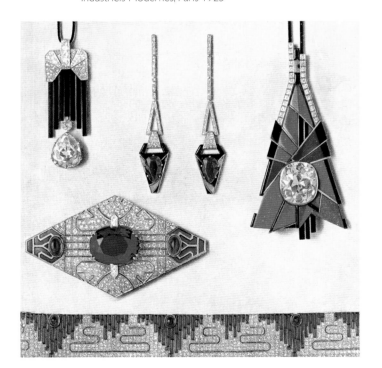

BELOW: Page showing Dusausoy jewellery in the catalogue for the Exposition Internationale des Arts Décoratifs et Industriels Modernes, Paris 1925

Jewellery design continued to flourish during the troubled political times of the 1930s, when dictators seemed to be as fashionable as outrageous hats. By the 1937 'Exposition Coloniale', storm clouds were gathering over Europe and the 'Années Folles' were just a distant memory. Into this fray came more names who were to bring their own originality and influence as jewellers: Line Vautrin, Vivianna Torun Bulöw-Hübe and Nanna Ditzel for Georg Jensen.

The Second World War

With the outbreak of the Second World War many of the great couturiers closed up shop. Those who did remain, became very discreet. Both Suzanne Belperron and Jeanne Toussaint stayed in Paris during the occupation, whilst tragedy struck Van Cleef & Arpels with the death of their great creative director Renée Puissant (daughter of Alfred Van Cleef). Little is known about this interesting person. Unfortunately, there is very little archival documentation that can lead us to say that Puissant designed this specific jewel or that particular piece. The importance of her contribution to Van Cleef & Arpels' design in the 1920s and '30s is beyond doubt and seems to have taken a similar route to that of Jeanne Toussaint for Cartier. Like Toussaint, she didn't draw, which meant that her input was through discussion and dialogue to put over her ideas. All we know for certain is that Puissant had a reputation for being extraordinarily talented and that she had an excellent working relationship with René Sim Lacaze, Van Cleef & Arpels' legendary bench jeweller before the Second World War; they worked together from 1926 to 1939. Perhaps one of the reasons for a lack of documentation is that she died at a tragically young age during the War in Vichy, 1942.

During WWII, platinum was requisitioned for the War effort, and gold was rare and expensive. For those who remained open, the client was obliged to supply all the gold and some of the gemstones. The Americans stayed away and Paris' influence on the world stage was on the wane, with America looking to home-grown talents, such as fashion designer Claire McCardell to fill the gap. The main jewellery houses continued to do business in the United States, but by this time there were some 'new kids on the block' as well.

ABOVE: Portrait of Renée Puissant (1896-1942 ; née Van Cleef), early 1920s
IMAGE COURTESY OF VAN CLEEF & ARPELS.

RIGHT: Cartier, Paris: Ball-bearing inspired bracelet, 1942 – silver, yellow gold
This bracelet was a gift from the French actor Jean Gabin to Marlene Dietrich.
IMAGE COURTESY OF DEUTSCHE KINEMATHEK - MARLENE DIETRICH COLLECTION, BERLIN

ALMA PIHL
The Ice Queen

It is only because of a series of unpredictable events, that Alma Pihl (1888-1976) did not fall into oblivion. During the Russian Revolution, a young worker, Oswald K. Jurison managed to smuggle out two of Pihl's sketchbooks from the Fabergé workshops; they were eventually sold to Wartski in London. In 1980, author and Russian court jewellery expert, Ulla Tillander-Godenhielm proved beyond doubt that two Imperial Eggs were conceived by Alma Pihl. Pihl's imaginative and skilled design work was finally given the worldwide recognition it deserved.

Fabergé

Alma Pihl was born in Moscow into a family of four brothers. On the death of her father, Knut Oscar Pihl (head jeweller for the Fabergé Moscow branch), her mother moved them all to St Petersburg. At the age of 20, Pihl started as an apprentice draftsman under her uncle, Albert Holmström, head designer at Fabergé in St Petersburg. Her job was to make accurate sketches of the jewels and *objets de vertu* that were being created in the Fabergé workshops. The sketches were archived in the accounts registers that detailed the cost of the gemstones and precious metals in a piece. Her skill was such that she was soon promoted to assistant designer.

In 1911 she was given the task of designing 40 brooches for Dr. Emmanuel Nobel, the oil baron, to give to the wives of his clients at a dinner party with a Winter theme. Pihl, inspired by the morning frost on her window, created a series of rock crystal brooches resembling snow crystals or frost flowers, touches of platinum and diamonds created flashes of light as the jewel moved. Her designs were a success and Nobel commissioned other jewels using Pihl's frost motif, including a rock crystal Easter Egg with a matching watch inside.

It was due to this success that Alma Pihl was given the honour of designing the Tsar's 1913 Easter Egg, which he would give to his mother, the Dowager Empress Maria Feodorovna. The

ABOVE: Pihl for Carl Fabergé, St Petersburg: Stylised six-pointed Snowflake brooch – diamond, platinum, yellow gold
An identical brooch is recorded in Albert Holmström's jewellery design ledger, dated 26 April 1913.
IMAGE COURTESY OF WARTSKI, LONDON

RIGHT: Pihl's sketch for the Fabergé accounts register of one of her own designs.
IMAGE COURTESY OF WARTSKI, LONDON

OPPOSITE PAGE: Pihl for Carl Fabergé, St Petersburg: Ice pendant – rock crystal, diamond, white gold
Signed: 'Fabergé'.
An identical design for this pendant is recorded in Albert Holmström's jewellery design ledger, dated 27 June, 1913.
IMAGE COURTESY OF THE HOUSTON MUSEUM OF NATURAL SCIENCE

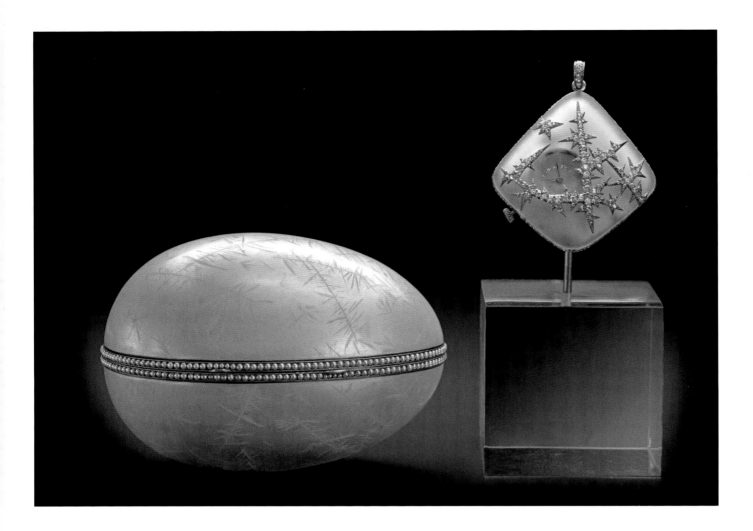

result is a stunning crystal egg covered in frost blossoms on the outside and the inside of the crystal to create the sense of depth. Touches of platinum and diamond 'snow crystals' give it an overall frozen effect. The quartz crystal base has a two-tiered effect of melting ice with rivulets of diamonds and platinum running down the sides, suggesting the end of winter is close. Within the egg sits an openwork diamond-set platinum basket, filled with white chalcedony spring flowers on a bed of gold moss; the stamens and the stems are crafted in yellow gold and set with demantoid garnets from the Ural Mountains and the leaves are carved in nephrite.

In 1914, Pihl designed the Tsar's Easter Egg for his wife. This time, Pihl's inspiration came from her mother's embroidery work to create the Mosaic Egg. The egg's form is created with cut platinum mesh into which is set carefully calibrated emeralds, rubies, sapphires, topazes, garnets, moonstones highlighted with rose diamonds, and brilliant-cut diamonds. The extraordinary feat was to create a 'hidden' setting, so that none of the platinum is visible. Inside the egg is a miniature ivory medallion painted with the portraits of the Tsar and Tsarina's five children. During her brief time at Fabergé, Pihl also designed 18th birthday gifts for Tsar Nicholas II's two daughters, the Grand Duchesses Olga and Tatiana.

Alma Pihl fled with her husband and brothers to Finland in 1921, settling in Kuusankoski, where she taught art for over 23 years before retiring in 1951; she never designed jewellery again.

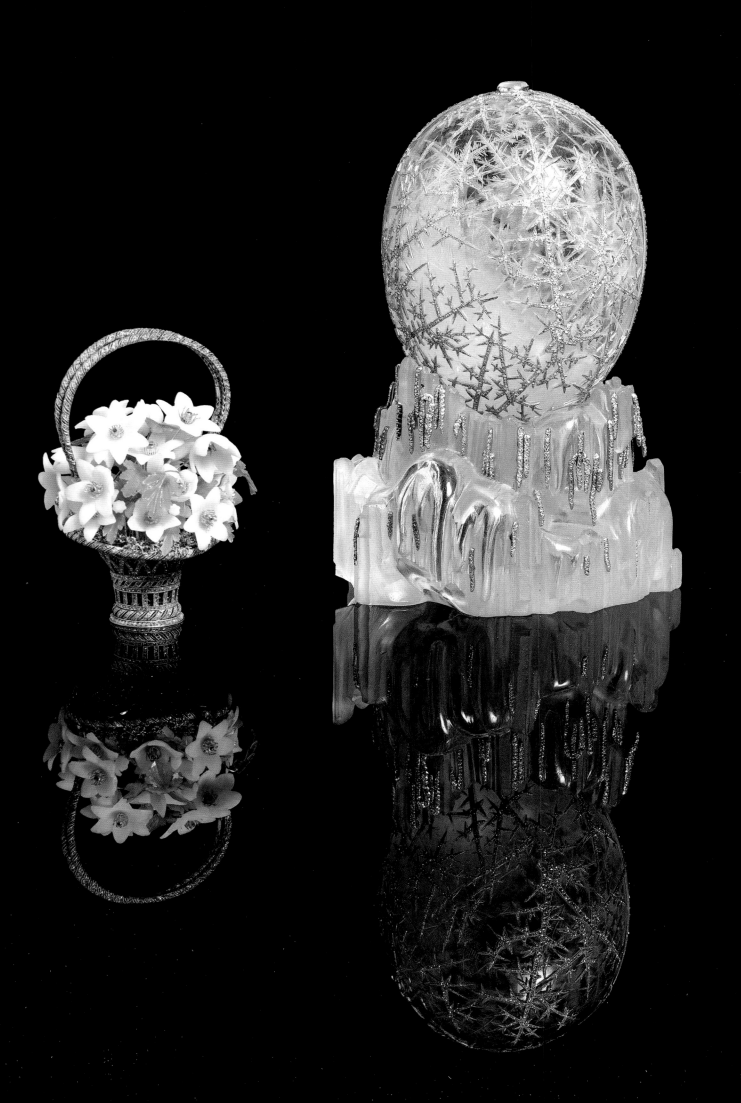

"In my profession, any means is legitimate, provided it is only used in the true spirit of fashion. I started creating costume jewelry because I felt it was refreshingly free of arrogance, during a period that tended towards ostentatious displays of luxury. This consideration faded into the background during the economic recession, when, in every sphere of life, there emerged an instinctive desire for authenticity, and amusing trinkets were once more put into their proper perspective."

Gabrielle Chanel, catalogue of the 'Bijoux de Diamants' collection, 1932

COCO CHANEL
Couture Chic

A visit to Gabrielle Chanel's apartments at 31 rue Cambon, Paris is to glimpse at the private life of this fascinating and elegant, wafer-thin woman whose instinct for business created her legend. Her home is a juxtaposition of mirrors and magnificent Cormandel screens that decorate the hallway, drawing room and dining room. The huge screens detailing an exotic faraway scene of the West Lake in Hangzhou, with fishermen and cormorants and small antique artefacts were a long way from her childhood days in the beautiful but austere Cistercian orphanage.

A large star hangs above her bed in her villa in the south of France. Stars are everywhere: carved in fans, on the spines of books on the shelves... All around, her astrological sign of Leo is represented by sculptures in wood and marble and brass. Transparent, colourless glass flowers glint in the light, on her desk sheaves of wheat support a small console, whilst another sheaf is carved in wood. A small painting by Salvador Dalí composed of an ear of wheat rests gently against the bookcase. They are all part of Chanel's DNA.

The Making of a Fashion Icon
In 1883, Gabrielle Bonheur 'Coco' Chanel was born into poverty in Saumur, France. At the age of 12, she and her sisters were sent to a convent orphanage after the death of their mother; it was here that Chanel learnt to sew. As a young woman she worked as a seamstress to make ends meet while pursuing her pipe dream of a career on the stage. Her inauspicious start in life and her career in the demi-monde of the Belle Époque did not augur well and yet by the beginning of the 1920s, Chanel was already a name to be reckoned with.

From the stage she became the mistress of wealthy textile heir, Etienne Balsan. Bored by the quiet monotonous countryside life Balsan offered, she occupied herself by designing hats. Her simple elegant style soon turned a hobby into a viable commercial success. Diversifying into clothing design, Chanel's first shops were financed by her new lover and muse, the sartorially elegant Captain Arthur 'Boy' Capel from the English upper classes.

Chanel understood what young fashionable women wanted, taking them away from corsetted restriction, transforming them into slender silhouettes of elegance and practicality.

ABOVE: Multi-gem brooch/pendant, 1930 – ruby, sapphire, emerald, diamond, yellow gold
Originally designed for Mrs George S. (Lydia) Gregory by her close friends, Coco Chanel and Fulco di Verdura.
PHOTOGRAPH © DAVID BEHL; IMAGE COURTESY OF VERDURA

OPPOSITE PAGE: Star brooch, 1932 – diamond, platinum
(Provenance: 'Bijoux de Diamants' exhibition, 1932.)
PHOTOGRAPH © DIDIER ROY; COLLECTION PATRIMOINE DE CHANEL; IMAGE COURTESY OF CHANEL INC.

Her master stroke was buying surplus jersey fabric, previously used mostly for men's underwear; Chanel transformed it into 'marinières'– a type of long sleeved T-shirt. In 1917, *Harper's Bazaar* stated that Chanel's garments were part of any fashionable lady's wardrobe. By the end of WWI, Chanel had a store in Paris, Deauville and Biarritz, employed 300 people and had already repaid Capel's investment in full. Her energy and her conviction had brought her a long way and she was ready to take on the couturiers in Paris, creating garments for a new woman and a new époque.

In 1919, tragedy struck. Capel was killed in a motoring accident in the South of France. Chanel's solution was to throw herself into her work and alongside her collections of clothes she started to include costume jewellery. Not knowing how to draw, Chanel would play with piles of gemstones and coloured crystals at her desk to find pleasing colour combinations and would shape modelling clay to create the desired forms. Despite her strong character and clear vision, she would often work in collaboration with other jewellery designers, such as Etienne de Beaumont, François Hugo, Paul Iribe, Fulco di Verdura and the atelier Gripoix.

Chanel: the Trendsetter

Costume jewellery was worn before this time but it had never been the deliberate choice of the well-heeled fashionable woman. Chanel changed all this. Her long affair with one of the richest men in Europe, the Duke of Westminster meant that she mingled with high society and was in full view of the press. Her outfits were remarked upon, as was her deliberate choice of mixing fine and costume jewellery. Real pearls sat next to artificial pearls – one, two, three strands at a time – complementing her dark, elegantly tailored garments. She designed chains and jewellery using coloured, cabochon gemstones, which at the time were not regarded as 'real' jewellery. So pink and green tourmaline, deep caramel citrines and pale violet amethyst cabochons, topazes and aquamarines were used to create colourful statements that could be mixed and matched.

Chanel took her inspiration from all around, including the exquisite jewels she received from the Duke of Westminster during their many years together, as well as the Romanov jewels she was given by another beau, Grand Duke Dmitri Pavlovitch of Russia, with whom she had had a brief relationship between 1920 and 1923. The Renaissance and Baroque periods with their rich heavy and colourful decorations were a constant inspiration to her. Her jewels were big, her sense of proportion commanded that they be even larger than those found in 'real' jewellery. Gilt chains, baroque crosses and big colourful artificial pearls were *de rigueur*.

Diamonds in the Sky

In 1932, with sales plummeting during the economic crisis, the diamond industry turned to Chanel for help to bring the gems back into popularity. The result was a stunning collection of 47 pieces of high jewellery that caused a seismic shift in people's attitudes to diamonds and parures. Jewellers of note came from across the Atlantic and from London to view the exhibition 'Bijoux de Diamants' held in her own Parisian home, 29 rue du Faubourg Saint-Honoré. She was quoted in *l'Illustration* as saying:

> *"If I have chosen diamonds, it is because they represent the greatest value in the smallest volume. And my love of things that glitter has inspired me to try to combine elegance and fashion through the medium of jewellery."*
> Gabrielle Chanel, catalogue of the 'Bijoux de Diamants' collection, 1932

In a time of recession the message was clear: these diamonds will keep their value and they can be worn. She wanted to popularise diamonds, showing not just huge stones for the wealthiest but also the potential of these bright, 'light-catching' gemstones. Platinum settings were chosen so they could be reduced to a minimum, keeping the focus on the gemstones themselves. Bringing her experience from the world of couture, she displayed her diamond jewels three-dimensionally on life like wax mannequins, showing how she envisaged her creations should be worn; this was in stark contrast to the usual conservative manner of displaying haute joallerie. Coco Chanel made diamonds a fashion item.

ABOVE: Invitation to Chanel's 1932 exhibition, 'Bijoux de Diamants'
IMAGE COURTESY OF CHANEL © CHANEL

RIGHT: Coco Chanel in her apartment at the Hôtel Ritz, Place Vendôme à Paris
Note that Chanel is wearing the Duke of Westminster's emerald necklace and her elaborate decorative cuffs.
PHOTOGRAPH BY KOLLAR FRANÇOIS (1904-1979)
© RMN - GESTION DROIT D'AUTEUR FRANÇOIS KOLLAR
PHOTO © MINISTÈRE DE LA CULTURE - MÉDIATHÈQUE DU PATRIMOINE

OPPOSITE PAGE: Press clippings from a period film of the 1932 'Bijoux de Diamants' exhibition, showing clockwise from left: Diamond Fountain Fall necklace and Shooting Star ornament/diadem; Shooting Star hairpiece/brooch; Diamond Bow choker; Floating diamond ring over three fingers
ALL IMAGES © UNIVERSAL / ALL RIGHTS RESERVED

Many of her designs were revolutionary at the time and remain as contemporary today as they were in 1932. The few photographs that survive of the exhibition show the extent of Chanel's ideas. The Fringe necklace was modelled as a bandeau with diamond fringes flowing down over the forehead, almost brushing the eyelashes of the model. There were sunbursts set as huge brooches weighed down with a plethora of yellow and white diamonds. Even a cigarette case covered in diamonds accompanied (in typical Chanel style) by a cigarette holder in diamond and red coral to disguise the smoker's lipstick. Rings were an innovation, they spiralled up the finger or appeared to float above three fingers. Necklaces were designed to hug and to gently trace the soft contours of the neck. Some of her jewels were transformable into other pieces:

> "Yet my jewellery can be assembled. See this necklace, you can instantly make it into three bracelets and a brooch for a blouse or a hat. Actually, this already existed, but I wanted to perfect and develop it."   Gabrielle Chanel, in interview, 1932

The main motif was one that had captivated her since her childhood at the Aubazine Abbey, the stars and the night sky:

> "I wanted to cover women with constellations. Stars! Stars of all sizes."

The iconic comet necklace leaves a trail of diamond tails that drape over the shoulder. Another necklace wrapped around the neck ending in two trailing stars, the weight of the stars keeping the necklace in place.

Coco Chanel did not stop at the night sky, she also included small bowtie and ribbon necklets, and pins entirely covered in diamonds. These were not the ribbons and bows of the 19th century, these were discreet and stylish and modern.

Chanel's claspless jewelled pieces — *"I have a horror of clasps!"* — included bracelets that could be slipped on and wrapped around the lower arm like ribbons. She also used the same effect for a wristwatch framed within a flush of diamonds that coiled shadows of diamonds sinuously up the arm. Another used black leather as the backdrop for the circular diamonds, creating extra contrast between the bright white light of the diamonds and the matt dark finish of the leather.

For the accompanying catalogue, Chanel chose the talents of a young photographer, Robert Bresson, who went on to become a highly acclaimed film director. His images capture the contrast between the delicate shadows and tones of the wax models and the sparkling hardness of the diamonds. His images, along with those of André Kertész for *Vogue*, capture this unique and fleeting moment in the history of high jewellery that otherwise would have been lost forever.

L'Affaire Chanel

The jewellery houses of Place Vendôme were scandalised that a mere "dressmaker" should have been chosen over them to represent the International Diamond Corporation. They held meetings and exercised their considerable combined power to stop any of the jewels from being sold, and insisted that after the exhibition the pieces be dismantled. However, two pieces are known to have survived — one original star brooch has been rediscovered by Chanel, and another piece is in a private collection. Knowing Chanel's strength of character and ingenuity, it is not impossible to imagine that other pieces may yet reemerge. (See Appendix 3: 'L'Affaire Chanel'. page 356.)

Legacy

Three weeks after France declared war on Germany, Coco Chanel closed the House of Chanel, leaving only the Paris boutique open to sell perfume, and accessories such as hats, gloves and scarves, and some jewellery. After the war, Chanel lived in semi-retirement in Switzerland. In her seventies, she was galvanised to reopen the House of Chanel to rebel against the prevailing 1950s fashion for the restrictive corsetted silhouette of the New Look; her clothes and jewellery appealing mostly to the American and British markets. She also continued to create some fine jewellery pieces for herself and select clients. Still working to the end, she passed away in 1971, at the age of 88. Known predominantly as one of the greatest couturiers, Coco Chanel's contribution to jewellery design should not be underestimated; she created some of the most interesting jewellery — both costume and fine — of the 20th century.

> *"She was an extraordinary person — absolutely fabulous. No age. I have known her exactly the same looking rather like a wonderful Japanese mask, like a Samurai mask. I think she has got more chic than any living woman I know. And the negation of fashion is always the same. I have known her always dressed the same, covered with jewels. I won't go into all the things that we all know, that she put on the map, costume jewellery."*
> Fulco Verdura, radio interview with Nan Garcia, New York, 1957

TOP: Original photography from the 'Bijoux de Diamants' exhibition catalogue, 1932, showing the Comet and Bow necklaces BOTH IMAGES © PHOTOGRAPH BY ROBERT BRESSON, 'BIJOUX DE DIAMANTS', CHANEL, 1932

RIGHT: Star brooch in its original étui, 1932 – diamond, platinum
(Provenance: 'Bijoux de Diamant' exhibition, 1932.)
COLLECTION PATRIMOINE DE CHANEL; IMAGE COURTESY OF CHANEL

SUZANNE BELPERRON
A Cut Above

Suzanne Belperron (née Vuillerme, 1900-1983) is truly one of the greats of 20th-century jewellery design. Strong minded and wilful, Belperron had a confidence and a conviction in her own style that belied her age, allowing her to trace a path independent of the dictates of the period. For years her work remained anonymous as, following Jeanne Boivin's example, she rarely signed any of her jewels, stating simply: "My style is my signature". Her star has shone all the brighter since her very special jewels designed for the Duchess of Windsor came to the public's attention at Sotheby's sale in Geneva in April 1987.

Belperron was born in the small town of Saint-Claude in the Jura Mountains of east France, a centre for gemstone cutting. She trained at the School of Fine Arts in Besançon, winning first prize in the decorative arts section in 1917-1918 for a yellow gold pendant watch decorated with white and black champlevé enamel work. The school was in the archaeological museum, giving her easy daily access to an extraordinary Egyptian collection, leading to her fascination with Egyptology.

The Belperron Style
Belperron's was a style that went against the main tendencies of the day. The silver bangle set with citrines in contrasting gold collet settings was made at the end of her training and was completely opposed to the diamond art deco jewels of the time; her jewels were curvaceous and round, they had an uncluttered simplicity about them.

Her jewels were made by many workshops in the early years. However, the main atelier with which she collaborated throughout her career was 'Groëné et Darde', from 1932 to 1955. In 1955, 'Groëné and Darde' changed its name to 'Darde et Fils' and then again in 1970 to 'Darde et Cie'. In effect, she worked with the same atelier from 1932, when she left Boivin, until 1974.

LEFT: Belperron for Herz-Belperron: Spire (Spiral) cuff, 1936 – calibré sapphire, diamond, platinum
IMAGE COURTESY OF PAT SALING, NEW YORK

OPPOSITE PAGE: Belperron for B. Herz: Geometric bracelet, 1934 – rock crystal, diamond, platinum
This was owned by Diana Vreeland, who can be seen wearing it in a photograph by Jérome Zerbe, 1938.
IMAGE COURTESY OF BELPERRON, LLC., NEW YORK

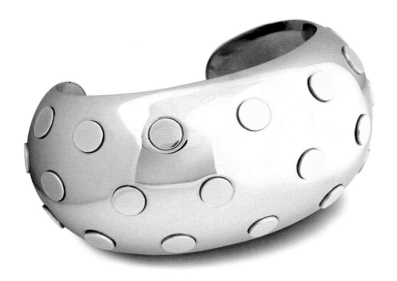

ABOVE: Belperron for Boivin: Clouté (studded) bracelet, 1933 – stainless steel, gold-plated copper alloy
IMAGE COURTESY OF L. COURTEILLE CREATIONS, PARIS

BELOW: Belperron for Boivin: Escalier earrings, 1929-33 – rock crystal, platinum
IMAGE COURTESY OF L. COURTEILLE CREATIONS, PARIS

House of Boivin

After the death of René Boivin, his widow, Jeanne employed Belperron in March 1919, at the age of 19, as a modelist-designer. Belperron was a natural; she used cabochon gemstones for their colour and their irregular outline to create jewels that were original, curvaceous and very different to the accepted style of the moment. Nurtured by Jeanne Boivin, she became creative director at Boivin in 1924. Jeanne Boivin followed her own instincts; not a fan of the Art Deco period, she used designs from her husband's time at the helm and reinterpreted them with Belperron, slowly introducing volume and colour to realise their ideas rather than being governed by the trends of the time.

Created in 1931 by Belperron, the 'Tranche' bracelet became a Boivin classic, and the inspiration for many different bracelets using an infinite array of gemstones and material combinations by Belperron and, later, her successor at Boivin, Juliette Moutard. They were made in rock crystal, wood and platinum; she even used steel, as daring then as it is today in high jewellery.

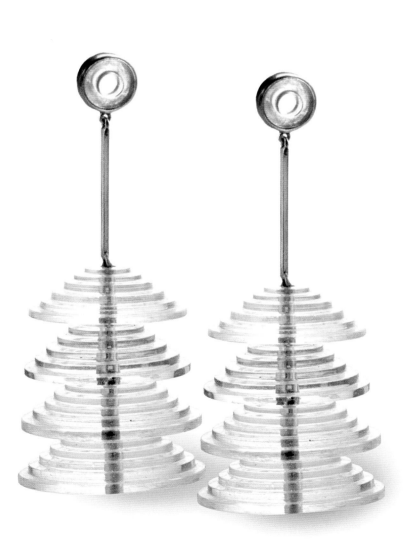

ABOVE: Belperron for Boivin: Torsade bracelet, 1930 – diamond, yellow gold
Belperron made several variations of this bracelet; amongst her celebrated clients who owned one were Elsa Schiaparelli and Millicent Rogers (Mrs Ronald Balcom).
IMAGE COURTESY OF SYMBOLIC & CHASE, LONDON

OPPOSITE PAGE: Belperron for Boivin: Spire (Scroll) necklace, 1935 – diamond, platinum
IMAGE COURTESY OF CHRISTIE'S INC.

Together, Belperron and Boivin designed bracelets and pendants inspired by world themes of African, Assyrian, Chinese, Egyptian, Etruscan, Indian (Mughal and Hindu) and Persian origins, such as the magnificent Cambodian bracelet designed by Belperron. First made in 1930 for Lady Duff-Cooper, it was a technical *tour-de-force*, inspired by an antique engraved bronze bracelet from Cambodia; another example of this design was bought by Princess Faucigny-Lucinge.

Herz

At the age of 32, Belperron left the House of Boivin to go to Bernard Herz, a well-known pearl and coloured gemstone dealer. At Herz she gained artistic freedom and developed a softer more sinuous style. She was a great success; from Elsa Schiaparelli to Daisy Fellowes, *everybody* was wearing Belperron. Very soon, advertisements in Bernard Herz's name changed from 'B. Herz Paris', in June 1934, to Herz-Belperron, as is evident in the advertisement placed in *Vogue* France, April 1936, which shows 'B. Herz' and in smaller print 'Mme Belperron'. Through the years, the advertisements in *Vogue* document the progression of Suzanne Belperron's importance within Bernard Herz's company.

Her reputation was international and in July 1939, the famous idiosyncratic jewellery designer to the stars of Hollywood, Paul Flato, approached her to suggest a collaboration. She declined the offer; preferring to stay in Paris and to remain independent.

The dark clouds of war were gathering. In occupied Paris, operating a business under a Jewish name was no longer legal. Of Jewish heritage, Bernard Herz was arrested by the Gestapo and questioned; he was saved on that occasion by the intervention of Belperron's friend Rika Radifé. To ensure his company's survival, Herz persuaded Belperron to register it under her own name; she traded under the name 'Suzanne Belperron SARL' from November 1940-December 1946. Herz was arrested a second time in November 1942; this time there was no escape. He was detained at the Drancy camp, before being deported to Germany in September, 1943. In a letter to Belperron, he entrusted his business and the future interests of his children to her.

Herz-Belperron

Though Herz did not survive the war, his son, Jean did return from Germany. Belperron automatically changed the name of the company to 'Jean Herz – Suzanne Belperron SARL', respecting the wishes of her former partner; it proved a successful business partnership, lasting until her retirement in 1975.

Belperron understood the link between fashion and jewellery. Designers of couture and fashion appreciated her use of volume and her great sense of proportion for each of her jewels. *Vogue* and *Harper's Bazaar* were quick to use Herz-Belperron for each jewel that was modelled with evening gowns by such fashion icons as Coco Chanel, Elsa Schiaparelli and, later, Nina Ricci and Christian Dior.

Exotic Fashions

New methods of travel had opened up the world and set a trend for the exotic. The Western world was fascinated by Lord Carnarvon and Howard Carter's recent discovery of Tutankhamun's tomb. Other than Belperron's trip to Egypt in 1923 on the occasion of her engagement, she herself does not seem to have travelled to any great extent. Much of her inspiration came from travel books and visits to museums.

Japanese and Chinese works of art were an integral part of interior design in the '20s and with this interest came an interest in lacquer. This Japanese technique *par excellence* was adopted by many jewellery houses and Belperron was no exception, though, of course, she used it in a totally original way. For her 'Lien' (link) necklaces, she covered thin metal (usually silver) chokers in black lacquer, which was easier to apply and more flexible than enamel, and was more resistant. Belperron also used lacquer to cover and emphasise parts of a jewel, be it the stem of a flower or leaf, or tracing the edge of a gold and diamond shell clip for example.

TOP LEFT: *Gouache of Suzanne Belperron's famous Sapin de Noel (Christmas tree) / feuille brooch. This motif was used in many different ways throughout Belperron's career.*
IMAGE COURTESY OF BELPERRON, LLC., NEW YORK

LEFT: Belperron for Herz-Belperron: Sapin de Noel (Christmas tree) brooch – diamond, platinum *See Harper's Bazaar, January 1939.*
IMAGE COURTESY OF PAT SALING, NEW YORK

BELOW LEFT: Belperron for Boivin: Pyramid cuff, 1929 – diamond, platinum
IMAGE COURTESY OF SYMBOLIC & CHASE, LONDON

BELOW RIGHT: Gouache study for torque necklace, 1935.
The design was executes in red and black lacquer and yellow gold.
IMAGE COURTESY OF BELPERRON LLC., NEW YORK

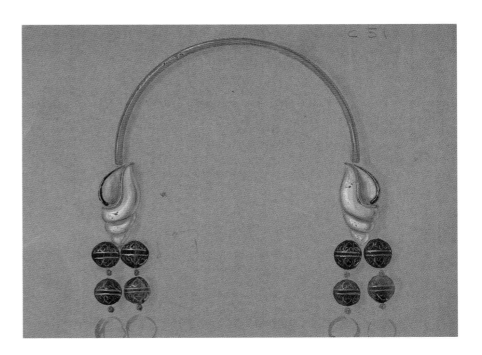

Throughout the 1920s, African art was making its way into the galleries and museums of Paris; the Colonial Exhibition of 1931 further encouraged this trend and the African colonies were well represented. Josephine Baker, although American, was a part of this renewed interest; she was the toast of the town and a celebrated client of Suzanne Belperron. Belperron, inspired by these African forms, used them to develop her own distinctive style creating slim torque-like necklaces and open double and three band cuffs. Metal techniques from the African continent were also used, such as hammered 22ct gold, to shape some of her simple earrings and rings, including her engagement ring. The resulting rich textures on the surface of the gold gave these jewels warmth and an intimate dialogue with the wearer.

Not only could those wealthy enough to afford it visit Africa and British colonial India, in turn, the princely Maharajahs of India came to Europe, bringing with them their extraordinary collections of gemstones. By the early 1930s everything Indian was all the rage. Although Belperron never designed a jewel that was overtly Indian in taste, she did incorporate some of the stylised shapes to be found in Indian art, such as her 'feuille' or the 'boteh'. Other pieces by her adopted India's wealth of colourful greens, blues and reds.

TOP RIGHT: Belperron for B.Herz: Gouache of carved ruby and emerald cabochon, diamond and gold Boteh brooch with nautilus-style earclips; inscribed "S.A. Duchesse of Windsor"
IMAGE COURTESY OF BELPERRON, LLC., NEW YORK

BELOW: Belperron for Herz-Belperron: Demi-Parure (clips and a bracelet), 1940 – sapphire, diamond, platinum, yellow gold
Note how Belperron has ignored the constraints of the outer edge of her jewels. A similar set was owned by Lady Cavendish (Fred Astaire's sister), she was photographed wearing her set in 1945.
PHOTOGRAPH © DAVID BEHL. IMAGE COURTESY OF THE NEIL LANE COLLECTION

Cut and Colour

Unusually for the time, Belperron used cabochon gemstones for their colouring. She was not very interested in the quality of these gemstones, just how their colour played in the light and how they interacted with their neighbouring gemstones. The result was a series of delightful bib necklaces. In April 1939 she took an order from Daisy Fellowes for a pair of 'mosaic ribbon' yellow gold bracelets using a multitude of differently sized oval and circular cabochons at a cost of 329,000 French francs. Rolled polished baroque beads of aquamarine, emerald and pale sapphires strung as long sautoirs were also a part of her repertoire.

Belperron used mixes of cuts from smooth beads and cabochons to the angular faceted cuts to add tension to her designs. Her stylised Fleur clips, for example, used angular lines for the stem. Bunches of grapes were given a similar treatment.

Coloured gemstones, such as kunzite, peridot and sapphires of all cuts and hues, were used in profusion to create colourful vanity cases and cigarette cases, which became all the rage; the Duchess of Windsor owned two famous versions.

As well as her multicoloured variations, Belperron returned repeatedly to certain gemstone/colour combinations: coral with emerald; blonde chalcedony with diamond and/or pearl; white metals, such as platinum, with the cold brilliance of white diamond and rock crystal; cabochon amethysts of varying colours set in yellow gold; pale blue aquamarine with dark blue sapphire; rose quartz with red garnet; ebony with rock crystal; and a blend of blues and greens from blue sapphires and peridot to jade and lapis lazuli.

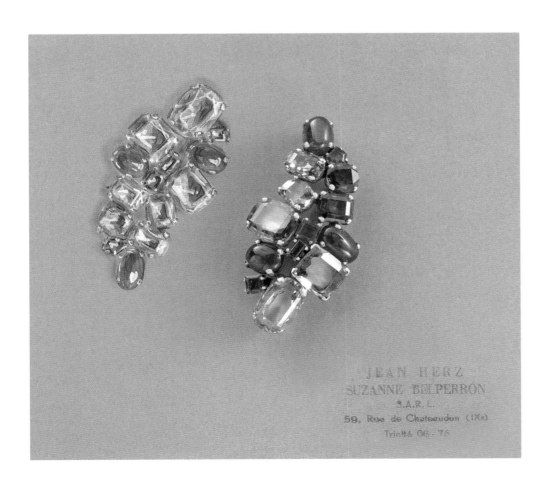

OPPOSITE PAGE: Belperron for B. Herz: Grappe de Raisin (Bunch of Grapes) brooch, 1935 – sapphire, rock crystal, white gold
PHOTOGRAPHY © DAVID BEHL; IMAGE COURTESY OF BELPERRON, NY

TOP RIGHT: Belperron for Herz-Belperron: Pair of Sakura (cherry blossom) brooches, 1936 – cabochon sapphire and vari-cut sapphire of varying colour intensity, yellow gold.
IMAGE COURTESY OF PAT SALING, NEW YORK.

BOTTOM RIGHT: Belperron for Boivin, Grappe de Raisin (Bunch of Grapes) brooch, 1932 – chalcedony, diamond, platinum, white gold
Grapes are a symbol of fertility and a similar brooch was commissioned by Suzanne Belperron's brother-in-law as a present to his wife upon becoming a mother.
IMAGE COURTESY OF THE FD GALLERY, NEW YORK

LEFT: Belperron for Jean Herz-Suzanne Belperron – Gouache and multi-gem brooch, 1950s – topaz, sapphire, cabochon ruby, emerald, yellow gold
PHOTOGRAPHY © DAVID BEHL; IMAGE COURTESY OF BELPERRON, LLC., NEW YORK

Quartz

Belperron started to work with lapidary Adrien Louart during her time at Boivin. By the time she joined the Maison Bernard Herz, Louart was recognised by all in the jewellery trade for his extraordinary carving talents. He carved rock crystal, smoky quartz, amethyst and chalcedony in its blues, browns and beige tones at the behest of Belperron, following her exacting instructions to the letter. The result was a series of iconic rings, their design very much part of the Belperron DNA. Arguably the most famous Belperron parure came from his atelier – the blue chalcedony parure, decorated sparingly with touches of blue sapphire and white diamond, for the Duchess of Windsor in 1935. The original clasp of two inverted 'feuille' clips was later replaced with the famous flowerhead clasp. The clips were transformed into earrings, which when worn do not follow the usual protocol of being mirror-images, as they are identical and no allowance had been made for left and right.

Of her iconic rings, the bibendum, 'nuage' (cloud), 'toit' (roof), 'clou' (screw), 'tourbillon' (swirl) and 'cerf volant' (kite) are some of her best known designs. Fluted, ribbed, double- and triple-bodied are other forms that were carved in quartz. Quartz, either in its crypto-crystalline form, as chalcedony or in its macro-crystalline form as quartz, gave the artist huge versatility. Lighter than gold, it could be carved into just about any form and Belperron saw its potential for large voluminous pieces of jewellery. It had the added advantage of being less expensive than noble metals, such as gold and platinum, and after the Wall Street crash of 1929, it became popular with many of the jewellery houses. Belperron started using quartz and developing her highly original forms at Boivin and on leaving to join Bernard Herz she continued to create her fascinating jewels. However, for many of the quartz-based jewels this now makes it difficult to be certain which jewellery house produced the piece for those few years during which her designs overlapped at Boivin and at Bernard Herz.

ABOVE: Casque (dome) ring, early 1930s – rock crystal, natural pearl IMAGE COURTESY OF THE FD GALLERY, NEW YORK

BELOW: Nuage (cloud) ring, 1933 – white agate, triangular-cut diamond, platinum
(Formerly the property of Suzanne Belperron.)
IMAGE COURTESY OF THE FD GALLERY, NEW YORK

TOP RIGHT: Tourbillon (swirl) ring, top and side views, 1933 – diamond, platinum
IMAGE COURTESY OF SYMBOLIC & CHASE, LONDON

BOTTOM RIGHT: Bibendum (Fluted) ring 1933 – smoky quartz, cabochon sapphire, platinum IMAGE COURTESY OF L. COURTEILLE CREATIONS, PARIS

OPPOSITE PAGE: Blue chalcedony demi-parure, 1935 – blue chalcedony, cabochon sapphire, diamond, platinum
Sold to The Duke and Duchess of Windsor. The petals of the clasp are articulated.
IMAGE COURTESY OF SIEGELSON, NEW YORK

Belperron for B. Herz: Grappe de Raisin cluster clip/brooch – natural pearls, white agate, yellow gold PHOTOGRAPH ©DAVID BEHL; IMAGE COURTESY OF NEWCAL GALLERIES

Belperron for B. Herz: Spire (scroll/spiral) earclips – diamond, platinum, white gold
IMAGE COURTESY OF BELPERRON, LLC., NEW YORK

ABOVE: Yin and Yang ring, 1923 – old mine diamond, hammered gold
This was Belperron's design for her own engagement ring in 1923.
IMAGE COURTESY OF PAT SALING, NEW YORK

OPPOSITE PAGE: Butterfly brooch, 1932-55 – pavé set cabochon ruby, yellow gold
Based on the original design by Suzanne Belperron for B.Herz.
PHOTOGRAPH © DAVID BEHL. IMAGE COURTESY OF BELPERRON, LLC/LANDRIGAN

The Belperron DNA

Certain forms and shapes appear regularly in Belperron's work, helping to define her style in design: snail or scrolls and her 'feuille' (leaf) motifs appeared very early on in her work as a student and they were to accompany her throughout her long career. An elongated fluted 'S' form was another shape that appeared over and over again, in many cases to underline the leaf motif, or used as a repeat to create gentle undulating organic shapes. Her simple barrel brooches and clips are an interesting consequence of this.

Nature was a constant companion. Flowers were a continued source of inspiration and yet Belperron always found her own interpretation, whether it be camellias, pansies, artichokes or pimento stalks. Butterflies, both angular and more naturally curved, were also favourites in her menagerie.

Legacy

Belperron's designs are as contemporary today as they were all those years ago, when she conjured them up in the 1920s and '30s. Some of her designs now seem so familiar, so ordinary, that they have entered into the global design encyclopedia of our minds. We have forgotten where they came from; in fact, we take them for granted, yet Belperron developed them years ago. Her Yin and Yang ring is one such example. Originally designed as her own engagement ring in 1923, it made the cover of Vogue in 1970, and it is still being used today.

Suzanne Belperron's contribution to 20th-century design has finally been acknowledged and it is only fitting that after years in the shadows, she has finally found her rightful place in the eyes of the arts and design world.

"With this audacious jeweller we are enthralled by heavy gold snakes moving with articulated scales, the digitalis with its visibly purple petals, diamond orchids wearily on the lookout for flies, the starfish covered in hundreds of stars, the brilliant stylised corolla. Jewellery which owes more to sculpture and to stories..." Jacques Audiberti (Exposition de 1946)

JULIETTE MOUTARD
Boivin's Artist

Despite being one of the great jewellery designers of the 20th century, Juliette Moutard remains in the shadows, known only to those who have a passion for jewellery. Having graduated first from the École des Arts Décoratifs in Paris and then the École de la Bijouterie de la rue du Louvre, Paris, she came to Boivin in 1933 after a stint working with the horologist Verger Frères. Naturally discreet, Moutard was a designer in the old sense, happy to consider herself part of a team, no more or less significant than her colleagues. She never felt the need to break out on her own, working as she did for nearly forty years under the umbrella of René Boivin, at first under Jeanne Boivin and then under Louis Girard.

Moutard worked well with Jeanne Boivin; they worked in tandem, Jeanne Boivin overseeing the fabrication of Moutard's designs up until her retirement in 1954. Moutard, an accomplished draughtswoman, sketched her ideas and those of Mme Boivin into a notebook before painting a final rendition in colour. Moutard rarely designed jewels for stock, concentrating on private commissions.

In the Footsteps of Belperron
When Moutard first started at Boivin, designs originally created by Suzanne Belperron were still being used. Conscious of staying true to the house style, she naturally studied what had gone before. Under Mme Boivin's guidance, Moutard used many designs from Belperron's time, making them her own by interpreting them differently, embellishing them with her own flair. For example, the Cambodian bracelet, first created in 1930 by Belperron in silver gilt for Lady Duff-Cooper, became more elaborate under Juliette Moutard. Moutard's Turban rings from 1934 are a modification of an earlier model called Tibia, and like other models this was repeated at Boivin through the years.

Crescent brooches were very popular in the 18th and 19th centuries; both Belperron and Moutard used their imagination to create their own interpretations of a familiar shape. Boivin's famous crescent brooches first appeared in 1934, taking their inspiration perhaps from the triple creole ear pendants which were already a part of the Boivin collection in 1925 and thus designed by Suzanne Belperron. Moutard continued producing these designs until the '50s. Unlike the crescent brooches of the 19th century, these brooches were worn 'upside down'.

LEFT: Moutard for Boivin: Gold leaf brooch – diamond, yellow gold
A reinterpreted design – based on an original design by Suzanne Belperron.
IMAGE COURTESY OF SYMBOLIC & CHASE, LONDON

OPPOSITE PAGE: Moutard for Boivin: Pineapple brooch, 1940 – ruby, peridot, diamond, platinum, yellow gold
Dimensions: 6.7 x 5.75cm
IMAGE COURTESY OF PAT SALING, NEW YORK

ABOVE: Moutard for Boivin: Bucrane (Longhorn) brooch, 1940 – purple sapphire, demantoid garnet, cabochon emerald, yellow diamond, diamond, yellow gold
Commissioned in 1938.
IMAGE COURTESY OF CHRISTIE'S INC.

OPPOSITE PAGE: Moutard for Boivin: Hippocamp brooch, 1939 – calibré-cut emerald, calibré-cut ruby, natural grey pearl (100 grains), yellow gold, platinum
Probably inspired by the Fontaine des Quatre Parties du Monde in the Jardins du Luxembourg, Paris, the brooch was commissioned by Millicent Rogers at the same time as the starfish.
IMAGE COURTESY OF LUCAS RARITIES, LONDON

Striking her own Pose

One of her earliest designs, and a huge success, was the Torque bracelet. Moving away from the fashion at the time of wearing two or three flat ribbon bracelets together, she created a large voluminous bangle set with gemstones and pearls in a multitude of different styles.

Moutard's imagination did not stop at the conventions of jewellery; she created her own path with the blessing of Jeanne Boivin, taking her inspiration from many different places. In 1939, Moutard designed a jewel from a drawing of a cow's skull. Her Bucrane (Longhorn) brooch is covered in diamonds with its horns entwined in a blue sapphire ribbon and garlands of flowers.

Her famous Hippocamp, composed of a horse's head and forequarters with a mermaid-like tail, is a symbol in Homer's poems of Poseidon, whose chariot was made of shell as is suggested in this jewel. Moutard may also have taken her inspiration from the fountain of the 'Quatre Parties du Monde' (the four corners of the world), in the Jardins du Luxembourg in Paris. The finished jewel was bought by Standard Oil heiress Millicent Rogers.

Garden of Flowers

Moutard used nature to create her own interpretations. Moutard's great interest in botany was a passion shared with Jeanne Boivin; she excelled in designs for gem-set flowers. Moutard's Queen Anne's Lace, Digitalis and Bouquet of Violets brooches are iconic.

Boivin's large 'Feuille' (leaf) brooch showed both Moutard's mastery of design as well as the extraordinary technical prowess of the Boivin workshops. The brooch was over 6cm long and had a flexiblitiy that meant it moved as the wearer moved, catching the light.

One of her most unusual floral creations must be her ear ornaments, which featured in *Vogue* in September 1934. Did their inspiration come from Indian jewellery? Possibly.

TOP LEFT: Moutard for Boivin: Queen Anne's Lace brooch – diamond, ruby, platinum
Mounted 'en tremblant'. According to Marie-Caroline de Brosses, Juliette Moutard designed this brooch in 1938 with only diamonds, the addition of the ruby was proposed by Jacques Bernard much later.
IMAGE COURTESY OF CHRISTIE'S INC.

BOTTOM LEFT: Moutard for Boivin: Ear ornaments, 1934 – diamond, yellow gold
Indian influence. See Vogue, 1 September 1934 for model wearing ear ornaments.
IMAGE COURTESY OF FD GALLERY, NEW YORK

ABOVE: Moutard for Boivin: Feuille (leaf) brooch, 1937 – cabochon ruby, cabochon emerald, diamond, platinum, yellow gold
The brooch has been made so that it is flexible. Dimensions: 6.3 x 6.5cm.
IMAGE COURTESY OF SYMBOLIC & CHASE, LONDON

OPPOSITE PAGE: Moutard for Boivin: Orchid brooch – citrine, yellow diamond, diamond, platinum, yellow gold
The bombé-shaped pistel is articulated.
IMAGE COURTESY OF CHRISTIE'S INC.

Birds and the Animal World

Moutard populated her jewelled garden with a menagerie of birds and animals. Her famous Pigeon's Wing brooch, set with diamonds and cabochon blue sapphires, was made for Daisy Fellowes in 1938; it was huge, certainly one of the most impressive jewels that Moutard designed. The blue sapphire Dove of Peace, designed in 1939, used cabochon and circular-cut blue sapphires. It had been ordered by the same client who ordered the 'Bucrane' clip in 1939 and it originally held a small diamond heart surrounded by an emerald olive branch. Unfortunately, because of the outbreak of WWII, the client never came to collect it and it was sold to a different customer in 1945 without the heart.

The Cockerel brooch is extraordinary for its large size. It was designed in 1945 to celebrate French liberation at the end of the Second World War. The crowing cockerel's tail feathers are decorated with ruby and sapphire calibre-cut gemstones, which together with the pearl body represent the patriotic red, white and blue of the French flag; the cockerel was the emblem of French resistance during Nazi occupation.

After the Second World War, jewellery saw a craze for panthers and tigers dressed in their diamond regalia at Cartier. Moutard introduced her own version of animal brooches at Boivin; she had a limitless supply of unusual, witty candidates: horses, elephants and sheep. Some could be worn on the shoulder such as a labrador or a lion's reclining form, its mane decorated with calibré-cut emeralds.

TOP RIGHT: Moutard for Boivin: Lion Shoulder brooch, 1960s – emerald, fancy colour diamonds, brown diamond, diamond, yellow gold
Articulated. Dimensions: 6.9cm
IMAGE COURTESY OF CHRISTIE'S INC.

RIGHT: Moutard for Boivin: Dove of Peace brooch, 1939 – varying shades of sapphire, diamond, yellow gold
In the original design, the dove carried a diamond-set heart surrounded by an olive branch in its beak. It was commissioned by the same client who had commissioned the famous Bucrane (Longhorn) brooch in 1938.
IMAGE COURTESY OF DAVID MORRIS, HISTORICAL DESIGN GALLERY, NEW YORK

OPPOSITE PAGE: Moutard for Boivin: Coq (Cockerel) brooch, 1944 – calibré-cut sapphire, calibré-cut ruby, natural baroque blister pearl (240 grains), diamond, platinum, yellow gold
Created to celebrate the liberation of France, the cockerel is patriotically dressed in the 'bleu blanc rouge' of the national flag.
IMAGE COURTESY OF LUCAS RARITIES, LONDON

Oceans Deep

Moutard found a wealth of ideas in the sea, from her extraordinary renditions of the starfish,
in its many moods and colours, to fish and dolphins with strong characters. Ammonite forms
were transformed into earrings as were shells, which were worn not only as ear pendants but
also tracing the long outline of the ear. Her first seaweed brooch was designed in 1962.

According to Françoise Cailles, the starfish was Moutard's favourite design, first produced for
Claudette Colbert in 1936 from a design completed in 1935. All her starfish are notable for
their use of brightly coloured gemstones. The ruby and amethyst starfish, the first of five
versions made by Boivin, was created in 1938 and purchased by socialite Millicent Rogers in
1939. Interestingly, this was the only starfish not to have articulated arms and it is also set with
baguette-cut and brilliant-cut amethysts. Two other starfish from this series were also made at
the Charles Profillet workshop, one in 1940 and the fifth, which came to life in the 1960s.
Each starfish has subtle differences and according to Moutard's successor, Marie-Caroline de
Brosses, Boivin's early starfish can be distinguished from their more contemporary versions by
the lack of gold visible between the settings.

Moutard took the maritime theme to the next level, creating pieces inspired not by the fish itself, but by its scales. The Profillet workshop in Paris used a setting that imitated the undulating shapes of fish scales to create gem-set links that easily transformed into a plethora of flexible bracelets and necklaces. Moutard's first Fish Scale necklace appeared in 1936 and remained a central theme throughout the 20th century.

The fish scale jewels produced one of the most emblematic of Boivin's rings: the Quatre corps (Four bodies). Marie-Caroline de Brosses, the last great Boivin jewellery designer, recalls a conversation she had with Louis Girard:

> "The inspiration came from a 'fish scale' bracelet which became flat when laid out. A client, whose husband had given her such a bracelet, brought it in because it was too long and it kept falling over her hand. She brought it back to Boivin to see if she could get it shortened. The workshop cut away four lines of gemstones and created a shorter version. Juliette Moutard didn't know what to do with the small piece which remained from the bracelet and not really knowing what to do with it, placed it on the side of large rose quartz ashtray on her desk. The piece of bracelet was set with blue sapphires, Moutard found the blue and pink of the quartz very attractive together. The gold and sapphire remains were stuck to the side of the ashtray, where it stayed for many years. One day the piece fell away from the ashtray, Moutard picked it up and started to nonchalantly play with it, she placed it on her finger and finding it attractive asked the workshop to create a back to it so that it would hold on the finger. At the time the workshop was very specialised in articulated and flexible mechanisms. They found the idea of an articulated ring interesting and created four bodies within, so that the movement was kept in the structure of the ring and hence the first 'Quatre Corps' in 1950."

The ring has since been made using diamonds, rubies, sapphires and just about every combination you can think of.

Passementerie

Passementerie was another theme which caught Moutard's imagination. There are countless examples of folded and pleated textiles, tied cords being transformed into gold gem-set bows, loops and cascades of flowing tassels. The gold and diamond necklace designed in 1945 is one such example.

Moutard also spent much of her time in Paris's museums, from the Louvre to the Musée Guimet seeking inspiration; it was here that she 'travelled' and sparked her imagination. The results of this inspiration can be seen in her Pampilles ring, created in 1956, her famous eight-strand pearl bracelet with pearl tassel, 'Hindu' bracelet in 1950 and her iconic tassel rings from 1956.

Juliette Moutard retired in 1970, leaving behind her an extrordinary body of work having made an immense contribution to the House of Boivin and to 20th-century jewellery design.

ABOVE: Moutard for Boivin: Passementerie ring, 1950 –
diamond, yellow gold
The ring is articulated.
IMAGE COURTESY OF SYMBOLIC & CHASE, LONDON

RIGHT: Moutard for Boivin: Noeud de Passementerie earclips,
1945 – sapphire, diamond, yellow gold
IMAGE COURTESY OF CHRISTIE'S INC.

BELOW: Moutard for Boivin: Indian Passementerie bracelet,
1955 – sapphire, blue chalcedony, diamond, yellow gold
IMAGE COURTESY OF SYMBOLIC & CHASE, LONDON

OPPOSITE PAGE: Moutard for Boivin: Passementerie necklace,
1945 – diamond, yellow gold
IMAGE COURTESY OF VERONIQUE BAMPS GALLERY, MONTE CARLO

"The people at Mademoiselle and Charm and Bazaar…had made finding 'the best in New York' their life's work. Some choices were obvious; others were not. I had thought, for instance, that if you wanted a pair of gold earrings, you should go to Tiffany's. Not at all. You went to a little place called Olga Tritt." Mary Cantwell, *Manhattan When I was Young*, 1995

OLGA TRITT
New York Chic

Olga Tritt was well known in New York social circles before and after the Second World War. She and her siblings – Reuben, George, Harold and Pauline – had emigrated to America from Russia before the First World War and well before the Russian Revolution. In Russia she had trained as a watchmaker, having started her seven-year apprenticeship at the tender age of eleven. After her arrival in New York, she set up shop in 1910, selling jewellery and watches. When jewellery sales were down after WWI, in order to make ends meet, she advertised in the back of *Vogue*, detailing her skills as a dressmaker; with time, she started to include announcements that she would buy antique and second-hand jewellery.

In time, she became the accepted go-to address for many of New York's society. She exhibited at the Chicago Arts Club in 1929 and 1930, and at the World's Fair in New York, in 1939, where she included a collection of jewels commissioned by the Brazilian government to show off the gemstones from their mines. She had become the quintessential American jeweller. Her jewels graced the pages of many *Vogue* issues during the 1930s, photographed by Horst P. Horst and later John Rawlings, and from 1937-1945, her pieces made the cover of *Vogue* several times.

Travel
Tritt led an adventurous life. She travelled the world, including South America, India and Russia, to find the big gemstones that became so synonymous with her name.

Though very few of Tritt's pieces have survived, the fashion pages of *Vogue* give us a great insight in to her design style.

Precious Jewels…
Ruby and diamond flower studded gold bracelet $400*, Matching gold ring $135*
(*20% Federal excise tax included)
Booklet on request

Olga TRITT
589 MADISON AVENUE
at 57th STREET
NEW YORK 22, N.Y

LEFT: Advertisement from the *New Yorker*

OPPOSITE PAGE: Aquamarine and diamond necklace – aquamarine, diamond, platinum
Commissioned by the Brazilian Government and believed to have been exhibited at the World's Fair New York in 1939 in the Brazilian Pavilion. It can be transformed to create two bracelets.
IMAGE COURTESY OF WARTSKI, LONDON.

"Olga Tritt, in the Heckscher Building makes the very, very, good variety. Many of her things use precious stones in a barbaric fashion. She has an antique Russian collar made of flawed emeralds and irregularly cut diamonds, tinkling with rough emerald drops. This is fantastic and perfectly beautiful. Another necklace has triple strands of emeralds, pearls, and onyx held by a medal of rough irregular diamonds. A Babylonian necklace is made of round robin's egg blue disks strung together. A long necklace is made of crystals carved in the shapes of elephants, Buddhas, fishes and every animal imaginable."

US Vogue, 10 November, 1930

Her preference was for the relatively new step-cut and her designs show a distinct geometry, amassing gemstones 'brick-style' for greater effect, such as in her Art Deco aquamarine and diamond platinum necklace. Her Indian Mughal-inspired necklace in the July issue of *Vogue* in 1937 is another excellent example.

An astute business woman and an expert at self-promotion, Tritt was often on radio and was obviously a well-known personality in her day; her name often appeared in the newspapers among the celebrities who were on passenger lists for liners crossing between Europe and the United States. During the 1930s, she opened a second shop in Palm Beach, opposite the prestigious Everglades Club. On her death at 81, her husband, amateur musician Mark Skalmer and daughter, Alva Davidson, took over the running of the shop, which continued as a viable enterprise until the end of the 20th century.

RIGHT: Demi-parure (cluster brooch and earclips), 1965 – sapphire beads, diamond, platinum
IMAGE COURTESY OF SOTHEBY'S INC.

OPPOSITE PAGE: Model wearing Olga Tritt jewels: large sapphire and citrine brooch as a head ornament; a multi-strand sapphire bead and diamond clasp bracelet and a Hindu-style sapphire and gold bracelet on her wrist. On her hand she wears a ring set with morganite and silver.
HORST P. HORST/VOGUE, SEPTEMBER 15, 1939 © CONDÉ NAST

"While Treskow's early work (1928-1950) interprets the ancient style, her later designs (1960-1980) incorporate granulation in a more abstract and streamlined way, reflecting the popular modern taste." Elise B. Misiorowsk, *JCK*, 1995

ELISABETH TRESKOW
Ancient Inspiration

Elisabeth Treskow (1898-1992) is one of Europe's best kept secrets. Her work is seen by many thousands, yet few people know who she is. Each year, in Germany the Bundesliga (Football League) is watched by huge television audiences and packed football stadiums, but as the winners raise the trophy for all to see, few realise that they are looking at Treskow's craftsmanship. In 1949, she and her students at the Kölner Werkschule were commissioned by the German Football Association to make the winners' trophy. Originally 50cm in diameter, in 1981 a 9cm ring was added around the edge by artist goldsmith Adolf Kunesch to allow more space for the winners' names to be engraved.

Influenced by the Bauhaus movement, Treskow instilled its pragmatic beauty in her creations, marrying this with her love of all things ancient to create jewels that nodded to the past but were very much of their own time. Throughout the 1920s, she studied the ancient and almost forgotten technique of granulation, patiently learning how to use the tiny grains of gold and how to keep them in place without using solder. Etruscans probably used a fusion method involving fish or cow glue with a copper carbonate, such as malachite. To create the tiny gold granules they may have used an iron file, the gold filings were then gathered and placed in powdered charcoal; it is a technique that Treskow was to recreate and master nearly three millennia later.

BELOW: Pendant, 1925 – zircon, yellow gold
IMAGE COURTESY OF THE RHEINISCHES BILDARCHIV, KÖLN

"H.A.P. Littledale in London, Hans Michael Wilm in Munich and Elisabeth Treskow in Essen synchronistically arrived at the same practical method of achieving this type of granulation, based on a theory proposed by Dr. Hans Joachim Wagner in 1913." Elise B. Misiorowski, *JCK*, 1995

Background
Based in Germany, Treskow's career spanned most of the 20th century including both World Wars. She trained at the Hochschule für Gestaltung (Higher Technical College for Precious Metals) in the town of Schwäbisch-Gmünd for two years in 1916 and 1917 before moving to Munich where she was apprenticed to the great goldsmith Karl Rothmüller, completing her final exams in 1918. She recounts how difficult these times were for her:

"I almost stopped three times, the skills were so difficult for me, inaccessible."
Rüdiger Joppien, *Portal Rheinische Geschichte*

OPPOSITE PAGE: The Bundesliga Shield – silver, yellow gold
The German football championship trophy is affectionately named 'The Salad Bowl'.
IMAGE COURTESY OF THE RHEINISCHES BILDARCHIV, KÖLN

ABOVE: Mussel Brooch with gold granulation, 1967 – cabochon orange sapphire, gold granulation, gold
(Provenance: Museum für Angewandte Kunst Köln / Museum of Applied Arts Cologne.)
IMAGE COURTESY OF RHEINISCHES BILDARCHIV, KÖLN

OPPOSITE PAGE: Fringe necklace, 1955 – cabochon ruby, cabochon sapphire, pearl, white gold
Treskow created this piece whilst she was a teacher at the School of Applied Arts in Cologne.
IMAGE COURTESY OF THE TADEMA GALLERY, LONDON

It was only when she started her apprenticeship that she started to enjoy her work with the discovery of how to use gemstones in her creations. With her apprenticeship certificate in hand, 1919 saw Treskow set up her own independent workshop in Bochum, in her parents' home. She reflected on those four years in Bochum and how difficult it had been: "distress and poverty were my teachers".

Moving to facilities in Margarethenhöhe, the new artist zone in Essen, gave her the opportunity to mix with other artists and creative people who were expressing themselves in different ways, among them the enameller Kurt Levy. In 1924, Treskow was awarded her master craftsman's title by the Chamber of Crafts in Düsseldorf.

During the 1920s her jewels were influenced by simple lines and shapes set with gemstones both ancient and new. On a trip to Paris, Treskow visited the Musée Cluny and was struck by the jewellery she saw there. It proved a turning point for her work and on her return to Germany, she started to research jewellery from earlier periods.

With hyperinflation in Germany in 1922-23 and then the global economic downturn after 1929, Treskow survived with orders from both the Church and the Essen municipality. Moving away from the expense of gemstones, she concentrated on granulation, first using it to decorate her jewels in 1928, including a pair of rings depicting Apollo and a Minoan bull, as well as a bracelet with the signs of the zodiac. Her jewels were simple, using the granulation as a means to create form and shadow to depict scenes from ancient Greek, Roman and Etruscan mythology as well as taking inspiration from flora and fauna. Hunting scenes were another favourite. She collected ancient jewels, often turning to them for inspiration for her own work.

Second World War

The war years were a struggle and after the bombing and destruction of her workshop in Essen she went to live with her parents in Dortmund and made ends meet by embarking on restoration work for the Prince Lippe-Detmold. At the end of the WWII, she was appointed the director of metalwork (silver and gold) at the Werkschulen in Cologne (Cologne School of Applied Art) in 1948. She stayed until her retirement in 1964.

During her time at the Werkschulen, she not only crafted the 'Salad bowl' but also took on the restoration of the Epiphany Shrine (also known as the 'Shrine of the Three Kings') with her students in 1954. The impressive medieval shrine was created between 1180 and 1225. Through its restoration, Treskow became reacquainted with the beauty of gemstones and especially those from medieval times and earlier. She started her own collection and began to reintroduce them to her own work. The jewellery that she crafted during her tenure at the college was made specifically for her clients, many of whom she knew personally and came from the influential families in the region; one particular commission in 1954 was to create the chain of office for the Mayor of Cologne.

Legacy

She took part in many exhibitions of which some had a huge influence on the direction of jewellery design. Amongst the most important were the International Exhibition of Modern Jewellery 1890-1961, Goldsmiths' Hall, London, 1961; 'Gold' exhibition at the Metropolitan Museum, New York in 1973; and the 'Retrospective – A Goldsmith's Art of the 20th Century', Museum of Applied Art, Cologne, 1990.

She produced pieces decorated with her own researched granulation technique, which led to accolades, including first prize from the German Society for Goldsmiths' Art in Berlin in 1933, 1935 and 1936. In 1936, she prevailed at the Triennale in Milan and at the World Exhibition in Paris in 1937, winning on both occasions a gold medal. In 1938, she became the first of just a handful of women jewellers to be awarded the 'Ring of Honour' by the German Society for Goldsmiths' Art, a great distinction and recognition from her fellow goldsmiths. She was awarded the Bavarian State Prize in 1963 before being awarded the Order of Merit at the time of her retirement.

In 1977 she left the bulk of her drawings and ancient jewellery and cameo collection to the Museum of Applied Arts in Cologne. She was a role model to many young women who were to follow in her footsteps, breaking into the male-dominated world of the goldsmith.

LEFT: Pendant, 1978 – chrysoberyl cat's eye, carved emerald, demantoid garnet, cabochon amethyst, cabochon sapphire, diamond, yellow gold IMAGE COURTESY OF THE RHEINISCHES BILDARCHIV, KÖLN

OPPOSITE PAGE: The Lord Mayor's Chain of Office, 1954-55 – antique gold, silver and bronze coins; bronze, silver, niello, gold granulation, garnet, enamel IMAGE COURTESY OF THE RHEINISCHES BILDARCHIV, KÖLN

MARGARET DE PATTA
Bauhaus Optical Illusionist

Margaret de Patta (1903-1964) was trained as an artist in San Francisco and then at the Art Students' League in New York, similar to Marie Zimmermann before her. So the story goes, de Patta turned to jewellery making in 1929 when she was unable find a wedding ring that she liked for herself. She taught herself from books, as well as visits to museums to study their collections of ancient and ethnic jewellery.

De Patta attended a summer course at the Mills College in Oakland, California in 1940, before going on to study for two terms at the Institute of Design in Chicago, under the directorship of László Moholy-Nagy. Hungarian-born Moholy-Nagy, who had been a Bauhaus leading light, brought with him an intellectual approach using practical techniques, skills and experimentation as well as the idea that artisan work was on the same level as fine art.

By the time that de Patta met Moholy-Nagy, she was already making interesting jewellery. She had exhibited at the International Golden Gate Exhibition in 1939 and she was experimenting with light, observing the effects of light at different levels within a gemstone and also on its external features. She explored photography and photograms and how they could work in jewellery, something she returned to often in her work. De Patta translated this study of opacity and transparency to gemstones, utilising the level of translucency in gemstones and their inclusions, and carefully studying their optical properties to create interesting jewellery using Bauhaus and constructivism principles. She also played with the distorted view of metal viewed through the gemstone, depending on the cut and the number of facets on her stones. Her collaboration with lapidary Francis Sperisen was essential for her designs; she would carve a template in wood or acrylic and then he would shape the stone to her design.

De Patta's jewels allowed the wearer to participate. None of her jewels dictated how they were to be worn, they used negative space and outlines with coloured gemstones that could be inverted to create something new depending on what the wearer decided. Pebbles from a river were transformed into beautiful studies of matt, opaque and shiny textures; later, she started to use diamonds and gold to highlight some of her work.

De Patta lived most of her life in San Francisco and was a founding member of the San Francisco Metal Arts Guild; she also taught at the California Labor School. She and her second husband, Eugene Bielawski were blacklisted in 1947 during the McCarthy era, which put an end to her teaching. She then tried her hand at limited editions in silver, with her husband, under the label 'Designs Contemporary'. Unfortunately, this was not the huge success that was anticipated and trading ceased in 1957. De Patta did continue on her own making highly individual pieces for special commissions.

De Patta's work stands alone for its principled adherence to the Bauhaus ideals on modern structural design and for her work on the visual appearance of her gemstones, developing new cuts – which she called 'opti-cuts' – in the process. On her death, many of her jewels were bequeathed to the Oakland Museum, California.

ABOVE: Studio ring 1950 – silver, oxidised silver
PHOTOGRAPH © 2009 BONHAMS & BUTTERFIELDS AUCTIONEERS CORP. ALL RIGHTS RESERVED.

OPPOSITE PAGE: Brooch, 1950 – quartz, silver, oxidised silver
(Provenance: The Daphne Farago collection.)
PHOTOGRAPH © MUSEUM OF FINE ARTS BOSTON

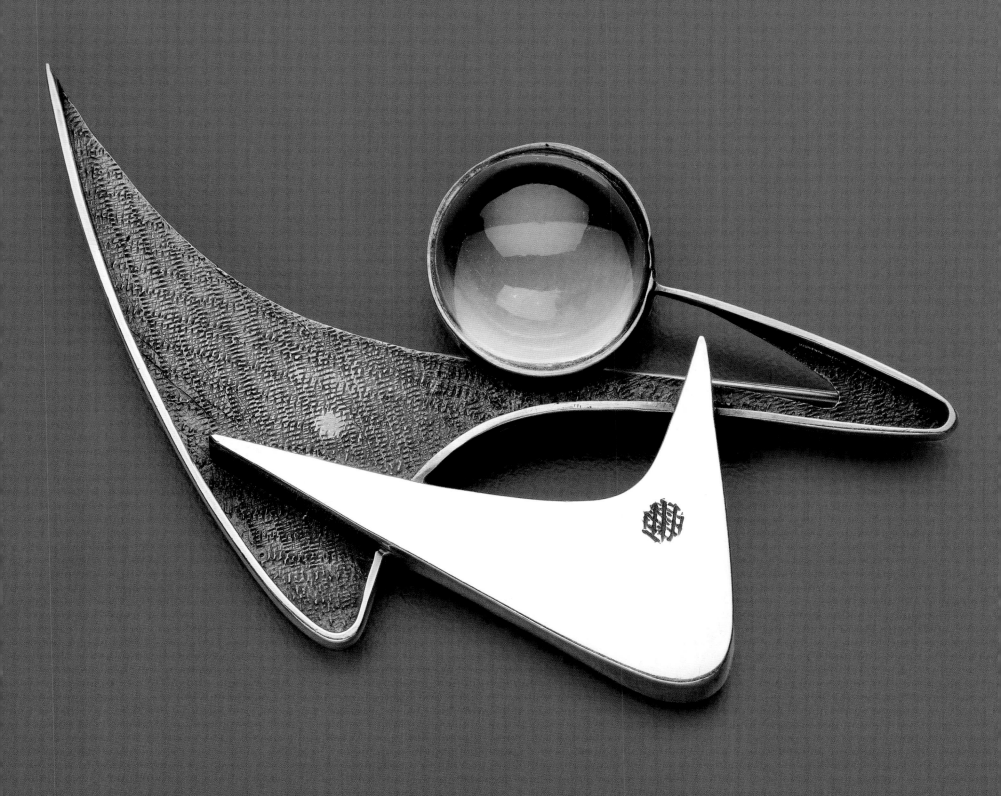

"She revolutionized luxury jewellery by rejuvenating and modernizing it, much in the manner of a great painter...she totally transformed jewellery by integrating it into contemporary fashion. She made the connection between jewellery, fashion and style... She devised a wholly revolutionary style...very personal, very particular, very Cartier."

Hubert de Givenchy

JEANNE TOUSSAINT
'La Panthère'

Arbiter of good taste, and guardian of Cartier's style for nearly forty years, Jeanne Toussaint (1887-1976) was no ordinary person. Jeanne Toussaint's life spanned most of the 20th century, she knew many of the icons of that century and counted them as friends from Jean Cocteau, Cecil Beaton, Misia Sert and according to the interviews conducted by Gilberte Gaultier for her book 'Cartier – The Legend', she was very close to Coco Chanel. Marlene Dietrich, Marilyn Monroe, Elizabeth Taylor and Grace Kelly were just a few of the 'greats' to have crossed Jeanne Toussaint's path.

No one seems to know exactly when Jeanne Toussaint started working with Cartier; most concur that it was shortly after the end of the First World War. However, Michel Aliaga, international deputy director of archives at Cartier, says that a letter has recently come to light written by a business associate, to Louis Cartier which states 'please pass on my regards to Mademoiselle Jeanne Toussaint'; the letter was dated 1916. Aliaga concludes, therefore, that:

> *"when you see this letter, you understand that Jeanne Toussaint must have already been part of the jewellery house, as by convention you would not have been permitted to write about private matters in a professional letter."*

Records also show that Jeanne Toussaint had been a customer of Cartier, since 1915.

She brought with her a new wave of ideas when she joined Cartier, first designing evening bags and then heading up the new 'S' department (S for 'soir') in 1924, which was to be Cartier's first venture into more affordable articles. With the support and encouragement of her mentor Louis Cartier, she joined the committee that presided over the choice of new designs to be created. As a member of the committee Toussaint was involved in the decision

LEFT: Cartier, Paris: Evening bag – onyx, enamel, diamond, platinum, black satin, black cord
IMAGE COURTESY OF CARTIER

OPPOSITE PAGE: Cartier, Paris: Suite of Gold bead cluster and tubogaz (gas pipe) jewellery, 1937 – sugar-loaf square-cut lapis lazuli, square upside-down step-cut diamond, diamond, yellow gold
Jeanne Toussaint made yellow gold and jewellery parures popular again; experimentation was in vogue. This suite consists of a bracelet, a brooch, a pair of ear clips, and a ring. The clusters of beads are attached to a base by a series of rings that allows them to move when worn.
(Provenance: 'Brilliant: Cartier in the 20th Century', Denver Art Museum, Denver, 2014)
IMAGE COURTESY OF SEIGELSON, NEW YORK

making for many jewels, well before her nomination as head of jewellery creation. In 1933, Louis Cartier chose Jeanne Toussaint over his most celebrated designer, Charles Jacqueau for the role of Creative director for Cartier haute joaillerie; Cartier's decision is recorded in a letter to his son-in-law, René Revillon (see Appendix II for translation).

Her Early Years

Her instinct was definite and her decisions were made with assurance, perhaps due to her difficult childhood, which had meant that she had had to make her own way in the world. Born in Belgium, in the town of Charleroi, to artisans in the lace-making business, Toussaint left home at a young age. She joined her sister, who had herself fled the Flanders home for Paris some years earlier, and proceeded to mix with the demi-monde and aristocracy who frequented Maxim's before the First World War, and where she eventually met Louis Cartier.

She and Louis built up a lifelong friendship, which was to produce some of Cartier's most important and sumptuous jewels. Louis Cartier had wanted to marry Toussaint, but at an ill-fated meeting with his family – 'the family council' – he was persuaded to marry someone 'more suitable'; and in January 1924, he married the Hungarian aristocrat, Jacqueline Almassy. Cartier's relationship with Jeanne continued until his death in New York, in 1942. They communicated constantly, writing about ideas, designs and about the running of Cartier. Toussaint eventually went on to marry Baron Hély d'Oissel in 1956, at the age of 68.

Toussaint had started out by creating accessories – tapestry handbags, perhaps influenced by her upbringing with lacemakers. Her instinct for proportion and design caught Louis Cartier's eye and it was he who honed her skills and taught her everything he knew about his world and the art world around them. She also had an extraordinary talent as a colourist, which led Christian Bérard to seek Toussaint's approval for his theatre sets.

A New Direction

Toussaint helped steer Cartier away from the Art Deco years to a period of figurative and floral designs, attracting the new independently minded and hugely wealthy women of café society. Heavy diamond jewellery of the pre-First World War era was transformed into flexible open diamond bracelets; and, in Cecil Beaton's words, she made

> "diamonds flexible, hanging them in little fringes, stalactites or tassels, creating chains of diamonds that are supple as beads of a rosary."

LEFT: A note written by Louis Cartier to his son-in-law René Revillon, 1932-33, announcing his decision to make Jeanne Toussaint his creative director. (See Appendix II, page 354 for translation)
IMAGES COURTESY OF CARTIER

BELOW: Cartier, Paris: Bracelet, 1938 – calibré sapphire, yellow gold
A pair of matching earclips were also made.
IMAGE COURTESY OF CARTIER

OPPOSITE PAGE: Cartier, Paris: Demi-parure (necklace with detachable palmette clip brooches and a pair of earclips), 1958 – brilliant and baguette diamonds, yellow gold
The five palmette motifs can be detached and worn as brooches.
IMAGE COURTESY OF CARTIER

From the flexible flowing ribbons of diamonds that she favoured, came her fascination for mechanisms. She has been credited with bringing back warmer feminine yellow gold to replace the exorbitantly expensive platinum settings of the end of the 1920s.
Toussaint found new ways to create jewels that were both figurative and more three dimensional. The simple outlines and flat jewels, as well as the cool blues and greens of Charles Jacqueau's time were replaced by the tutti-frutti Indian-inspired colours of the end of the 1920s. Reds, blues and greens were set together with diamonds, such as in the iconic Hindu necklace created in 1936 for Daisy Fellowes. The blue pendant sapphires take on an interesting form – taweez – where the oval facetted beads are placed on their 'sides'.

This period from 1934-35 was known as Toussaint's 'Qajar' period. Before the 1930s, mere touches of fine gemstones such as coral, onyx and jade had been used, whereas now larger sculpted pieces of such stones were abundant. Coral, jade and lapis lazuli beads were popular, and turquoise, aquamarine and amethysts were used to create large statement jewels. The new colour combinations found on vanity and cigarette cases of the 1920s, were now being translated to jewellery in imaginative and more playful forms.

Toussaint oversaw the work of up to ten designers at Cartier, who would interpret ideas from such eclectic sources as books; souvenirs from her travels; animals she had observed at the zoo at Vincennes, Paris; flowers and the tiniest of creatures. Ladybirds in coral, dotted with diamond or onyx spots were introduced in 1935 followed by tortoises and birds.
From 1937, Jeanne Toussaint also became interested in watches and clocks as a way of offering her clients an alternative to expensive commissions, in a time of devaluation and increasing unemployment and political instability.

A-List Ladies
Under Toussaint, Cartier became a compulsory stop for any woman of fashion and, ultimately, taste. Toussaint would also discuss the commissions with her clients, involving them at each stage of the design process. From socialites Daisy Fellowes and Mona Williams (later Countess von Bismarck) in the 1930s, to Princess Nina Aga Khan (formerly Nina Dyer) and the Mexican actress María Félix of the 1960s. One of her most famous collaborations was with the Mexican actress Maria Felix conceiving the famous alligator necklace which was a technical tour de force. It was articulated and wound around the neck snugly hugging Felix's throat.

However, Toussaint's most successful collaboration must surely be with Wallis Simpson, the Duchess of Windsor. She helped design some of the most iconic jewels in the Duchess of Windsor's collection. Many which were made during the war years using other jewels, that were broken up. The Duke of Windsor gave Toussaint three conventional line bracelets in calibre ruby, sapphire and emerald respectively, so that she could create the wonderful three-dimensional 'flamingo' brooch with its red, blue and green ruffled feathers, which demonstrates to perfection Toussaint's imagination and her use of volume.

ABOVE: Cartier, Paris: Ladybird earclips, 1936 – coral, black lacquer, diamond, platinum, white gold.
IMAGE COURTESY OF CARTIER

BELOW: Cartier, Paris: Chimera bangle, 1954 – fluted coral beads, buff-top coral cabochons, marquise diamond, brilliant diamond, platinum, white gold
The diamond 'eyes' are set in reverse.
IMAGE COURTESY OF CARTIER

OPPOSITE PAGE: Cartier, Paris: Hindu Tutti-Frutti necklace, 1936 (altered in 1963) – carved beads and leaf shapes in ruby, emerald, sapphire, 13 sapphire taweez, baguette-cut diamond, old-cut diamond, platinum, white gold.
Commissioned by Daisy Fellowes.
IMAGE COURTESY OF CARTIER

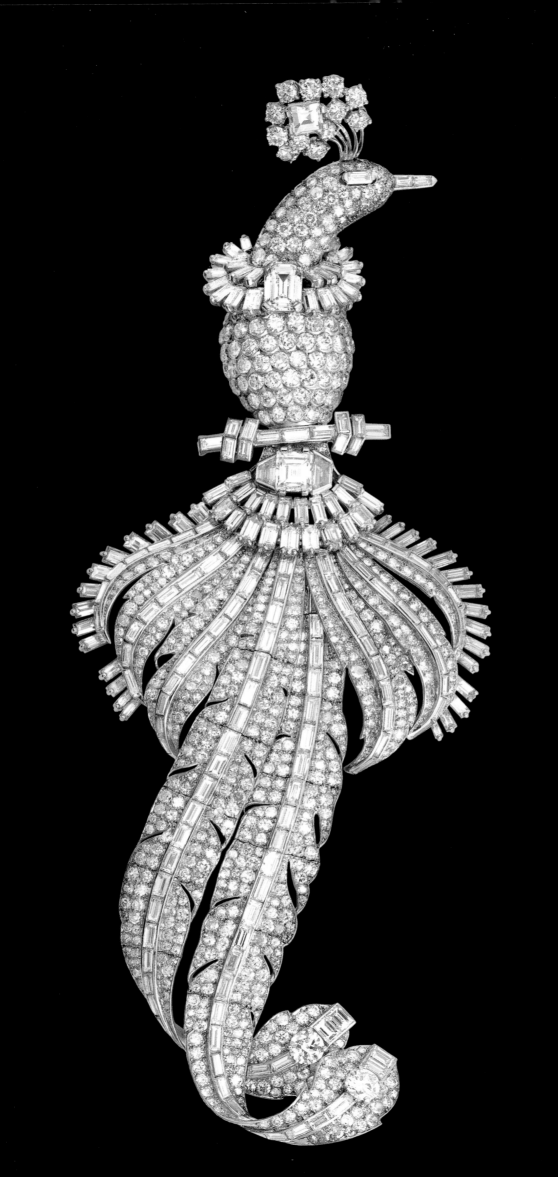

Toussaint's Aviary

Birds of all shapes, sizes and species had a special place in Toussaint's heart and under her aegis and designer Peter Lemarchand's pen, some spectacular jewels were created. The Paradise Bird brooch (1948) set entirely with white diamonds of differing cuts was one such example.

Smaller examples had been part of Toussaint's aviary since the 1930s. Indeed, she once displayed a jewel in the form of a caged bird to represent occupied France in the Cartier window on the Rue de la Paix, which earned her a visit from the Gestapo. In happier times, she designed birds nesting looking after their eggs represented by tiny pearls, and small song birds opening their wings in celebration on the liberation of Paris in 1944.

TOP LEFT: Cartier, Paris: Flamingo brooch, 1940 – square-cut emerald, ruby, sapphire, citrine, cabochon sapphire, brilliant-cut diamond, platinum, white gold
The Duke of Windsor supplied the gemstones for this special order, which he commissioned as a gift for his wife, The Duchess of Windsor (form. Wallis Simpson).
PHOTOGRAPH BY NILS HERRMANN; IMAGE COURTESY OF CARTIER

TOP RIGHT: Cartier, Paris: Bird clip brooch, 1944 – cabochon emerald, sapphire, ruby, diamond, platinum, yellow gold
The bird's wings and tail are articulated.
CARTIER COLLECTION; PHOTOGRAPH BY NICK WELSH; IMAGE COURTESY OF CARTIER

RIGHT: Cartier, Paris: Oiseau libéré brooch, 1944– sapphire, coral, lapis lazuli, platinum, yellow gold
During WWII, Cartier designed various brooches featuring caged birds to symbolise occupied France. When Paris regained its freedom the 'bleu blanc rouge' of the French flag were used as the plumage of the freed bird singing with joy.
CARTIER COLLECTION; PHOTOGRAPH BY NICK WELSH; IMAGE COURTESY OF CARTIER

OPPOSITE PAGE: Cartier, Paris: Exotic Bird brooch, 1948 – step, square, baguette, brilliant and fancy-cut diamonds
The client supplied many of the diamonds for this special order brooch.
CARTIER COLLECTION; PHOTOGRAPH BY NILS HERRMANN; IMAGE COURTESY OF CARTIER

Liberation

There was a certain euphoria after the Second World War drew to a close, it was a time of great innovation in jewellery design and new bold jewels were designed for an ever demanding clientele. In 1947, the Duke of Windsor brought Cartier a collection of 28 amethysts which he presented to Toussaint, the result was a new colour combination for Cartier – blue turquoise with purple amethysts and twisted yellow gold cords. The effect was a magnificent display of contrasting textures of gold cord and smooth gemstone surfaces and of course the resulting contrasts in opaque turquoise and transparent amethyst lustres. A necklace and pair of earrings using the same combination of colours and gemstones was sold to Marjorie Merriweather Post in 1950, in a very different style, and a braided gold necklace sold to Daisy Fellowes in 1953.

The Palm Tree brooch, which had first appeared in 1939 using different cuts of diamond to add depth and texture, was revitalised in 1950, using more baguette diamonds and including pear-shaped diamonds to represent coconuts. In 1957, a variation of these designs used highest quality cushion-cut rubies as the coconuts among the diamond fronds.

Throughout the 1950s and '60s, small gold animal and bird brooches were constantly being added to an already overflowing pool of ideas. To such an extent that Toussaint brought back some of the creations of the 1920s, Chimera bangles with lion and dragon heads were once again 'de rigueur'. Coral, a favorite material for Toussaint reappeared as did tortoise shell adorned objects.

OPPOSITE PAGE: Cartier, Paris: Necklace, 1953 – amethyst beads, cabochon amethyst, cabochon turquoise, braided yellow gold
Sold to Daisy Fellowes.
CARTIER COLLECTION; PHOTOGRAPH BY NILS HERRMANN; IMAGE COURTESY OF CARTIER

ABOVE: Cartier, Paris: Palm Tree clip brooch, 1957 – ruby, baguette diamond, brilliant-cut diamond, platinum, white gold.
The trunk is articulated.
CARTIER COLLECTION; PHOTOGRAPH BY VINCENT WULVERYCK; IMAGE COURTESY OF CARTIER

RIGHT: Cartier, Paris: Twin Chimera Head bangle, 1960 – ruby, emerald, marquise diamond, baguette diamond, brilliant-cut diamond, yellow gold, white gold
The heads swivel to open the bangle.
IMAGE COURTESY OF CARTIER

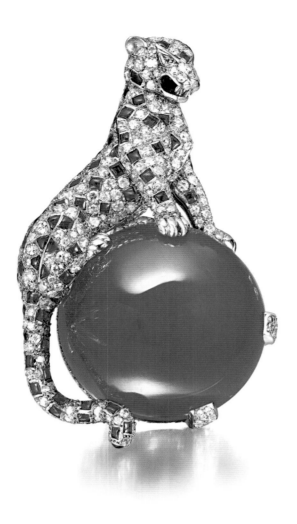

The 'Feline Club'

Toussaint's passion for the feline form earned her the nickname 'La Panthère' from Louis Cartier. In actual fact, it was Charles Jacqueau who first used the panther theme on a wristwatch in 1914, placing onyx spots amongst the rose-cut diamonds. Under Toussaint, the panther's distinctive spots were soon to be found on the clasps of evening bags, and on cigarette and vanity cases, as well as on jewellery. Toussaint recounted in a letter to Louis Cartier how she had encountered a stuffed panther with a mechanism that enabled it to pounce with extended claws in the hallway of Marchesa Luisa Casati's rose palace in Le Vésinet to the west of Paris:

> "The sight of the stuffed panther has confirmed me in my desire to create a panther-jewel; if we manage, it will be something quite different from the one we designed in 1922, and which I now refuse to wear."
>
> Gilberte Gautier, *Cartier, The Legend,* 1983

Toussaint had for a long time nurtured the idea of a sculptural panther jewel, but it wasn't until 1948 that she finally managed to have it executed in gold, perched upon a large pale cabochon emerald. It was bought by the Duke and Duchess of Windsor, who would also snap up a diamond and sapphire panther sitting regally on a huge cabochon sapphire, which had been created for stock. Panther bangles, bracelets, clips and brooches followed, each with its own expression and posture.

The panther was not the only big cat that inspired Toussaint. Barbara Hutton, the Woolworth's heiress, had a formidable eye for jewels, and in 1957 she bought a tiger clip brooch to be followed by the purchase of tiger ear clips in 1961. In the usual Cartier/Toussaint fashion, the tigers were articulated and would move seductively with the wearer's own movements.

Legacy

Toussaint was neither a technician, nor an artist – Louis Cartier actively discouraged her from learning to draw. But she knew exactly what she wanted in a jewel. Jacques Coziot, a jeweller who worked alongside Toussaint in the 1960s reminisced to Michel Aliaga that she was extremely demanding and her instructions had to be followed to the letter. In 1970, at the age of 83, Jeanne Toussaint retired.

> "Jeanne Toussaint – her great era was the '40s and '50s, without her, would Cartier have survived?"   Harry Fane – Obsidian Gallery, London

ABOVE: Cartier, Paris: Panther clip brooch, 1949 – cabochon sapphire, 1 sapphire cabochon weighing 152.35ct, fancy yellow diamond, diamond, platinum, white gold
This was the second three-dimensional panther clip to be made by Cartier. It was sold to The Duchess of Windsor.
PHOTOGRAPH BY VINCENT WULVERYCK; IMAGE COURTESY OF CARTIER

FAR LEFT: Design for a panther jewel front and side views, 1967 – graphite and gouache on tracing paper
The design was executed in onyx, emerald, diamond and platinum.
CARTIER PARIS ARCHIVES.

LEFT: Cartier, Paris: Panther clip brooch, 1948 – 1 emerald cabochon weighing 116ct, emerald, black enamel, yellow gold
This was the first three-dimensional panther clip to be made by Cartier. It was sold to The Duchess of Windsor.
CARTIER ARCHIVES; PHOTOGRAPH BY NICK WELSH; IMAGE COURTESY OF CARTIER

OPPOSITE PAGE: Cartier, Paris: Tiger ear clips, 1961 – fancy yellow diamond, onyx, emerald, yellow gold
Sold to Barbara Hutton. The head, legs and tail are articulated.
CARTIER COLLECTION; PHOTOGRAPH BY NICK WELSH; IMAGE COURTESY OF CARTIER

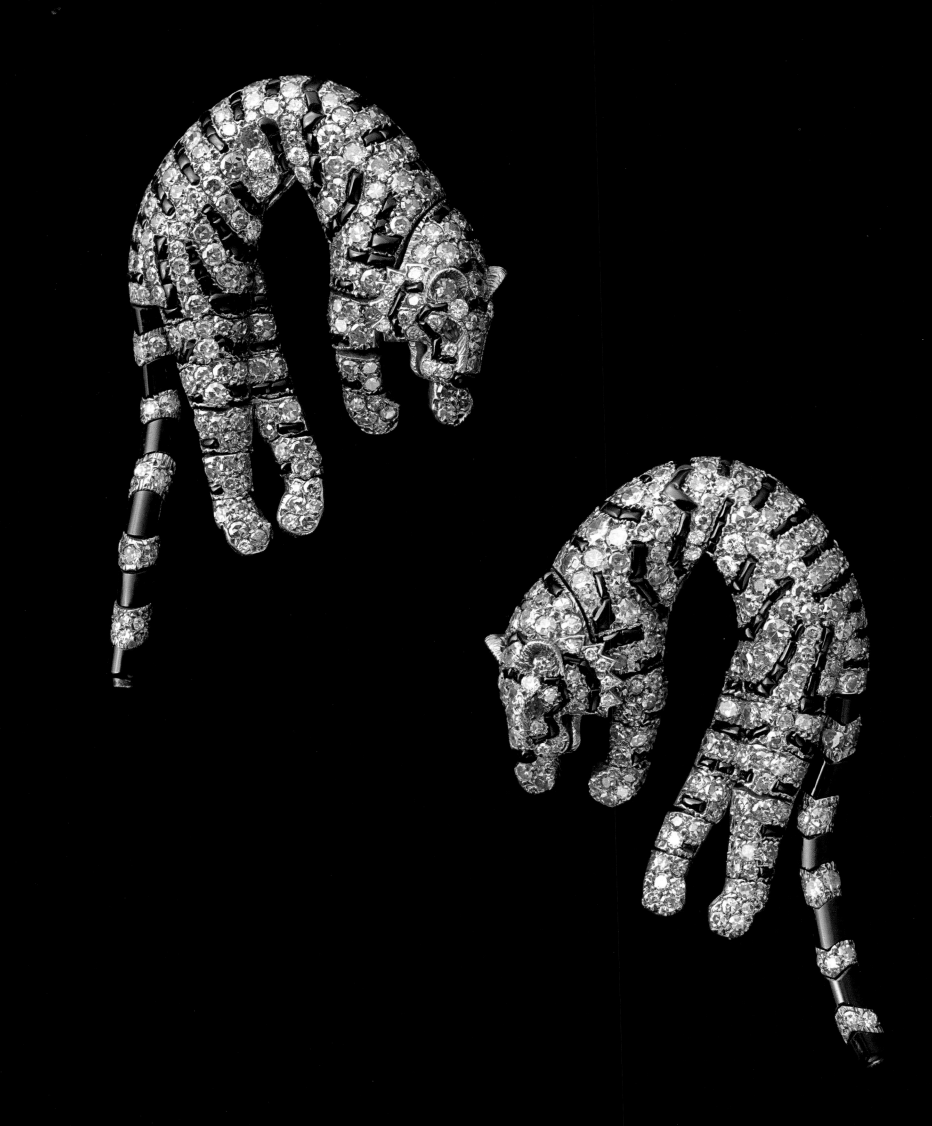

PART TWO
Full Steam Ahead:
The Search for the Perfect Design

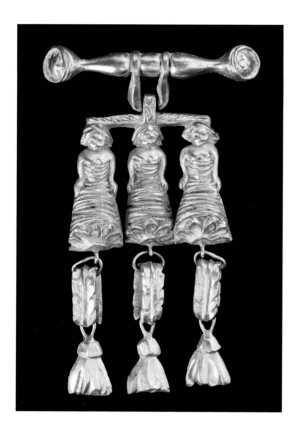

The Post-war Boom

The Second World War was a massive jolt for the world at large; it changed everything. After the war, societies – shattered both economically and culturally – had to be rebuilt from the ground up. But that rebuilding brought with it a sense of purpose and optimism, an idea that anything was possible.

The Marshall Plan was put into place in 1948 to help Europe get back on its feet and to ward off the perceived attractions of Communism at the time. Films, magazines and exhibitions abounded to show the advantages of the new technologies that had been developed during the War years and how they could enrich people's lives. The reconstruction of Europe was an opportunity for new ideas and new designs. Inevitably, the funds that were poured into staying one step ahead in the Cold War with the Soviet Union, particularly during the 1950s, had a trickling down effect and gave architects and designers a chance to adapt inventions, technologies and initiatives, increasing comfort in the home. In France, this period was referred to as 'Les Trente Glorieuses' (The Thirty Glorious Years) by Jean Fourastié; it was a time that brought a new-found sense of wealth and optimism to Europe.

As the years of rationing and restrictions came to an end, this was reflected in the dramatically changing fashions. Pencil skirts gave way to full skirts luxuriating in the amount of material used, and the 'New Look' by Dior defined the silhouette. New fashion designers emerged, dominated by such names as Cristóbal Balenciaga, Jacques Fath, Hubert de Givenchy, Jacques Heim and Mainbocher, and, by the end of the fifties, Yves Saint Laurent. Amongst female fashion designers to become big names were Sybil Connolly, Claire McCardell and Pauline Trigère; and Coco Chanel was back, making very few concessions to the new age. Glamour returned in the 1950s, with clothes for work, the home and evening wear. New York usurped Paris as the mecca of fashion; if Paris was keeping its own for haute couture, then *pret-à-porter* was holding sway in the United States, democratising fashion.

Jewellery was no longer just for the super rich, though during the '50s it remained relatively conservative – pearls were iconic, even imitation pearls. Ear clips became popular and costume jewellery was the rage, helped by their adoption in photo shoots for the fashion magazines. Jewellers such as Marianne Ostier were winning accolades and jewellery competitions, including the Diamond International Awards an astonishing five times. During the 1950s and early '60s, Ostier helped transform the conservative perception of what a jewel should be; she even marketed the idea of 'skin jewels', which were stuck directly on to the wearer.

During and after WWII, *Bijoux fantaisie* (fantasy jewellery) saw a resurgence and was called 'couture jewellery' or 'art jewellery'. When great artists of the 1940s and '50s, including Georges Braque (1882-1963); Jean Cocteau (1889-1963); Alexander Calder (1898-1976); Max Ernst (1891-1976), Les Lalannes (François-Xavier: 1927-2008; Claude: b.1924) and Pablo Picasso (1881-1973) tried their hand at the medium, it became known as 'artist jewellery'. As well as Line Vautrin, others who explored the concept of artist jewellery and its rapport with the body were Vivianna Torun Bülow-Hübe, Nanna Ditzel and Astrid Fog, all three of whom designed silver jewellery for Georg Jensen in Denmark.

1960s

The sixties brought an optimism and a freeing from social restrictions. Adolescents were now an important new social group; television and cinema were at the forefront of this change. Youth was celebrated, their ideas counted as never before. Mary Quant introduced the iconic miniskirt and made Carnaby Street in London the centre of the fashion universe. Men wore their hair defiantly long, while women had their tresses dramatically bobbed. For those with long hair, the style was voluminous and bouffant, or worn as a beehive or bun.

Jewellery in the sixties took its cue from the fifties: gold and diamonds were still *de rigueur* but experimentation was the mainstay of this decade, with textured and matt gold surfaces. With experimentation came new materials, including paper and plastics. Gemstones were not only faceted, they were also set in their natural state and using more informal outlines; large bold hoops, bangles and brooches were transformed using geometric shapes. There was a feeling of design freedom and an 'anything goes' attitude.

The hippie lifestyle became synonymous with the decade, technology was advancing in leaps and bounds. The Cold War had reached the stratosphere; the Soviets won round one of the Space Race in 1961 by putting the first man, Yuri Gagarin, into orbit.

This was also a big year for the jewellery world. Graham Hughes, at the Worshipful Company of Goldsmiths, and Shirley Bury, at the Victoria and Albert Museum collaborated to stage the

ABOVE: Model wearing paper jewellery by Wendy Ramshaw, 1960s IMAGE COURTESY OF THE LAKELAND ARTS TRUST

Barbara Anton: Anton Crazy ring – multi-gems, sapphire, aquamarine, garnet, yellow gold
COURTESY OF KIMBERLY KLOSTERMAN AT KKLOSTERMAN JEWELRY, CINCINNATI, OHIO

Astrid Fog for Gerg Jensen: Rectangular link bracelet, 1970s
– silver IMAGE COURTESY OF GEORG JENSEN

renowned International Exhibition of Modern Jewellery 1890-1961. With over 900 pieces showcasing jewellery artists from 33 countries, the exhibition proved a major influence on jewellery design during the 1960s and '70s and is still referred to today, more than fifty years on.

One of the jewellery designers featured in the exhibition was Gerda Flöckinger. She was a master of fusion (electroforming), which created thin hollow spheres, like 'bubbles' of metal, allowing her to create large light jewels. (Today both Ornella Iannuzzi and Jacqueline Cullen use this method, creating very different styles.) Tension setting was another advancing technique, in which a gemstone was suspended between two pieces of metal, using only pressure to hold it in place. Only diamond and corundum are hard enough to withstand this pressure without fracturing.

By the close of the decade, lifestyles had changed and there was no going back. But this created tensions. Around the world, there was a wave of anti-authoritarian activity, such as civil rights movement in America, anti-war protests in response to the conflict in Vietnam, and the rise of feminism to promote gender equality. But the world united in awe as America moved ahead in the Space Race and Neil Armstrong took his first steps on the moon.

1970s

This was a decade of inflation, unemployment and civil unrest, which all dramatically changed the political and social landscape. In contrast, flight prices dropped and international travel was no longer the reserve of the few. For the first time, it was possible to make dreams a reality for the majority, who travelled afar and returned with ethnic jewellery from exotic sounding places around the globe. Authenticity was important, and jewellery using unusual woods, stones and shells were all the rage. Maxi dresses, flared jeans, ascot blouses, and jumpsuits in big floral patterns, 'à la Pucci', were popular with platform shoes taking fashion to dizzying heights. Jewellery of the '70s took on the hippy feel with heavy textured gold chains and large pendants.

There was a freedom to think differently, which in turn created some great jewellery. Vivianna Torun Bülow-Hübe was exploring the use of light and metalsmithing in her work; Nanna Ditzel was studying form and translating it into different mediums. In particular, designers were exploring different materials. Wendy Ramshaw, and later Catherine Noll, experimented with acrylics and perspex to create new interpretations of what they felt jewellery should be. Influenced by the moon landing, Ramshaw and others considered meteors as possible material. Remaining true to the essence of her own culture whilst experimenting with her man-made talosel resin, Line Vautrin included rebus and poetry in her work. It was an exciting time for new designers with such diverse ideas with which to express themselves, and they found a wide audience ready to accept their offerings. Elsa Peretti for Tiffany's turned the concept of expensive jewellery on its head; she brought back an acceptance of silver jewellery, which had been fashionable in the 1930s.

In 1977, *Saturday Night Fever* starring John Travolta became an overnight sensation, and the jewels followed suit; big dangly earrings were a part of the look as the fashion world was influenced by night clubs and the disco scene.

1980s

Ronald Reagan and Margaret Thatcher were about to transform the political and economical landscape on both sides of the Atlantic as the Western world suffered a recession. The economy recovered and business flourished; computers started to make inroads into people's consciousness; banks were making fortunes and there seemed to be no end to the spending and consumerism. Confidence was there in spades. This was the decade of power dressing, shoulder pads and big heavy gold jewellery popularised by Bulgari, and the Greek jewellery houses, Zolotas and Ilias Lalaounis. Paloma Picasso's large, simple, gemstone jewels for Tiffany's defined the era.

It was no longer enough to be an artist, artists needed to be businessmen and women; branding had become a serious concern. Designers became multinational businesses from Giorgio Armani, Ralph Lauren and Donna Karan to Azzedine Alaïa and Vivienne Westwood. *Dallas* and *Dynasty* were the undoubted television successes of the '80s, portraying big costume jewellery, which became a part of the mainstream fashion look for the decade. Madonna, Michael Jackson and HRH Diana, Princess of Wales all defined this period, as did Bob Geldof's *Band Aid* in 1984, which was the beginning of a collective moral consciousness.

There was however a flip side to the coin; the spectre of AIDS reared its ugly head for the first time and the Iran-Iraq war was in full swing. Then in 1986, the Chernobyl disaster shook the world and opened the ethical debate about the environment and what was sustainable. The world left the eighties behind, with the fall of the Berlin Wall in 1989, and entered into the nineties in a more sober mood.

Paloma Picasso for Tiffany & Co.: 1985 Blue Book Collection, Paloma's 5th Anniversary necklace is an extraordinary creation of gemstones – green tourmaline, tanzanite, precious topaz, pink topaz, peach tourmaline, rubelite, peridot, aquamarine, indicolite, platinum-set diamonds yellow gold *The 'X' motif references her first design for the company.*

"Sensuality is translated by modelling… A model must when touched offer satisfaction to the finger; it shouldn't collide with it. The hand must judge as much as the eye."

LINE VAUTRIN
A Reflective Mind

A pair of turtledoves swing back and forth, perched from their vantage point, they survey the Parisian streets keeping the wearer company; earrings which hark back to antiquity; suns glow with pointed arms and others with twisted flames; the daughters of Zeus pass by; secret codes are whispered and rebuses are handed from one to the other; 'Je t'aime en silence' *(I love you silently)*; Adam and Eve look on hand in hand… This is the world of Line Vautrin.

Line Vautrin (1913-1997) left school early, having had very little motivation to continue. After several unsatisfactory jobs, including selling industrial photographs, Vautrin decided that design was where her destiny lay. With the insouciance of youth, she started designing and making her first pieces of jewellery using the basic techniques of gilding and engraving that she had learnt from her metalsmith father, who had in turn inherited a foundry from his father.

For the first four years, she sold her pieces by going door-to-door. Vautrin also designed buttons, which were used by Schiaparelli on her outfits, bringing her to the attention of fashion editors and enabling her to sell them to retail. With the money she earned from this venture, Vautrin hired a booth at the Universal Exhibition in Paris in 1937 to show her jewellery.

Her pendant depicting Adam and Eve eating from the Tree of Life was a particular success. It was the break she needed; she built up a substantial clientele and by the following year she was able to rent a tiny showroom in rue de Berri in Paris.

Her profits financed trips to Heraklion in Crete and to Cairo in Egypt, which provided inspiration for many of her later works. It was not long before the Second World War broke out and Paris succumbed to the sombre shadows of the evening. Despite the problems she increasingly encountered procuring materials, her bronze gilt jewels and boxes became ever more popular. The Lorraine cross and the cockerel became patriotic themes during this period.

In 1942 she moved to 63 rue Faubourg Saint-Honoré, in the very centre of Paris. In those uncertain times, she showed belt buckles, buttons, powder compacts, embroideries, mules, foot warmers and umbrella handles in her windows, in fact anything she could make or invent and that she thought she could sell. Women could not easily buy new clothes but they could buy something small, a trinket with which to brighten their ensemble.

LEFT: Pair of Turtledoves earrings – bronze gilt; hoop in canon de fusil (gun metal steel)
PHOTOGRAPH BY JEAN-CLAUDE MARLAUD; IMAGE COURTESY OF MARIE LAURE BONNAUD VAUTRIN

OPPOSITE PAGE: Les Filles de Zeus bracelet – bronze gilt
PHOTOGRAPH BY JEAN-CLAUDE MARLAUD; IMAGE COURTESY OF MARIE LAURE BONNAUD VAUTRIN

Labyrinthe brooch – beige talosel encrusted with fire-coloured mirrors

In 1943, she and her husband Jacques-Armand Bonnaud set about restoring and decorating the abandoned Mégret de Sérilly Hotel in the historic district of Le Marais. Vautrin set up her workshops with over forty artisans in the hotel. She used the main reception rooms to entertain and to show her work to her clients, whilst a 16th-century polychrome wooden statue of Venus displayed her necklaces of small enamel beads.

In 1949 she left everything behind to follow her husband to Morocco (a French protectorate at the time). However she returned to Paris in 1952 with her daughter.

Work Ethic

Vautrin had a strict work ethic, setting herself the rule of one object a day. Vautrin employed diverse techniques, such as sand smelting, as well as the lost wax method; some of her pieces required both techniques. Enamel was applied by using a flame and the gilding was done by electrolysis. She was just as open to using a variety of materials:

> "All materials interested me, at the beginning metal; ceramic, spun glass, mother of pearl and sculpted ivory followed. Finally I found my preferred material: resin which determined my later life and introduced me to decoration."

She loved to play with images and words, creating rebuses, allegorical symbols and simple messages, which led to *Marie Claire* naming her the 'poet of metal' in 1946.

Talosel

In 1950, Vautrin started using a form of cellulose acetate, a synthetic resin, which came in sheets from which she cut out the patterns. A gas-heated iron was used on the pieces in order to scarify, carve and twist them into the shapes desired, which were then polished and patinated in an acid bath to give them a finished look. This process and the resulting appearance was unique to Vautrin and she patented it under the name Talosel. She used it with coloured glass, which she had treated using mercury silvering (a process which is now illegal) to give them a mirrored iridescent effect and which she then cut into tiny mosaic-like pieces. She used this technique to decorate lamps, tables and convex mirrors, as well as in her jewellery.

By the end of the 1950s, Vautrin opened a boutique at 3 rue de l'Université on the Parisian Left Bank; unfortunately the adventure didn't last for long due to high overheads and she was forced to close shop in 1962. Vautrin continued to experiment and create, but on a smaller scale.

From 1963 onwards, she introduced a small copper mosaic with the word 'Joux', which she placed on her jewels; this was accompanied with a Roman numeral beside her signature to help identify the artisan who had made the piece. In 1967, she started a school, the Association for the Development of Manual Arts (A.D.A.M.), to transmit her know-how to the next generation of artists as well as to inquisitive amateurs.

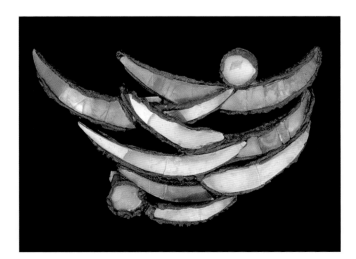

Furet (Ferret) necklace – bronze gilt
'Il court, il court le furet' (The ferret: he runs, he runs) inspired by the French nursery rhyme.
PHOTOGRAPH BY JEAN-CLAUDE MARLAUD; IMAGE COURTESY OF MARIE LAURE BONNAUD VAUTRIN

There were several important exhibitions and retrospectives of her work towards the end of her career. In the late 1980s, she sold off many of her creations at two sales organised by the auctioneer Briest at Hôtel Drouot, Paris. At the second auction, in 1987, she met London-based gallery owner and collector David Gill. As well as holding several exhibitions of her work and promoting her work abroad, he encouraged her to continue and to make new designs. She adjusted designs from the past: a policeman chasing a thief theme for a belt buckle was transformed into a bracelet; a bronze chain belt was shortened to make a choker with ferrets holding the clasp referencing the French nursery rhyme, *'il court, il court le furet'* ('run, ferret, run'). In 1992, she was awarded the National Arts and Crafts Prize for her work in decoration and she was made Chevalier of Arts and Letters by Jack Lang.

Legacy

Two years after her death in 1997, a retrospective of her work was held at the Musée des Arts Décoratifs, entitled 'Line Vautrin: Secrets de Bijoux'. In 2003, there was an exhibition of her work at the Museum für Kunst und Gewerbe (Arts and Crafts Museum), Hamburg.

Vautrin's mirrors fetch soaring prices at auction and her poetic boxes, compacts and jewellery are now favourites among an ever-increasing number of collectors.

Vautrin's jewellery stands out for its originality. She conceived many new inventive links for her chains, necklaces and bracelets. Her clever use of rebus and symbols instead of gemstones creates intrigue and mystery. Her jewellery is just as precious for the words she has crafted and the messages that she has sent the wearer through her style of figurative jewellery.

LEFT: Marchand de Ballons (The Balloon Seller) round powder compact – bronze gilt
PHOTOGRAPH BY JEAN-CLAUDE MARLAUD; IMAGE COURTESY OF MARIE LAURE BONNAUD VAUTRIN

OPPOSITE PAGE: Les Planètes necklace – canon de fusil (gun metal steel), gilt
The central medal is a rebus for 'Line Vautrin'
PHOTOGRAPH BY JEAN-CLAUDE MARLAUD; IMAGE COURTESY OF MARIE LAURE BONNAUD VAUTRIN

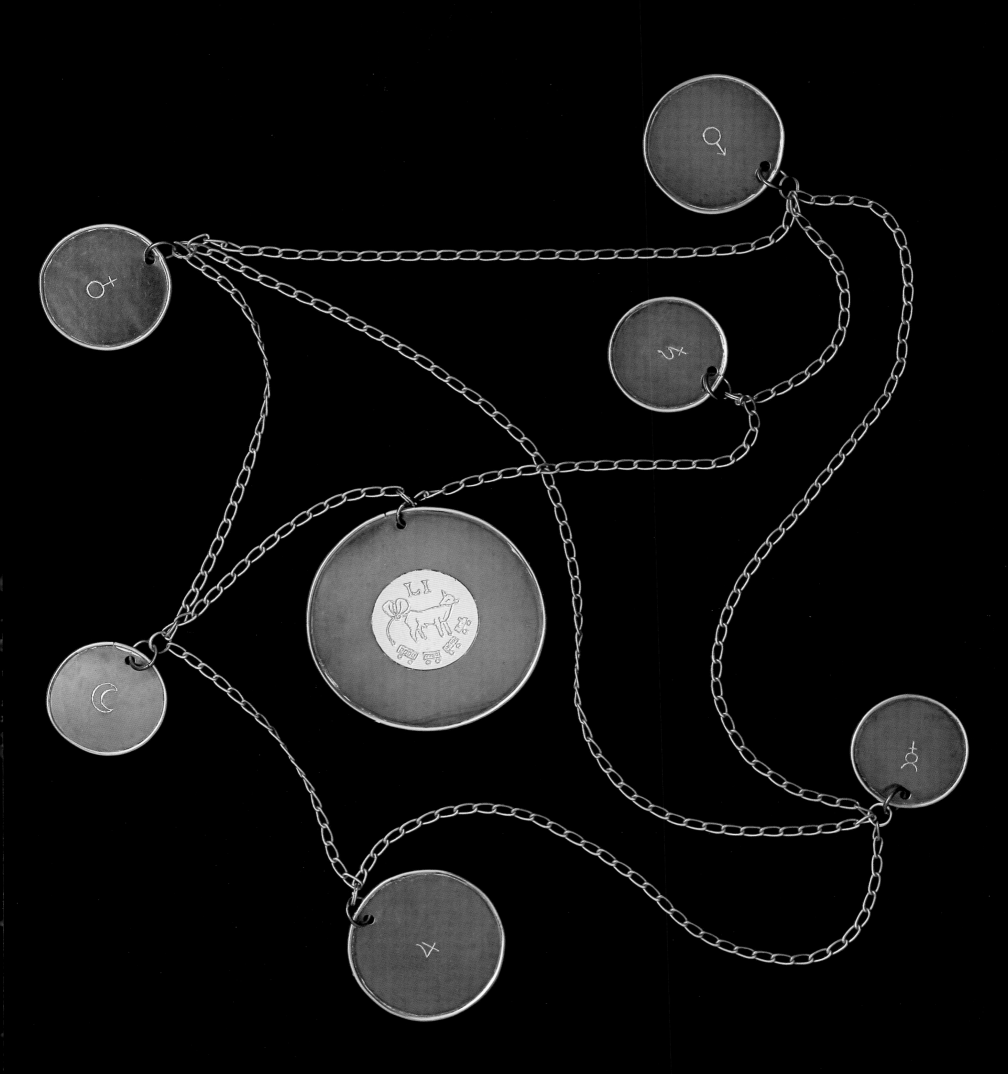

MARGRET CRAVER
The Creative Teacher

Born in Kansas City, Missouri, Margret Craver (1907-2010) was to have a great influence on a generation of hollowware and jewellery designers. Barbara Cartlidge said that her "contribution to the craft revival was crucial to the later flowering of the art." (*Twentieth-Century Jewelry*, Abrams, New York, 1985).

On graduating from the University of Kansas, Craver became deeply interested in metalsmithing and studied under Arthur Neville Clark at the Cranbrook Academy of Art in Michigan. Unable to find formal classes on soldering, she taught herself and learned to make her own tools with the help of the Armoury curator at the Metropolitan Museum of Art. She moved to Sweden where she studied under the aegis of Baron Erik Fleming (silversmith to the King of Sweden). By 1938 she was back in the United States teaching the techniques she had learnt and working as a part-time curator at the Wichita Art Museum, in Kansas. During WWII, she became a volunteer nurse and in association with the metal refinery Handy & Harman she set up a rehabilitation metalwork program for wounded war veterans under the supervision of General Kirk, Surgeon General of the US army.

She trained occupational therapists and organised workshops to teach her metalsmithing techniques to art teachers, thus spreading her knowledge as far and as wide as she could after starting out at the renowned Rhode Island School of Design and the Rochester Institute of Technology. She became a major influence on the American Studio Jewellery Movement. She also wrote about her techniques as well as filming them for students to learn from. This was followed by an exhibition at the Metropolitan Museum in 1949, entitled 'Form in Handwrought Silver'.

En résille Enamelling
On seeing a pin using *en résille*, Craver dedicated many years to researching, experimenting with and perfecting this particularly difficult enamelling method previously popular in 17th-century France. The technique involves etching the design onto glass, this is then lined by a thin piece of gold foil, covered with enamel powder, and fired. Craver's *en résille* jewels have an intimacy that has been described by the famed fashion journalist and editor, Suzy Menkes as "colours floating like oil drops on a surface".

A member of the Gold and Silversmith Guild, Sweden, Craver became a fellow of the American Crafts Council and recipient of their gold medal for excellence. Notable exhibitions of her work include Museum of Contemporary Crafts, New York (1959), 'Objects USA', Smithsonian Institution (1969), and 'Margret Craver and her Contemporaries', Museum of Fine Art, Boston (2002).

OPPOSITE PAGE: Time neck pendant, 1963 – *en résille* enamel, glass, yellow gold
PHOTOGRAPH © 2017 MUSEUM OF FINE ARTS, BOSTON.
THE DAPHNE FARAGO COLLECTION

BELOW: Brooch, 1945 – gold wire
PHOTOGRAPH © 2017 MUSEUM OF FINE ARTS, BOSTON. GIFT OF MARGRET CRAVER WITHERS

"It should be possible to hang up the washing while wearing my jewellery!"

VIVIANNA TORUN BÜLOW-HÜBE
Balanced on the Edge

Vivianna Torun (1927-2004) was a leading light in silver jewellery design and was one of the first women jewellery designers to gain an international reputation. Even today to copy a Torun design presents a challenge for the most talented of silversmiths.

The Mastery of Balance
As a child, she loved figure skating:

> *"It took a lot of discipline and physical awareness to make those fine curves; a continual balancing of the outer and inner edges of the blades. . . . the daily hour-long practice in using body balance, to describe patterns in the ice, double figure of eight, looping and back on a backward inner edge stroke and feeling a gradual mastery of all these counter-balancing elements, that have slowly been instilled like ABC, while one moves faster and faster over the ice, turning and jumping. The one without the other is impossible. It's rather like writing: if you can't form all the letters properly, you can't write a long fluent story."*

She applied this self-discipline to her work as a silversmith and was ever-conscious of the counterbalances required in creating and forging her silver creations. Her Mobile necklace, made from one continuous piece of silver, balances freely on its own axis; it is a masterpiece, and earned her a Gold Medal at the Milan Triennial in 1960. It was for this pioneering work that she was awarded the Lunning Prize that same year. An example of the Mobile necklace is in the permanent collection of the Musée des Arts Decoratif, Paris.

The figure-of-eight can be seen in Torun's Two become One wedding ring – a folded figure-of-eight or Möbius-strip – which symbolises infinite love.

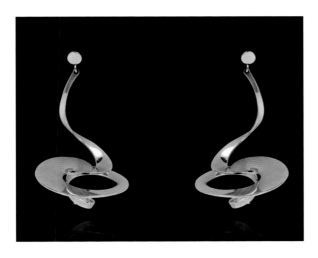

LEFT: Torun for Georg Jensen: Vortex earrings, 1987 – silver IMAGE COURTESY OF GEORG JENSEN

OPPOSITE PAGE: FROM TOP TO BOTTOM:

Torun for Georg Jensen: Water-Lily Leaf ring – silver
This is a contemporary reissue of Torun's original 1973 design, which was inspired by her first trip to Indonesia.

Möbius ring – silver
This is a contemporary reissue of Torun's original design.

Möbius Strip ring – silver
This is a contemporary reissue of Torun's original design.

Two become One ring – silver
This is a contemporary reissue of Torun's original 'folded figure-of-eight' design.

ALL IMAGES COURTESY OF GEORG JENSEN

"The Möbius-strip … after that came the 'spiral', and it is these two forms that I have been developing for 40 years. The spiral evolved into the double swirl, or vortex, in the '80s, to become an independent mobile sculpture in 1989."

Her fascinating twisted silver torque comes from the simple observation of ordinary things, for example, the swirling motion of milk as it is poured.

"The rhythmic patterns of flux inherent in nature and the universe."

The Beginning

Torun was the youngest of five children, born in 1927 in Malmö, Sweden. Her family was artistic: her mother, Runa, was a sculptress and her maternal grandfather was the artist Knut Ekwall. It was her sister Günlog who encouraged her to work with silver and to meet the silversmith Wiwen Nilsson. Afterwards, visiting another sister, Sigrun in Stockholm in 1943, she met the silversmith Sigurd Persson. From these chance encounters, she decided to learn how to work silver; starting at her kitchen table with a blowtorch and a sheet of silver, she progressed to being an apprentice for Dahlgren and Co., in Malmö in 1945.

At 18, Torun was studying at the Konstfack, School of Arts, Crafts and Design in Stockholm, as well as looking after her daughter, Pia. Struggling to make ends meet, she transformed cane and brass wire that she had found in the college's furniture department into African-inspired rattan chokers. She showed them to Estrid Ericson at Svenskt Tenn, a well-known interior design shop in Stockholm, and started to sell her jewellery there, displaying them on leopard skin.

On leaving the Konstfack she set up a small 10m^2 workshop in a rented laundry room and borrowed 2,500 kroner (about 300US$) from a friend to buy a lathe. Within a year, she was able to repay her friend from the sales of her wood and rattan jewellery.

France

By 1950, Torun was married to her second husband, Jean-Pierre Serbonnet, a French architect. She continued to sell through the Svenskt Tenn and in Paris in 1952, at the Cercle des Arts Gallery, on the boulevard de Saint Germain. From 1954 to 1968 she exhibited continuously at the Galerie du Siècle, on the opposite side of the street.

During this period, she was creating some of her most innovative pieces of jewellery. She used pebbles for her necklaces as single stone pendants and as abstract designs with wooden shapes. Some were worn down the nape of the neck and others in front, as choker pendants. In 1955, using tubular ceramic beads, she created a simple lace-like collar as well as her silver hair comb with rock crystal teardrops that Billie Holiday would go on to wear at her concert in Paris in 1957.

Torun settled in Paris in 1956 with her third husband, the Afro-American painter Walter Coleman.

"We moved mostly in jazz circles: there was Bud Powell and Billie Holiday…"

Left: Portrait of Billie Holiday wearing Vivianna Torun's hair comb, ear pendants and neck pendant, during her famous concert in Paris, 1957 Photograph by Jean-Pierre Leloir; Image courtesy of Archives Leloir

Opposite Page: Multi-gem hair comb – glass, rock crystal, amethyst, citrine, paste, silver Image courtesy of Drucker Antiques, New York

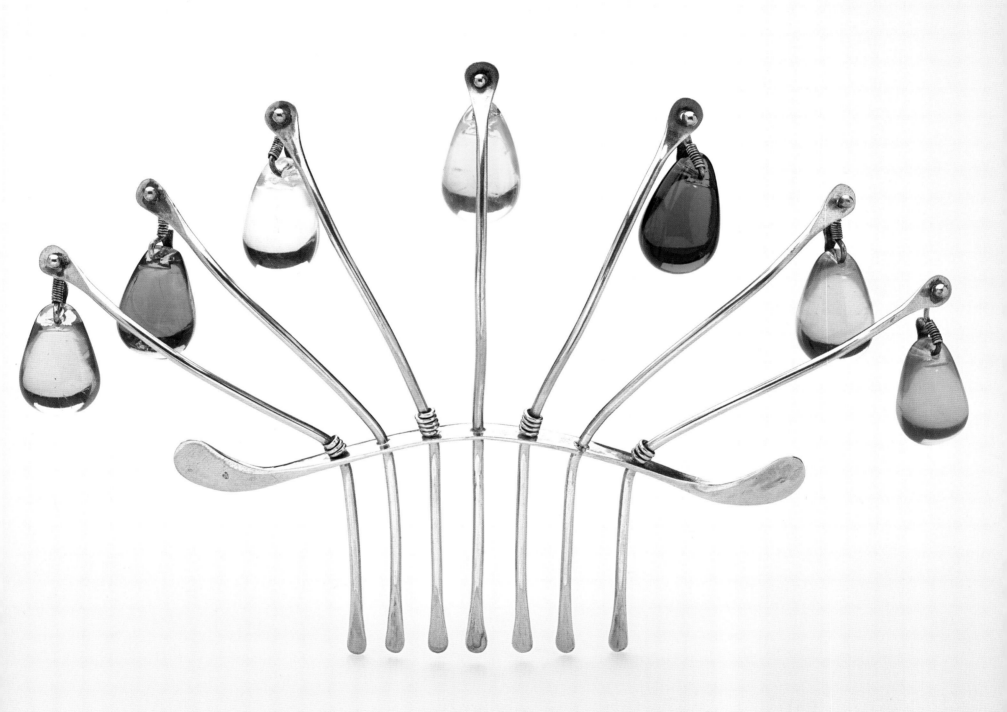

By 1958, she was a well-known artist and, following an exhibition of her jewellery at the Picasso Museum in Antibes (1958-1960), she was cited in an article on new artist jewellery in *Connaissance des Arts* magazine, 1961. She was amongst illustrious company with the likes of Braque, Calder, Dalí, Ernst, Giacometti and her friend Picasso; notably, she and Calder were the only craftsmen. (She had first met Picasso in 1948 as she gathered pebbles on the beach for her jewellery whilst on holiday in the Riveria with other artist friends.) She also showed at the hugely influential exhibition at the Goldsmith's Hall, London, in 1961.

Torun and Coleman had moved their family to Biot, on the Riviera to escape racial tension in the city during the war with Algeria. Torun encouraged young Swedish silversmiths to make the journey to see her, including Urban Bohlin and Bengt Liljedahl. She recalls in Ann Westin's book how it was:

> *"Great fun and instructive for me when they tried out techniques that were quite new to me."*

Georg Jensen

Torun's great break came in 1967, when Georg Jensen took over her entire production of silver designs. Torun's collaboration with Georg Jensen gave her an economic stability and, therefore, the freedom to experiment. It coincided with her stay in Germany and a newfound desire to understand herself spiritually and the world around her. Not only did she create more jewellery, she also looked at hollowware, cutlery, glassware and handbags.

Indonesia

In 1973 after a visit to Indonesia, she created her famous armband based on the shape of giant lotus leaves, alongside her Water-lily Leaf ring and her Leaf brooch. She set up a workshop in 1976 with a young geologist Mansur Geiger, in Indonesia, making simple pearl and mother-of-pearl jewels with the profits being invested into the community and the training of young people. This project was the impetus she needed to move to Indonesia in 1978.

LEFT: Torun for Georg Jensen: Bangle – amber, silver
This is a contemporary reissue of Torun's original design.
IMAGE COURTESY OF GEORG JENSEN

OPPOSITE PAGE: Neckring with Pebble pendant – pebble, silver
IMAGE COURTESY OF MODERNITY, STOCKHOLM

The Wristwatch

Torun's most iconic design, which has been continued by Georg Jensen, is the stainless steel wristwatch originally conceived for the 1962 exhibition 'Antagonism II - l'objet' at the Musée des Arts Décoratifs. It was Torun's absolute dislike of the "relentlessness of time" that inspired her watch:

> "With no numbers; it was to be an ornament, not a chronometer. At first it only had a seconds hand, but when Georg Jensen began producing the watch in 1967, we added both the hour and minute hands. The bracelet did not completely encircle the wrist but was left open at the outside so as not to feel oneself a prisoner of time..."

The simplicity of the watch was continued in the dial; there were no markings, only a mirror so that when you looked at the dial you would only see yourself:

> "A reminder of the present moment... the very second."

Her own woman

Torun never followed a trend and, except for a cover page for *Elle* magazine in 1955, her work was largely ignored by the world of fashion at the time.

> "The haute couture in France never showed the slightest interest in me. During the time I lived there nothing was ever written about my jewellery in the fashion magazines."

Part of the 'anti-status' generation, looking for something different, she wanted young working women to be able to go to work and on to the theatre or to a dinner in the evening, without having to worry about what they were wearing.

> "I wanted to make things 'pour être, non pas pour paraître' – to be, not to seem! ... I wanted it to be natural, anatomical: adapted to the movements of the human body, to slide up and down, back and forth on the arm."

Her philosophy was that the functional should also be beautiful, as seen in her treatment of clasps and links, which are an integral part of her design.

Looking always to the future, teeming with new ideas, Torun had many retrospective exhibitions in her life time, with perhaps the most prestigious, at the Musée des Arts Décoratifs in Paris, from October 1992 to January 1993. She died in 2006, leaving behind a volume of work that is still of the moment and has been brought back to the fore by the relaunch of Georg Jensen when it was taken over in 2011 by David Chu.

LEFT: Torun for Georg Jensen: Bangle – diamond, silver
This is a contemporary reissue of Torun's original design with an added embellishment of diamond.
IMAGE COURTESY OF GEORG JENSEN

OPPOSITE PAGE: The Iconic wristwatch – stainless steel
(Provenance: 'Antagonism II – l'objet' Exhibition, Musée des Arts décoratifs, Paris, 1962.)
This is a contemporary reissue of Torun's original design. IMAGE COURTESY OF GEORG JENSEN

"The pieces have to state what they are. Of course there should be an element of surprise, but the pieces have to be credible."

NANNA DITZEL
Light and Shadow

Born in Copenhagen, Denmark, Ditzel's design career started in furniture. Nanna Ditzel (née Hauberg, 1923-2005) attended the School of Arts and Crafts in Copenhagen before going on to study at the Danish Royal Academy of Art, where she met her husband, Jørgen.

> *"We met in the dark days of the war, in the autumn of 1943 at the furniture school, which was then in the loft of the Museum of Decorative Art... he was in his third year and I was in my first."*

They participated in a Cabinetmakers' Guild exhibition in 1944 before officially becoming furniture designers in 1946. After the War, they got married and set up business together. They made an extraordinary team, creating pieces not only in wood but also in glass, enamel and ceramics, as well as designing textiles. Together, they produced many prize-winning and iconic pieces, including the Hanging Chair (Egg chair) in 1959, before Jørgen's untimely death in 1961.

Nanna Ditzel continued to design furniture for the rest of her life, and also broadened her scope to include textiles and jewellery. She began to design jewellery while she was caring for her first child. In 1950 she submitted a necklace, bangle, brooch and an asymmetrical ring to the National Board of Goldsmiths' competition; out of 148 participants, she won first prize. Made by the court jewellers, Anton Michelsen, the silver gilt necklace comprises a double row of concave spoon-like links, constructed so as to create a 'light trap' around the wearer's neck. The ring was designed for the left hand and in such a way as to appear to elongate the finger. (She went on to design several award-winning pieces for Michelsen, many of which were signed 'A. Michelsen' rather then Nanna Ditzel.)

At that time, jewellery was not regarded as serious art in Denmark. Designers were looking at functionality above all else; Ditzel's designs took a new approach. The competition board noted that Ditzel's pieces stood out because they were elaborate, personal and showed a good understanding of the metals used, and that they were realistic yet innovative.

LEFT, CLOCKWISE FROM TOP LEFT: Nanna Ditzel for A. Michelsen: Brooch, 1950 – gold
Signed: 'A. Michelsen'. Winner of the National Board of Goldsmiths in Denmark
IMAGE COURTESY OF DENNIE DITZEL, NANNA DITZEL DESIGNS, DENMARK

Nanna Ditzel for A. Michelsen: Ring, 1950 – gold
Signed: 'A. Michelsen'. Winner of the National Board of Goldsmiths in Denmark
IMAGE COURTESY OF DENNIE DITZEL, NANNA DITZEL DESIGNS, DENMARK

Nanna Ditzel for A. Michelsen: Double row necklace, 1950 – silver gilt
Signed: 'A. Michelsen'. Winner of the National Board of Goldsmiths in Denmark
IMAGE COURTESY OF DENNIE DITZEL, NANNA DITZEL DESIGNS, DENMARK

OPPOSITE PAGE: Nanna Ditzel for A. Michelsen: Necklace – silver
Signed: 'A. Michelsen'. IMAGE COURTESY OF MODERNITY, STOCKHOLM

Nanna Ditzel for Georg Jensen: Hollow silver bracelet – silver
This is a reissue of Nanna and Jørgen Ditzel's original design, which won the silver medal at the Triennial in Milan in 1957 (DANSK KUNSTHÅNDVÆRK no. 10, 1957).
IMAGE COURTESY OF GEORG JENSEN

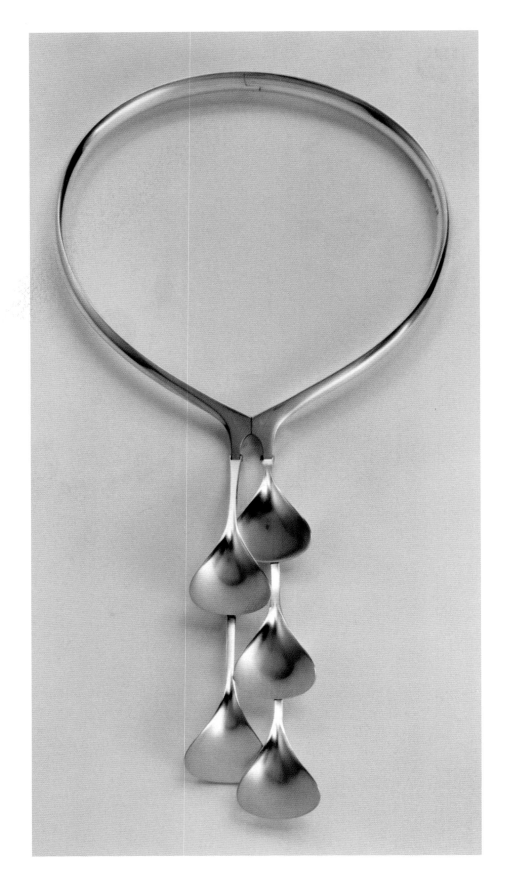

Scallop Pendant necklace, 1957 – silver
The organic shapes echo those of Nanna and Jørgen Ditzel's famous Egg chair.
IMAGE COURTESY OF DENNIE DITZEL, NANNA DITZEL DESIGNS, DENMARK

Georg Jensen

Nanna and Jørgen Ditzel joined forces with the silversmith Georg Jensen in 1954. One of the first jewels that Nanna designed was a large hollow bangle, which was a statement in itself; its triangular and ovoid outline referenced a piece of jewellery dating from the Iron Age that Ditzel had seen at the National Museum of Finland in Helsinki.

For the exhibition of Georg Jensen's 50th Anniversary, Ditzel created another hollow bangle with accompanying earrings and an asymmetrical ring. The fluid lines of the voluminous bangle stretch and fan out to create a rounded hinged form with a simple opening system, which is an integral part of the design. The great originality of the bracelet is that the 'centre of interest' is worn on the side rather than in the middle of the wrist. The set won Ditzel the silver medal at the Triennial in Milan in 1957.

Her well-known bracelet with its solid looking hollow silver links won the gold medal at the Triennial in Milan, in 1960. The full-bodied convex links were reflected in the neighbouring links almost as if two mirrors were facing each other and creating an infinity of shadows and forms. The play of light on the surface of her jewels was almost as accidental as it was deliberate; she knew the properties of the metals she used, but as she started the process with a wax model it was not easy to see where and how the light would react to the surface of her rounded forms. Thus experimentation was very much a part of her initial work for each piece of jewellery.

ABOVE: Nanna Ditzel for Georg Jensen: Hollow gold bracelet – yellow gold
The cuff was inspired by a piece of jewellery dating from the Iron age.
This is a reissue of Nanna and Jørgen Ditzel's original 1957 design
IMAGE COURTESY OF GEORG JENSEN

LEFT: Modern version of iconic ear screws – yellow gold
This is a contemporary reissue of Ditzel's original design, which won the Silver
medal at the Triennial in Milan 1957 with the hollow bangle.
IMAGE COURTESY OF GEORG JENSEN

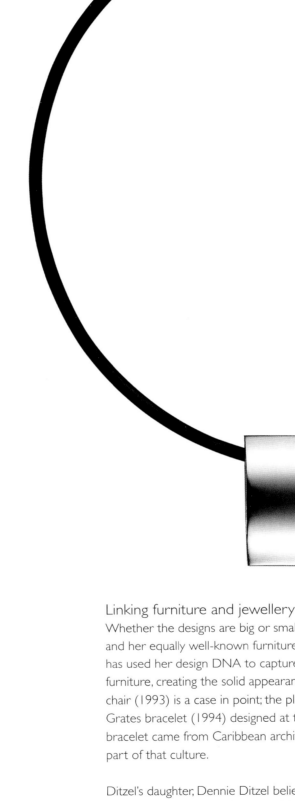

RIGHT: Surf necklace, 1999 – silver, leather
Inspired by Nanna Ditzel's Seashell chair.
IMAGE COURTESY OF GEORG JENSEN

BELOW: Surf bracelet, 1999 – silver
Inspired by Nanna Ditzel's Seashell chair.
IMAGE COURTESY OF GEORG JENSEN

Linking furniture and jewellery

Whether the designs are big or small there is a definite correlation between her iconic jewels and her equally well-known furniture designs, each feeding off the other for inspiration. Ditzel has used her design DNA to capture the outlines and the concept of overall volume in her furniture, creating the solid appearance of her jewellery forms. Her prize-winning Trinidad chair (1993) is a case in point; the play of shadows was introduced into her silver openwork Grates bracelet (1994) designed at the same time. Inspiration for both the chair and the bracelet came from Caribbean architecture, its grates and shutters, which were so much a part of that culture.

Ditzel's daughter, Dennie Ditzel believes the Surf bracelet (1999) was influenced by the Seashell armchair (1996). The undulating form deliberately plays with the movement of light and shadow on the silver's surface. A similar process can be attributed to her necklace from 1961, which works on a series of overlapping and convex plaques.

Her collar, formed with a double row of alternating polished cornelian plaques, highlights a regular outline. It can be seen later in her set of formation benches, Tema, which she created for Fredericia Stolefabrik in 2002, as well as the outline of her Nanna easy chair of the same year.

Ditzel's gold Oyster brooch not only takes its inspiration from the mollusc, it also echoes the outline of the Oda chair, which she designed with her husband, Jørgen in 1956.

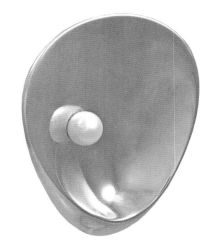

Gems

In 1962 the new artistic director for Georg Jensen, Soren Georg Jensen asked Ditzel to include gemstones in her jewellery designs. The result was a fascinating bracelet set with various coloured cabochon tourmalines. The stones appear to float above the yellow gold hinged bangle, and the light plays with the reflections of the gemstones on the surface of the gold below; there is also a lively display of colour as the wearer moves. Only one bangle was made with tourmalines, others have been crafted set with cabochon amethysts.

TOP: Oyster brooch – pearl, yellow gold
This is a contemporary reissue of Ditzel's original design.
IMAGE COURTESY OF GEORG JENSEN

ABOVE: Light Reflecting bangle, 1962 – tourmaline, yellow gold
IMAGE COURTESY OF GEORG JENSEN

RIGHT: Grates bracelet, 1994 – silver
Inspired by Nanna Ditzel's Trinidad chair. IMAGE COURTESY OF GEORG JENSEN

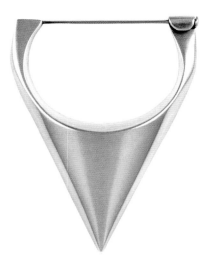

ABOVE: Iconic silver brooch, No. 326 – silver
IMAGE COURTESY OF GEORG JENSEN

BELOW: Nanna Ditzel for Georg Jensen: Hollow Convex Link
bracelet – silver
*This is a reissue of Nanna and Jørgen Ditzel's original design, which
won the gold medal at the Triennial in Milan in 1960 (DANSK
KUNSTHÅNDVÆRK no. 10, 1960).* IMAGE COURTESY OF GEORG JENSEN

OPPOSITE PAGE: Overlapping Convex Plaque necklace, 1961 –
silver IMAGE COURTESY OF GEORG JENSEN

Colour and form

She loved bold colours and was inspired after being exposed to the rich array of colours in Mexico's culture and everyday life. Nanna Ditzel believed firmly that silver jewellery should be worn with dark and cold colours and that gold jewellery was the preserve of pale and warm colours. Her taste was simple: well-made clothing with powerful jewellery to balance the look. She preferred one large voluminous jewel to many smaller pieces. For her, there was a dialogue between the body and her jewellery and what was near the body should be curvaceous, fluid and comfortable.

Ditzel's jewellery is all about form, outline and simplicity; she studied how green plants were structured, discovering their geometrical make up. She did away with decoration of any kind, looking purely at the essence of the form, its volume. Without working the metal into textures, she used the reflections of light on the metal's surface to tell the story. Her work echoes that of the great sculptors of the time, such as Jean Arp and Henry Moore.

Ditzel's style, alongside that of the sculptor Henning Koppel opened the way for new ideas in metal jewellery, from playing with the light on the metal's surface to its matt or burnished finish.

"According to Nanna everything was possible. Life was so great with Nanna, because she had such a loveable way of pushing things one step further all the time. The work she produced in the '90s and the speed at which she worked and the way she dared to use new materials made her highly popular, becoming 'the grand old lady of modern design'."

Thomas Graversen, director of Fredericia Furnitures.

"The sparkle of the diamond necklace suits any complexion and enhances the glow of any skin."

MARIANNE OSTIER
Jeweller to the Stars

An artist of many talents, Marianne (1902-1976) studied sculpture at the Arts and Crafts school in Vienna for three years. Her husband, Otto Oliver Oesterreicher, was a third generation Court Jeweller. The family business, situated at Graben in Vienna, were jewellers to Queen Marie of Romania and Queen Geraldine of Albania, as well as the Maharani of Cooch-Behar and the Maharani of Baroda. They emigrated to the United States, via Rio de Janeiro, from Austria after the Anschluss in 1938. In New York, they changed their name to Ostier.

Pioneers
It is a credit to their endeavour and hard work that Marianne and Otto set up Ostier Inc. at 724 Fifth Avenue in 1941, and soon became a popular jeweller in New York, with Marianne designing classically modern jewellery. Ostier's contribution to jewellery design in the United States was recognised early on; she has been attributed with introducing three-dimensional jewellery design, although this was really more of a reintroduction after years of voguish flat diamond jewellery. Ostier did come up with a series of new ideas, which found their way into the annals of jewellery design history: her pin cushion brooch, for example, which was inspired by looking at ...a pin cushion! Another, which is as contemporary today as it was when she developed it, was her skin pin – jewels that were stuck directly to the skin using a suction technique and a brown fluid made from a 'secret formula'. Dorothy Roe, fashion editor for the Associated Press, described Marianne Ostier's attendance at a gala:

> *"...A decorative redhead with creamy-white skin, recently startled her public by appearing at a formal function with a US$25,000 diamond clip fastened to her bare shoulder. It stayed firmly in place all evening, and so intrigued the onlookers that people left the dance floor to gather round for a closer look."*

Publicity
Ostier had all sorts of ideas for creating a loyal following. In 1948, the *Dunkirk Evening Observer* reported how Hollywood men could join Ostier's club at a cost of US$10,000 a year, in exchange for which, once a month they could choose a jewel for their girlfriends or wives to wear and then change it the next month. A great self-publicist, Ostier even filmed a short newsreel topic for Warner-Pathé news at her home, in 1953. Journalists would regularly ask her about trends in jewellery; she spoke on the radio about gemstones and what the etiquette was for wearing jewellery and, more to the point, what it *should* be.

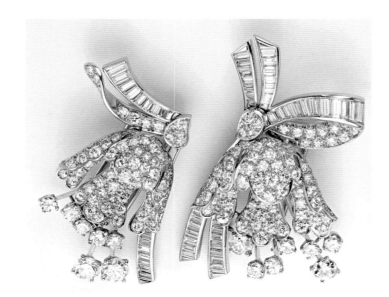

LEFT: Canterbury Bell double-clip brooch, 1950 – diamond, platinum IMAGE COURTESY SOTHEBY'S INC.

OPPOSITE PAGE: Gold oval link necklace, 1960 – diamond, textured yellow gold IMAGE COURTESY WARTSKI, LONDON

Hollywood

Ostier was one of the first to understand the promotional power of lending jewellery to film stars for special occasions. She would recount how she saw Hedy Lamarr at the opera in Vienna. Having decided that the Hollywood actress's jewellery was not very becoming for her features and style, Ostier sent some design sketches to Lamarr. It was the beginning of a fruitful relationship and Lamarr started to wear Ostier's designs. Marlene Dietrich was another fan of Ostier's work. Ostier even won herself a contract at the Enterprise film studios by walking in and telling the executives what she thought of their choice in jewellery for their stars. She once stated:

"It is amazing, Hollywood has fashion experts and make-up experts but no one supervises jewellery! An actress can ruin the entire effect of a beautiful gown simply by wearing the wrong jewellery."

She is reported as having given a diamond and gold disc bracelet with a 'replica of the Arc de Triomphe', to Ingrid Bergman. The inspiration for the bracelet came from Ingrid Bergman's forthcoming film, *Arch of Triumph*, for the Enterprise Studios; naturally, it was all over the press.

Advice for the Wearer

And it was not just the Hollywood stars she sought to influence. Ostier had strong opinions about how jewels should be worn and was keen to voice her point of view. In 1958 her book *Jewels and the Woman* (Horizon Press, New York) explained to every woman the proper art of adorning themselves.

She was always conscious of the body and how her designs would sit, as well as the complexion of the wearer. She discussed how she used a black pearl's dark lustre to accentuate a pale complexion. Indeed, Ostier had very fixed ideas of who could wear certain gemstones and what type of woman could wear a specific jewel; for instance a woman with black hair and blue eyes should wear aquamarine in red gold or golden topaz with yellow gold and both of these should be combined with blue sapphires. For those with brown eyes, aquamarines with rubies in a platinum setting is a must. For a blonde with fair skin, Ostier advises that "*rubies, amethysts and aquamarines will do wonders*" but that the "*plain metallic look of gold and silver should be avoided; little of any metal should be seen and coloured stones should be dispersed throughout the earclip.*"

She was very fond of ear clips, which in her opinion were the focal point of jewellery in the late 1950s and, of course, she was all for 'the bigger the better'.

Multifunctional Jewellery

Whilst still in Vienna, Marianne Ostier had designed jewellery for Queen Geraldine of Albania. In 1939, King Zog I was deposed by the Italians, and his wife Queen Geraldine sold some of her jewellery at Ostier Inc. in 1959, including her coronation tiara and some other bridal jewels, many of which had been designed by Marianne Ostier. One such jewel was a 30-inch long necklace that could be adjusted and worn as a short necklace or as a choker. It also had a detachable pendant. (*The Troy Record*, 7 April, 1959). In *Jewels and the Woman*, Ostier explains jewellery conversions:

"The problem is complex, because it is not simply a question of what other jewels a main piece can be broken into. The major concern is how well all the transformations fit the personality of the individual who is to wear them."

Target brooch, 1947 – lapis lazuli, turquoise, pink sapphire, diamond, yellow gold rope twist

She describes her most challenging commission, for a Viennese ballerina, who wanted a
necklace that could be separated into a bracelet and five clips of varying sizes:

> *"Two of these were to form an assorted pair of dress clips; two were to be
> matched for the ears; one was to be larger, to serve as a brooch but with an
> attachment so that it might also become a hair ornament."*

Ostier rose to the challenge and the finished jewel was awarded the Gold Medal *für Schönheit
und Kunst* ('Beauty and Art') at the Künstlerhaus.

Themes and inspiration
Her jewels had several interesting themes. Her yellow gold jewellery was set with brilliant-cut
and marquise-cut diamonds, coloured gemstones and invariably would have a twisted yellow
gold cord that traced the outline of the stones, giving the pieces a light openwork feel. She
created gold openwork lace-like bib necklaces with gem-set quatrefoils. She had a talent for
composing diamonds into interesting varied cut necklaces and brooches. Cascades of pearls
would tumble from the ears and her diamond compositions were a mix of baguettes,
brilliants and marquise cuts.

Queen Geraldine of Albania's Coronation tiara by
Marianne Ostier for Oesterreicher, Vienna – diamond,
white gold IMAGE COURTESY SOTHEBY'S INC.

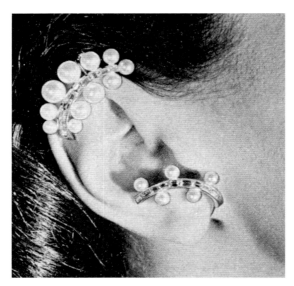

Re-appearing New Moon earrings – pearl, diamond, platinum
Winner of the Diamond USA Awards in 1956.
ILLUSTRATED IN *JEWELS AND THE WOMAN: THE ROMANCE, MAGIC AND ART OF FEMININE ADORNMENT* BY MARIANNE OSTIER.

Textured gold and abstract forms were another more avant-garde style. Bark-like surfaces cropped up in brooches and as links for bracelets and necklaces; one, her diamond and cabochon emerald 'Voodoo' necklace, was illustrated in *Art Magazine* and was chosen to represent the United States at the 'Art in Precious Jewelry' exhibition at the Finch College Museum in 1966. It was a huge accolade for Ostier who found herself in the rarified company of other artists such as Georges Braque and Salvador Dalí.

The natural world as well as the abstract were a continual inspiration to her: pine cones, leaves, molten lava, starbursts and bubbles were all given the Ostier treatment. Passmenterie fringing, lace and sewing stitches were given a similar lease of bejewelled life.

Legacy

The death of her husband Otto in 1968 meant that she had to take on increasing administrative duties for the company. In 1969, she decided she could continue no longer and Ostier Inc. ceased trading. The company's stock was sold off at the Parke-Bernet Galleries in New York on 19 November 1969, including all of Marianne Ostier's jewellery designs.

During her remarkably successful and high-profile career, Ostier's work was recognised with many honours, including the Diamond USA Awards in 1954, 1955 and 1956. Her three winning pieces in 1956 were her Star Performer platinum cuff buttons and shirt studs, set with baguette diamonds; a pair of Cherry Blossom earrings crafted into a bouquet of small brilliant diamonds tied together with a small baguette diamond ribbon; and a pair of ear clips, entitled Re-appearing New Moon. The latter were designed as two crescent moons that trace the top and the bottom of the ear, set with baguette diamonds and pearls, and held in place by a platinum wire behind the ear. The earrings were reversible, with the heavier crescent being interchangeable with the smaller crescent. Ostier went on to receive the International Diamonds Award five times and, in 1960, she became the first ever lifetime member of the Diamonds International Academy.

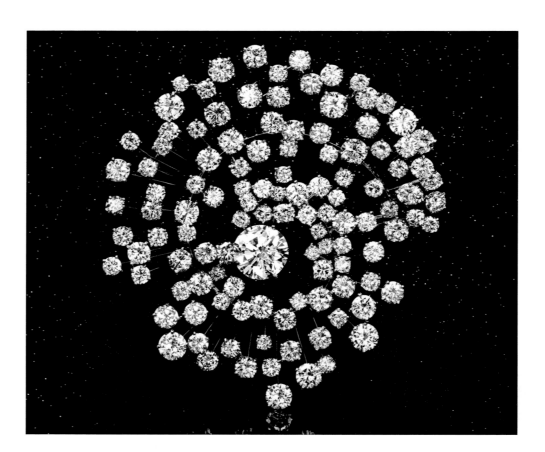

RIGHT: Constellation (Galaxy) brooch – diamond, platinum
IMAGE COURTESY SOTHEBY'S INC.

OPPOSITE PAGE: Voodoo necklace – cabochon emerald, diamond, yellow textured gold IMAGE COURTESY SKINNER'S INC.

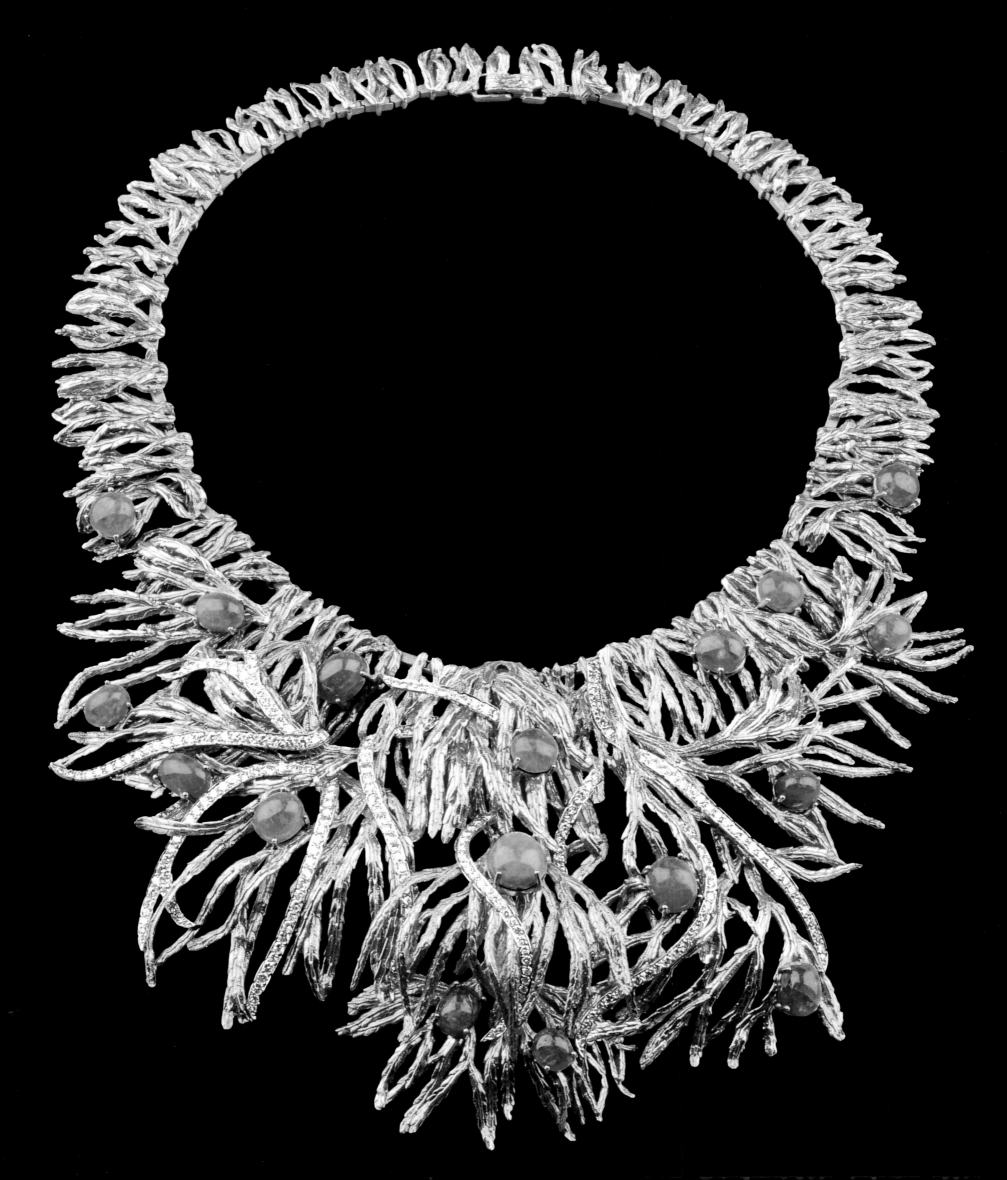

"Oils seemed such a fragile means of expression ... I decided to work in a more enduring medium: gemstones, gold and platinum."

The Pocono Record (Stroudsburg, Pennsylvania) 12 November, 1969

BARBARA ANTON
From Painting to Pearls

Pennsylvania-born Barbara Anton (1926-2007) followed in the tracks of Olga Tritt. Just as Tritt designed jewellery for the Brazilian Pavilion at the 1939 New York World's Fair, so Barbara Anton designed jewellery for the Pakistan Pavilion at the 1964 New York World's Fair. One of Anton's pieces on show was a hand jewel set with natural pink pearls; it decorated the back of the hand with a large medallion from which radiated five rings worn one on each finger. Another show-stopping jewel from the same collection covered the entire finger with tendrils of flowers set, again, with natural pink pearls. Anton christened it the Branch of Life ring.

Anton had initially studied engineering at Antioch College before going on to study acting and oil painting at Columbia University and at the Ridgewood School of Art. She painted in oils for many years before becoming a gemmologist at the GIA alongside her husband, Albert, and studying jewellery design at the Museum of Modern Art, New York.

In 1963, her Pagoda clasp, created using 6 baguette and four round diamonds set in yellow gold, won the De Beers Diamonds International Award. The clasp transformed a strand of pearls or beads and could also be worn as a ring, charm or as a pendant.

Pearls were a predilection of Anton's. She received an astonishing 23 international jewellery awards during her career, including awards from the Cultured Pearl Associations of America and Japan in 1966 and 1967. Her winning jewel in 1967 was as inspired as it was eccentric; she designed a knee bracelet using blue and white cultured pearls to be worn just below the knee, decorating the leg as it peeked from below the hem of a 1960s dress. The jewel could also be converted and worn as an arm bracelet or transformed into a brooch or hair ornament. In 1968, she took away their most prestigious award.

Barbara Anton was a hugely talented jewellery designer whose work defined the style and designs of high jewellery in the 1960s. She experimented with gold textures, bringing a well-honed sense of randomness to her gold forms set with gemstones and pearls. As well as designing jewellery, Anton was an actress and a writer. She was a contributing editor on fashion and design for the *National Jeweler* on a monthly basis and the *Journal Suisse d'Horlogerie et de Bijouterie*, was appointed to the design panel of the famous *Jeweler's Circular Keystone* trade magazine, and she published many plays, songs and several works of fiction.

Anton worked with her husband from a small boutique/workshop in New Jersey. After her death, many of her landmark designs came up for sale. Her work can now be seen in the permanent collection of the Museum of Fine Arts, Boston.

Fish ring – moss agate, pearl, pale emerald, diamond, yellow gold
COURTESY OF KIMBERLY KLOSTERMAN AT KKLOSTERMAN JEWELRY, CINCINNATI, OHIO

OPPOSITE PAGE: Bib necklace – cultured baroque pearl, pearl, diamond, textured yellow gold
(Provenance: From the Estate of Barbara Miller Anton, Sarasota, Florida.)
COURTESY OF KIMBERLY KLOSTERMAN AT KKLOSTERMAN JEWELRY, CINCINNATI, OHIO

"Once I began to fuse I also started on increasingly complex ideas and my work gradually took me longer and longer to evolve ... I was really trying to see how far the metal could be pushed."

GERDA FLÖCKINGER
Fusing Texture and Light

In England, Gerda Flöckinger creates her own bridge between art jewellery and more mainstream jewellery. She experiments with metal and pushes the boundaries of what is possible; talking about her fusion process, she has said:

> *"The technique is one of total risk at all times, of total melt-down or irreparable damage. The secret is to go to the edge of that, and stay there."*

Beginnings
Born in Innsbruck, Austria in 1927 she came to England as a child in 1938. After attending Saint Martin's school of Art for five years painting, she was very influenced by the work of Jean Fouquet on a trip to continental Europe in 1951. This proved to be a turning point for her.

On her return, Flöckinger did a stint working with a costume jewellery factory in London and went back to the Central School of Arts in the evenings. Here she created jewels that Grahame Hughes, Art Director of the Goldsmiths' Company, described as a *"two-dimensional approach to a three-dimensional art"*. Her pock-marked designs were built up with gold dust and small hollows, onto which she fused metal, just as a painter would build up an image using oils. On this lunar terrain she set her gemstones, creating contrasts in texture and light.

During the 1950s, she was influenced by the many new technologies, from micro-photographs of cell structures to high speed photography, such as the famous Milk Drop Coronet by Harold Edgerton in 1957.

Flöckinger had a huge influence on the first generation of art jewellers to appear on the '60s design scene in England. In 1962, she ran a now-famous course at the Hornsey School of Art, which concentrated on basic design and technical skills. The purpose of building this skillset was to enable the application of ideas.

Dr Elizabeth Goring of the Royal Scottish Museum says of Flöckinger:

> *"She proved to be an inspirational teacher ... her importance extends far beyond her influence on others, however, for her output is of the highest calibre both technically and aesthetically ... a unique contribution has been the development of new techniques using fusion of gold and silver."*

She became the first living woman artist to have her own exhibition at the Victoria & Albert Museum in 1971, and then again in 1986.

OPPOSITE PAGE: Gold ring and Disc Link necklace, 1962 – mother-of-pearl, cabochon aquamarine, onyx, gold
IMAGE COURTESY OF THE WORSHIPFUL COMPANY OF GOLDSMITHS, LONDON

BELOW: Sleeve ring – natural pearl, diamond, yellow gold
COURTESY OF KIMBERLY KLOSTERMAN AT KKLOSTERMAN JEWELRY, CINCINNATI, OHIO

ASTRID FOG
Sculptural Simplicity

Having started out as a fashion designer and then working as an editor, Astrid Fog (1911-1993) came late to jewellery. She, like many designers before her, couldn't find jewellery that she liked and that she felt would enhance her fashion designs. With this in mind, she turned her creative skills to creating sculptural, simply formed jewels that had an impact as well as making a fashion statement.

Her heart pendant/necklace was a huge success when it appeared in 1969. The fashion at the time was for polo neck sweaters, low waists and tight fitting shirts. This necklace dressed the outfit perfectly, with its long sautoir-style chain with its signature links and huge silver heart suspended from it. In 1970, she created a variation on the theme with an open circle of four rounded hollow bars replacing the heart.

Her use of simple geometric shapes was her signature. Silver hollow bars were composed in a multitude of different ways, from articulated links to curved convex/concave links creating bracelets, pendants and rings. Square shapes created a dynamic as the light moved across their textured surfaces, as did overlapping rounded plaques, which became a Fog icon.

Though little is known about this artist and archival information is slim, her simple lines and block shapes had a great impact on design towards the end of the 1960s and the beginning of the '70s. Fog is credited with revitalising the Georg Jensen jewellery department and helping to double their sales in the 1970s. Her designs are still being produced by Georg Jensen and are as popular today as when they were first created.

It is interesting to note that she also worked for the Royal Copenhagen Porcelain Manufacturers as a designer for many years, and with Just Anderson, a Danish metalware manufacturer. She was also a costume designer for the Danish film *Grau ist alle Theorie,* directed by John Jacobsen in 1956.

LEFT: Fog for Georg Jensen: Heart pendant and chain — silver
IMAGE COURTESY OF GEORG JENSEN

OPPOSITE PAGE: Fog for Georg Jensen: Silver bangles, 1966 — silver
IMAGE COURTESY OF GEORG JENSEN

"I believe in using ancient techniques in modern forms to show that old and new can mix."

CORNELIA ROETHEL
Tracing with Gold

Cornelia Roethel trained from 1964-67 with Johann Wilm Jr., with whom she learnt the subtle beauty of granulation. She developed her own technique using flux in the glue so that she was able to fix the gold granules to curved surfaces without having to worry about the grains rolling away, before she fired the piece.

Roethel started to work with Max Pollinger as an apprentice in 1967. Together, they created a collection of 15 pieces inspired by Wassily Kandinsky's jewellery designs, recently discovered by Roethel's father, Hans Konrad Roethel, a renowned art historian and the conservator at the Pinakothek Art Museum, Munich.

From Kandinsky's painting 'Trente', Roethel and Pollinger chose a series of six squares, which they transformed into six gold plaques, playing with the surface to create etched and textured reliefs in accordance with the chiaroscuro technique that Kandinsky had used in the original oil painting; these in turn were the interchangeable design at the centre of three bangles.

Amongst Roethel's other jewellery designs, some of her most impressive ideas include hollow gold beads, decorated on the surface with shapes and patterns using tiny granules that are highlighted with small circular coloured gemstones and diamonds. They in turn, were placed on complex gold chains woven in yellow gold. Pendants of carved emerald cabochons depicting flowers and other foliage are set apart with elaborately decorated frames using once again her signature granulation technique. She uses the gold grains to heighten the texture and the three dimensional aspect of both her flat designs and her more sculpted jewels.

In 1970, she was awarded the accolade Master Goldsmith, and two years later she opened a workshop in New York, gaining a reputation in the artistic community for excellent workmanship and intricate designs. Some of her work, including the Kandinsky pieces, were included in the Exhibition 'Gold' at the Metropolitan Museum in 1973. She returned to Munich in 1992, where she opened a new atelier.

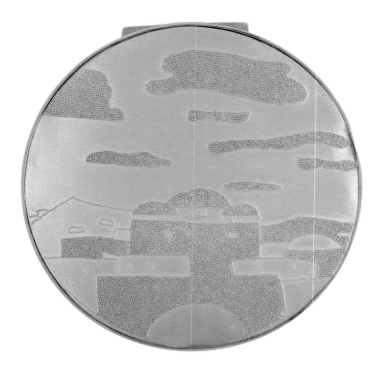

LEFT: Roethel and Pollinger: Pill box – gold granulation, yellow gold
(Provenance: exhibited at the Leonard Hutton Galleries, 1968.)
One of the 15 pieces inspired by Kandinsky's jewellery designs. IMAGE COURTESY OF LUCAS RARITIES, LONDON

OPPOSITE PAGE:
Miró Bracelet, 1970 – cabochon ruby, cabochon sapphire, cabochon emerald, cabochon aquamarine, pearl, gold granulation, gold
This jewel is similar to Roethel's Diploma piece in 1968, the Miró necklace. IMAGE COURTESY OF CORNELIA ROETHEL

Spiral bracelet, 1974 – natural pearls, gold granulation, yellow gold IMAGE COURTESY OF CORNELIA ROETHEL

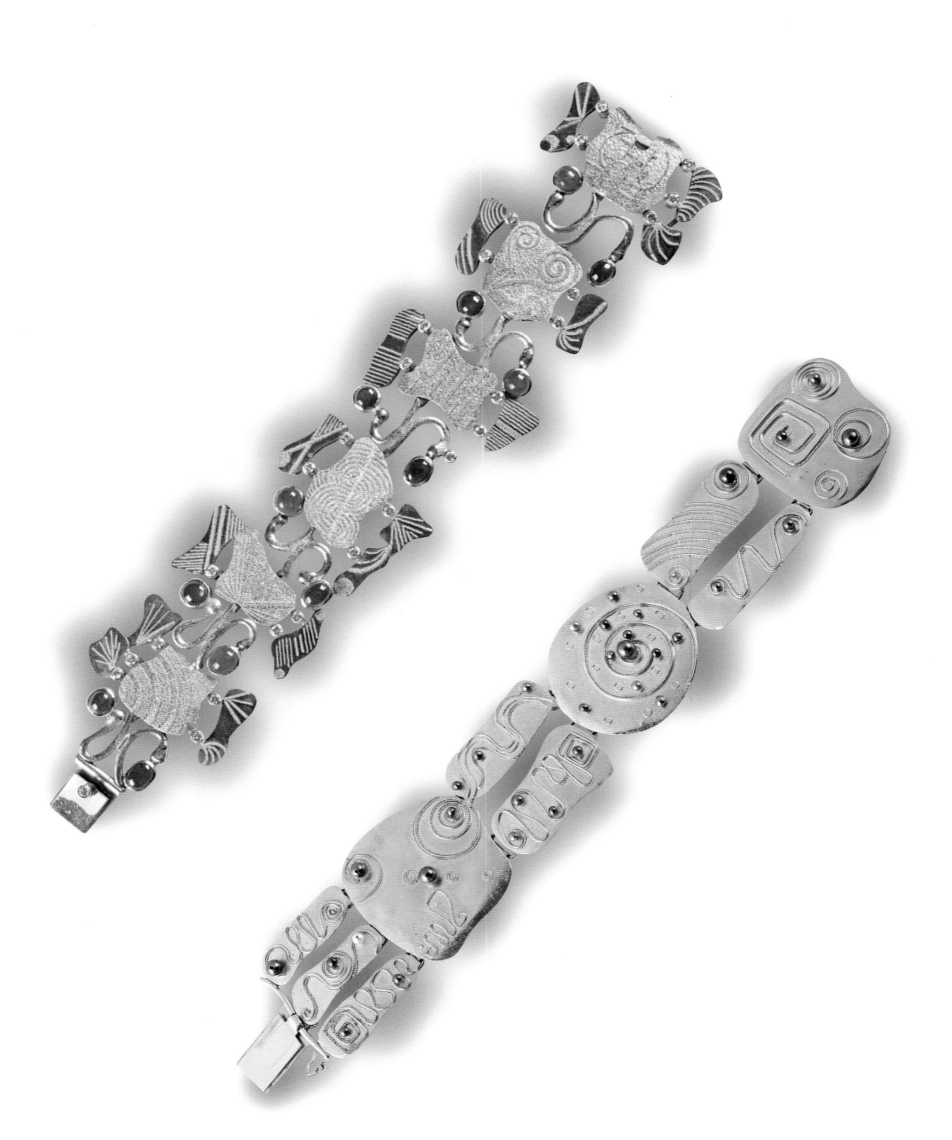

"My best jewellery creations are round, curvaceous, if it is a success, it will become timeless and live on through different periods ... they are designs which are between sculpture and jewellery."

CATHERINE NOLL
The Beauty of Wood

Catherine Noll (1945-1994) was a jeweller who explored the concept of jewellery art and its rapport with the body, alongside such jewellers as Line Vautrin, Vivianna Torun von Bülow-Hübe, Nanna Ditzel and Astrid Fog. Noll worked with light and contrasts, as well as solid ovoid forms and crescent, concave and convex silhouettes. Cuffs, honed in ebony and ivory, are asymmetrical like the bias on a dress; they are gently sloping, immensely elegant understatements of outline.

Materials
Her favoured material was wood – African ebony, wonderfully striated Macassar ebony, the dramatic feline markings of coconut and red palm wood derived from densely packed fibres, rosewood, sandalwood, the reddish Asian wood padauk, and the heavenly purpleheart wood, amaranth.

Shortly after graduating from the Ecole Nationale des Arts Décoratifs in Paris in 1972, she began to experiment with plexiglas, lucite and altuglas, which are all forms of acrylic glass and are known for their very high capacity to transmit light. What makes them so interesting to work with is that they can be opaque or transparent and they come in different colours, as well as being anti-reflective, matt or mirror-like. Noll also worked with ivory, shell, quartz, lapis lazuli and turquoise, as well as imitations in plastic of lapis lazuli and malachite, and matt and transparent resin.

RIGHT: Multi-coloured bangles – plexiglas
IMAGE COURTESY OF HARRY FANE, OBSIDIAN GALLERY

OPPOSITE PAGE: Bangles – ebony, padauk wood, acrylic
IMAGE COURTESY OF HARRY FANE, OBSIDIAN GALLERY

RIGHT, TOP TO BOTTOM:
Beaded bangle – ivory, elasticated cotton

Torque – ebony, mother-of-pearl

Bangles – ivory, acrylic, brass; ebony, acrylic, brass

OPPOSITE PAGE: Carved toggle/pendant – ivory, cotton

ALL IMAGES COURTESY OF HARRY FANE, OBSIDIAN GALLERY

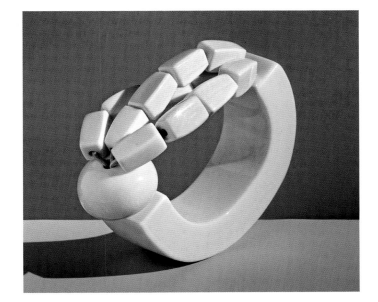

Background

On his death in 1970, Catherine Noll's grandfather, the famous furniture artist Alexandre Noll, left her his workshop in Fontenay-aux-Roses, with all its tools. As a child, she had watched her grandfather and then her mother Odile work and sculpt the different woods in Alexandre Noll's atelier. She had learnt how to choose woods, how to sense and feel them, how each wood had a different character and what was necessary to get the most out of each specimen. Most of the woods Noll used were hard with a high density and they had a high lustre making them ideal for jewellery. Others, such as palm wood, were tricky to work due to the differences in hardness between the fibres and the lighter cellulose structure of the wood.

Collaborative Work

Noll collaborated with Tiffany's in New York and Bergdorf and Goodman at the beginning of her career, and presented her jewels at Bijorhca, Paris, a professional salon that helped introduce her work to such fashion houses as Chanel and Christian Dior. Her first exhibitions were at the Chéret Gallery in Paris. In 1982 she founded a small group of artists and jewellery designers with four other friends; they called themselves Héphaïstos, after the god of fire and volcanoes and, by extension, the god of metallurgy. Later, she joined her friend Maté Lapierre, exhibiting in Lapierre's gallery in the Marais. Lapierre was an artist who worked in glass creating sculptures, as well as jewellery, forming a link between the glass jewellery of antiquity and that of the modern day. Lapierre's work most certainly had an influence on Noll's work and it is probably no coincidence that Baccarat, the famous crystal manufacturer, commissioned Noll to create their first collection of glass crystal jewellery – the Coquillage Collection in 1993. Noll took part in the 1987, 1990 and 1993 triennials for jewellery in Paris (Triennales européennes du Bijou).

Legacy

Catherine Noll's designs are strong curved forms. She had a great sense of proportion and dimension; her artisan approach to these shapes and outlines set her apart from other jewellery designers working on similar lines. She worked as one with her tools and shared with sculptors a form of creating, by taking away from the material to achieve what she was looking for. The deliberate gestures she used whilst wielding her tools formed the simple primitive concave and convex shapes.

"Tactile, organic, she is creative and bold! Her pieces are big but it is never the wrong size." Harry Fane, founder of the Obsidian Gallery

"I have come to the conclusion that the beauty in nature is not there simply to be beautiful… it is there because it has meaning. Living near the mountains, I do a lot of hiking and I am constantly in awe of nature – always thinking could I do something special with this or that?"

ANGELA CUMMINGS
Turning Nature into Gold

A passionate nature lover and artist, Cummings evokes the natural world in her jewellery, be it in a deliberate fashion or in more subtle references, using opaque coloured fine gemstones with iridescent mother-of-pearl and opal to create her compositions. The play of light on the surface of the metals she uses is just as important in each of her designs.

Background

Cummings was born in Klagenfurt, Austria in 1944, but spent her childhood on the outskirts of Washington DC before returning to Europe to study fine art in Perugia, Italy, at the Accademia di Belle Arti, and then gemmology and jewellery making at the Staatliche Zeichenakademie in Hanau, Germany. As a young student, Cummings recalls stopping off at Tiffany's in New York, to visit an exhibition of Jean Schlumberger's work. It was to be a watershed moment for Cummings and she instantly decided that she would become Schlumberger's assistant (without consulting Schlumberger about her decision!).

> *"Right after I graduated, I went straight to Tiffany's and of course Mr. Schlumberger already had a wonderful team in place."*

She did, however, get a job with Tiffany's in 1967, with the head designer at the time, Donald Claflin. She absorbed everything that she was told and from the very start she designed special orders for Tiffany's clients.

> *"He really taught me everything about fashion and the concept of marrying fashion with timelessness; it's a difficult balance to get, to be of the moment and yet to have the timeless quality which means that it will be worn years later. He taught me so much about the importance of fashion and the unimportance of fashion."*

LEFT: Snakeskin Wave bracelets – diamond, matt yellow gold COURTESY OF CHRISTIE'S INC.

OPPOSITE PAGE: Orchid necklace, 1985-87 – opal inlay, yellow gold COURTESY OF CHRISTIE'S INC.

ABOVE: Cummings for Tiffany & Co.: Fish necklace – diamond, platinum, matte yellow gold COURTESY OF CHRISTIE'S INC.

LEFT: Dragonfly bangle – mother-of-pearl, yellow gold COURTESY OF CHRISTIE'S INC.

OPPOSITE PAGE, TOP: Cummings for Tiffany & Co.: Multi-stone Inlay bangle – coral, blue lace agate, aventurine, ice quartz, yellow gold COURTESY OF CHRISTIE'S INC.

OPPOSITE PAGE, BOTTOM: Cummings for Tiffany & Co.: Multi-stone Inlay earclips – coral, blue lace agate, aventurine, ice quartz, gold COURTESY OF CHRISTIE'S INC.

Tiffany's

In 1975, she designed her first jewellery collection under her own name for Tiffany's. Fallen leaves, petals and dried sunflowers were to become her inspiration. From these realistic representations of nature, she interpreted what she saw with negative space to create light butterflies and fallen leaves using outlines of shapes that she found. Clouds, Chinese lanterns, feathers, scales of lizards, snakes and fish, and splashes in diamonds were themes to catch Cummings' attention. She was particularly inspired by the patterns in nature, from lotus roots to hydrangea and rose petals, to the round cross section of citrus fruit and nothing escaped her observant eye. Textiles were another source of inspiration: how they fall, individual stitches and knots were all investigated, turned into gold, inlaid mosaic and diamond interpretations.

Mosaics

A visit to Venice's most famous buildings led to some of Cumming's most durable designs. On viewing their beautiful 'Pietra Dura' marble floors and their 'trompe l'oeil' perspectives, she created her inlaid mosaic bangles and necklaces. The stunning hardstone colours, with veins which shot through them, struck a chord within her; the juxtaposition of these stones, alongside opals and mother-of-pearl, have spanned her career, both during her time with Tiffany's and afterwards.

> "I know a lot about stones… I just have a mental paint box, I know the colours of my stones. I had a brilliant teacher in Germany; he had a basket full of stones and it was passed from student to student and we had to identify a stone from the basket. There were all these colours, it was like a game."

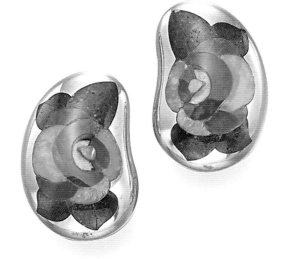

Opal is a favourite because of its play of colour and its wonderful versatility; Cummings found a stone cutter in Hong Kong who understood what she wanted and had the talent to execute the shapes and forms she needed for her mosaic bangles.

After leaving Tiffany's in 1984, Cummings set up on her own, and allowed herself a free rein to explore in different directions, not only creating jewellery but also moving into flatware and tabletop accessories. She distributed through the main department stores of the time, from Bergdorf Goodman to Neiman Marcus and Harrods, London. She retired and closed her company in 2004.

The Ocean

As a child, Cummings was fascinated by the oceans. She dates this back to a book her father gave her, which recounted the exploration of the sea and what lay beneath the surface of the waves. She was amazed by the photographs in the book, and although she never became the oceanographer of her girlhood dreams, she nurtured her passion through scuba diving and snorkelling for pleasure.

After taking an extended break, in 2013 she returned to the world of jewellery, in association with Assael, a purveyor of South Sea pearls; this collaboration takes full advantage of the great attachment that Cummings has to the sea.

She continues in 2016 to design jewellery for Assael, working from her home in Park City, Utah, enabled by the gift of modern technology to follow the progression of her jewels in workshops far away. Always concerned with the portrayal of nature in simplified forms, her designs are classical with a hint of the original; they are as discreet as they are refined in taste.

BELOW: Cummings for Assael: Coral branch necklace, 2013 – baroque South Sea pearl, diamond, white gold
PHOTO BY STEVEN HAAS, IMAGE COURTESY OF ASSAEL

OPPOSITE PAGE: Cummings for Assael: Seahorse pendant with detachable pearl, 2015 – baroque South Sea pearl, diamond, white gold, yellow gold
PHOTO BY STEVEN HAAS, IMAGE COURTESY OF ASSAEL

"I am not an artist, I am a craftswoman"

ELSA PERETTI
The Sensual Magician

Peretti – model, artist, philanthropist, businesswoman – but above all, a craftswoman whose creative imagination has forged a philosophy of style that is as relevant today, perhaps even more so, than when she started at the beginning of the 1970s. With the simple stroke of a pen and sleight of hand, Peretti has introduced simplicity and form to jewellery that is trendy, classic and iconic.

"The shape of my objects has to be clear. I want them to be simple and natural."

In her hands, the ordinary takes on a different purpose from beans, hearts, apples, teardrops and pumpkins to scorpions, starfish and claws. All are given the Peretti treatment, transformed into simple, fluid lines. She takes the mundane and looks at it differently, she takes little parts of our lives and creates fleeting moments in time caught forever.

Her jewels not only have a visual quality; they are also sculptural and tactile. Her influence and success is such that when in 2012 Peretti was thinking of leaving Tiffany's, along with her designs, they were obliged to inform the New York Stock Exchange. In the end, both parties came to an agreement, which will perpetuate her designs at Tiffany's with a new 20-year licensing agreement.

Background
After completing an interior design degree in Rome at the Volbicela School, she left her native Italy in 1966 and moved to Barcelona, which was the cultural hub of Europe at the time, attracting many artists. It was here, whilst working as a fashion model, that she met many extraordinary people who were to populate her life, including Salvador Dalí, for whom she modelled at his home in Port Lligat.

"I never regretted this decision. Spain was so different, Franco was still alive and Barcelona was full of very interesting individuals. Gaudí was an inspiration that lasted a long time in my mind."

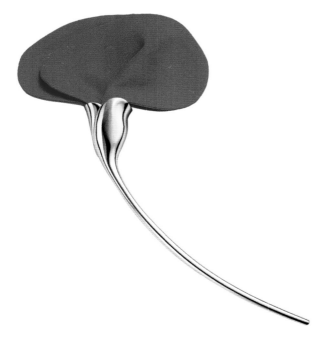

LEFT: Elsa Peretti® Amapola brooch – red silk, yellow gold
PHOTOGRAPH BY JOSH HASKIN © TIFFANY AND COMPANY

OPPOSITE PAGE: Elsa Peretti® Bone Cuff – yellow gold
PHOTOGRAPH BY HIRO; © HIRO; IMAGE COURTESY HIRO STUDIOS

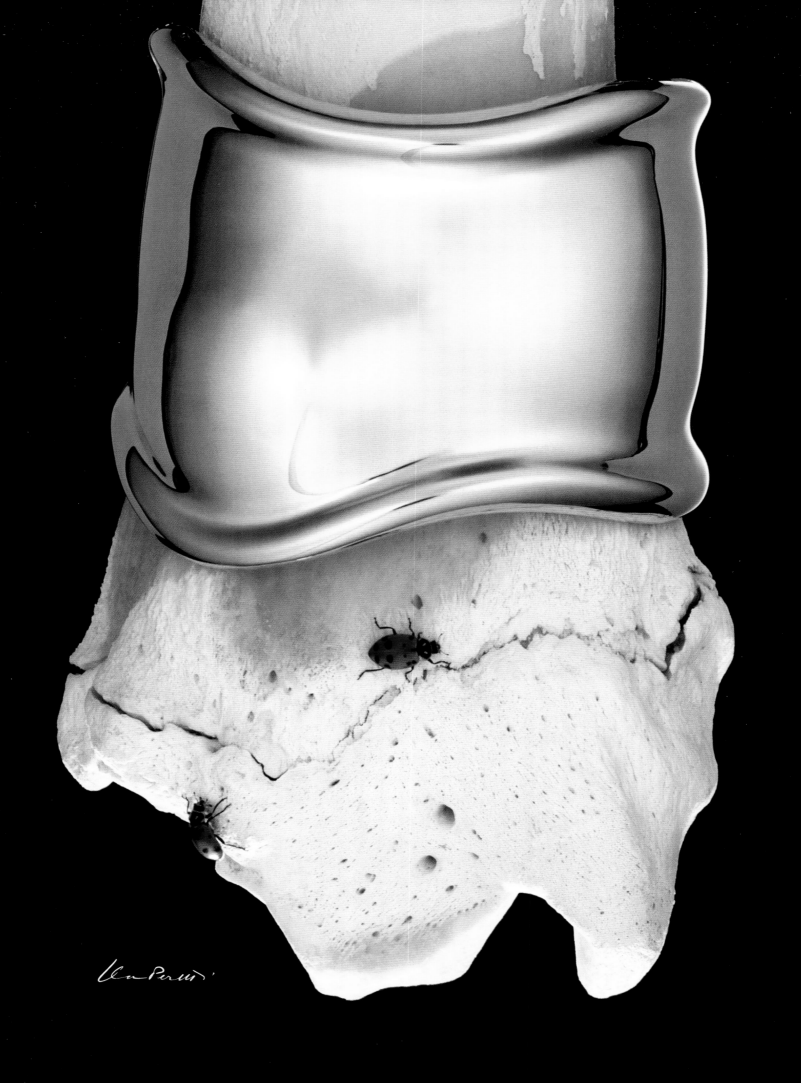

TIFFANY & Co.

At first Peretti worked with the sheets of silver herself, covering any shapes that she found inspiring. These were usually wooden carvings that were whittled into shape until the right form was found. Later, she would sit with the craftsman and watch as he produced her ideas.

"A beginning of a reality... what was important was his advice, which gave me hints to eventual problems in the production process – to change a line then was easy."

Inspiration can be ever-consuming, and sharing that conversation with the craftsmen was exhilarating:

"It is a great satisfaction to work as a whole, to have an understanding and share the same enthusiasm. This MAGIC happened with everybody I have worked with, it is like singing together in unison."

First Jewellery Design

Peretti's very first jewellery design originated in Portofino, Italy in the 1960s. She designed it for her dear friend, fashion designer Giorgio di Sant'Angelo:

"Portofino in the sixties was magic. All the women were stunning figures in shockingly beautiful Pucci silks, each with a gardenia in her hand."

Peretti found a vase from a Rolls Royce in a bric-a-brac shop, and from this came her first 'bottle' design. She made some sketches and back in Spain she hammered silver metal under the eye of a silversmith, creating a miniature silver bud flask that could be worn with a leather thong.

"Of all the bottles I fashioned, the first was the most magical."

Sant'Angelo sent the pendant out onto the catwalk with a small rosebud peering out from the vase and success was assured!

Her bottles and flasks were made in many different materials including rose quartz and jade. Jade was a special gemstone for Peretti, she used it for many of her pendants and in many different forms from her bottles to her open heart and teardrop shapes. It had the tactile quality that she sought for each of her forms; not only did the sensual curves and changing thickness of her jewels and objects matter, but also how they felt to the touch.

"Jade for me is maybe the most beautiful stone, between emeralds and imperial jade, I go for the jade every time. Jade also brings good luck, at the touch it is as smooth as a baby's skin."

ABOVE: Elsa Peretti® Open Heart pendant on mesh chain – yellow gold
PHOTOGRAPH BY JOSH HASKIN © TIFFANY AND COMPANY

LEFT: Elsa Peretti® Cabochon rings – black jade, turquoise, green nephrite, yellow gold, sterling silver
PHOTOGRAPH BY JOSH HASKIN © TIFFANY AND COMPANY

That same year she designed her famous eternally contemporary belt which was inspired by the leather girth of a horse which she had seen on a visit to Mexico. The resulting silver belt was the beginning of many:

"But the horse, that handsome, strong, noble animal, inspired my first one."

Peretti collaborated with the sculptor silversmith Xavier Corbero, and her works were soon to be found in Bloomingdale's, New York. By 1971 she was already a name to be reckoned with, and that year received the prestigious Coty Award, the first of many awards.

The New York Crowd

On a visit to Paris, Peretti met the Dutch supermodel Wilhelmina Cooper, who had recently set up a model agency in New York. Encouraged by Cooper, Peretti moved to New York to start a new chapter in her life. During this period, she enjoyed notoriety as a Studio 54 acolyte and for her role as one of the 'in' nightclubbing crowd, which included such names as Andy Warhol, Helmut Newton, Halston himself, Bianca Jagger and Liza Minnelli. She was Halston's muse, friend and model.

During this hectic period, she still managed to design and produce intuitively beautiful, minimalist works of art. It was at this time that she met the great fashion photographer Hiro (Yasuhiro Wakabayashi), with whom she was to collaborate throughout her career as a jewellery designer. Halston advised her about the proportions for her jewels, he said to create everything in small, medium and large.

It was Halston who introduced her to Walter Hoving of Tiffany's in 1974 and from that moment on, she created exclusively for Tiffany & Co. As Harry Platt, former president of Tiffany & Co. explains: *"We were looking for somebody who could capture the mood of the young woman as well as the older woman ... someone who could make jewellery that women could wear with jeans and sweaters as well as with their ball gowns."* (*New York Social Diary*, 7 December 2009, Jill Krementz Photo Journal – Elsa Peretti.) Peretti was the obvious choice: she was well known on the party scene, she had a rebel image, she was already in her thirties and she could design – she was a gift for Tiffany's.

She introduced silver jewellery to Tiffany's jewellery line. It was a brave move, prestigious jewellery houses had not used silver since the 1930s and it was a gamble for everyone concerned. Tiffany's created a range of affordable luxury, which even a secretary could afford. It was also the beginning of branding, as we know it today. People were buying into a universe, they were part of a special club.

ABOVE: Elsa Peretti® Bottle pendants – sterling silver
PHOTOGRAPH BY JOSH HASKIN © TIFFANY AND COMPANY

RIGHT: Elsa Peretti® Equestrian belt buckle – sterling silver, leather
PHOTOGRAPH BY JOSH HASKIN © TIFFANY AND COMPANY

Japan

Peretti's passion for Japan and all things Japanese, began with a visit to this intriguing country in 1969:

> "The impact I felt on my first trip to Japan was the speed and technology of a train from Tokyo to Kyoto and the exquisite craftsmanship of the things I saw."

Lacquer bangles – red, black, brown and inky blue – are witness to her respect for this culture, and the artisans who make her ideas a reality. She was obsessed with getting the technique correct, so much so that she tracked down an artisan who was able to execute the fabled 77 steps in the ancient *urushi* (lacquer) process.

The lacquer beans are a shape that Peretti returns to frequently: the organic shape fits the hand and was transformed into lacquered clutch purses using magnolia wood. It took Peretti a long time to find the right craftsmen who understood her need to perfect the simple smooth shape:

> "The hollow for the hand does not detract from the primary shape and thought, a bean, a seed, the origin of life."

Linked with the tea ceremony from ancient times, Elsa also worked with Japanese bamboo artist, Watanabe Chikusei, to create delicately perfect bamboo baskets, the product of dexterous hands.

> "I managed to persuade the best craftsmen to manufacture some of my forms. Behind them lie centuries of culture and a long process of loving production."

Her iconic gold, silver, lapis lazuli, and black jade beans are central to Peretti's philosophy and design. The simplicity of its outline means that the bean has been used repeatedly for bracelets, charms, cufflinks, earrings, leather boxes, necklaces and many more.

Iconic Inspiration

Many of Peretti's ideas begin with nature, while others come from the street, and also "from something inside, a link with the subconscious". Her talent is to transform "symbols into dimensions". Amongst her best known designs is the Open Heart pendant; she found her inspiration from a huge Henry Moore sculpture. In its central void, she could see the outline of a heart there, where there should have been nothing,

> "No one else saw a heart there. Just me."

The problem was how to hang the heart as a pendant, how should she attach it? The head of Tiffany's jewellery, Mr. Kalich came to the rescue, suggesting the solution of putting the chain *through* the heart, creating a jaunty, off-the-cuff statement.

Diamonds by the Yard

Synonymous with affordable luxury, and iconic in the history of jewellery, Diamonds by the Yard represents the absolute essence of a gemstone and its relationship with the person who wears it. At first, the idea was:

"to put the smallest diamond on a thin gold chain and then I kept adding different diamond sizes with different chain lengths."

Her diamonds come in round, oval outlines attached to a single gold chain allowing people to choose the length of chain and the size of the diamonds they wished to wear.

"A yard will go around a girl's neck three times... we plan to show them in yard, yard and a half and three yard lengths but they can be ordered as long and with as many diamonds as anyone wants."

Harry Platt, former president of Tiffany & Co. (*The Times*, Shreveport Louisiana, 22 June 1974)

Mesh jewellery

"Inspired by the beautiful atmosphere in Jaipur, I thought about a gold bra."

On her travels in India, Peretti was inspired by the beauty of Jaipur to create a gold bra; this was the beginning of her mesh jewels. The original piece was made in India; on returning home, the challenge was to find a workshop in the USA that had the expertise to make gold mesh, which had last been popular for evening bags at the end of the 19th century and the beginning of the 20th century. Peretti turned to her friend Samuel Beizer, the first director of the FIT's jewellery department for help. Beizer tracked down a company called Whiting and Davis who had been known for their work with pressure metal mesh. Peretti and Beizer

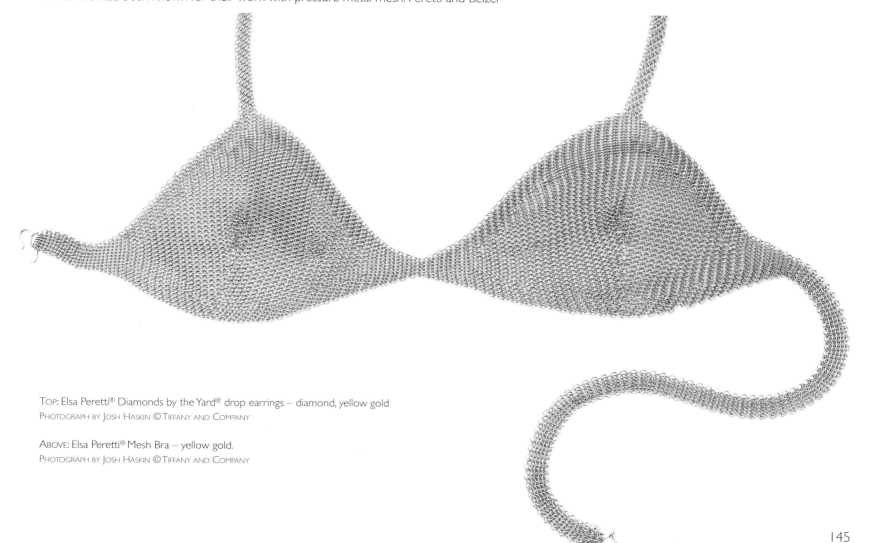

TOP: Elsa Peretti® Diamonds by the Yard® drop earrings – diamond, yellow gold
PHOTOGRAPH BY JOSH HASKIN © TIFFANY AND COMPANY

ABOVE: Elsa Peretti® Mesh Bra – yellow gold.
PHOTOGRAPH BY JOSH HASKIN © TIFFANY AND COMPANY

collaborated to rescue the old machines and with the help of an 80-year-old retired worker, they learnt how to make the gold mesh. Peretti's scarf, earrings and chains were cut and created by hand. One mesh scarf is composed of approximately 43,000 links, and is knitted like a stocking, avoiding seams, using solder-filled wire.

The Peretti Cut

In 1977 Tiffany's introduced The Peretti Cut diamond. It has a deeper pavilion than the usual brilliant cut and 54 facets instead of 58. The result is that the diamond has a larger surface of brilliance; it is also identical on both sides. What makes this a remarkable idea, is that at the time there were very few new cuts due to the traditional culture of the diamond industry and the difficulty of cutting diamonds, a process which did not use computers or lasers at the time.

Bone cuffs

Bones have been a fascination to Peretti ever since she was a child, not for their macabre aspect but for their shapes and unusual forms. As a child, Peretti would visit a 17th-century Capuchin church in which all the rooms were decorated with human bones.

Peretti's Bone cuffs have a very sensual simplicity, they were there almost from the beginning, first seen in 1971. They have been part of Tiffany's collection ever since, made in sterling silver, yellow and rose gold.

The Animal Kingdom

In Elsa Peretti's animal kingdom, snakes and scorpions have been stripped to reveal their articulated gold or silver bone structures. The scorpion's magnificent exoskeleton has been immortalised by Peretti's construction of her scorpion necklace. The creature's body and tail hangs as a pendant, whilst its pincers grip the wearer's neck. Peretti saw numerous scorpions scuttling around the medieval village of Sant Martí Vell, in Spain a special place where she visits. Their arthropod aesthetic and their mechanisms fascinated her, thus launching her research and keen observation for the unseen.

The Sea

Perretti's relationship with the sea is multifaceted; memories of gathering worn glass 'pebbles' and shells from the beach as a girl sit beside more emotional and sensual souvenirs of the ocean.

> "What instilled my profound respect for the ocean was to dive into it, to feel myself inside it and at the same time under it ... I pay homage to those hours beneath the waves by recording some of them in my small portraits."

More recently, Peretti has introduced new forms such as the Bean in the Net pendant; her delightful Amapola brooch and her Comma earrings; The Sevillana – an elliptic "O", which comes from a hazy memory of an earring she saw on a Flamenco dancer many years ago.

The accolades have never ceased: in 2001 she was awarded an honorary degree from the FIT (Fashion Institute of Technology) in New York.

The last word should be left to Mr. Shimofuri, an *urushi* craftsman, who sent Peretti a poem to celebrate her 'Fifteen of My Fifty Years' exhibition:

> "A golden carp, swam against the muddy torrent
> a thousand miles upstream
> met a barrier of a waterfall,
> struggled, and suddenly leapt clear, transformed into a shining dragon
> to fly free into the translucent air."

ABOVE: Elsa Peretti® Scorpion necklace – yellow gold
PHOTOGRAPH BY JOSH HASKIN © TIFFANY AND COMPANY

OPPOSITE PAGE: Elsa Peretti® Teardrop pendant – pavé diamond, platinum
PHOTOGRAPH BY HIRO; © HIRO; IMAGE COURTESY HIRO STUDIOS

TIFFANY & Co.

"It's about complication and how far you can push an idea."

WENDY RAMSHAW
Poetic Minimalist

Artist, jeweller, designer – it is difficult to define Wendy Ramshaw; her impact on the world of jewellery has been huge over the past forty years.

Ramshaw is inspired by and incorporates many ideas from the man-made world of machinery and engineering. Antique scientific instruments, precision tools and optical paraphernalia are but a few of Wendy Ramshaw's pools of influence. In the narrow confines of high jewellery, strictly speaking her jewels cannot be defined as such; however, she has over the years created an essential bridge between artist jewellery and high jewellery, pushing the boundaries of what is acceptable and producing the jewel as a total art form.

Ramshaw uses colour in blocks of translucent and opaque enamels and acrylics. Her gemstones are set either with a unity of colour, or with a slight variation and gradation. Iridescence is part of a panoply of devices she uses to bring light and interest to her settings.

Her pair of non-matching earrings is typical of Wendy Ramshaw's work as a jeweller; it is an abstract geometry, a composition of spirals, angles and extruding radiant arms suspending gemstones as if part of a pendulum clock mechanism.

The Beginning

Ramshaw has come to jewellery from the stance of an artist. Born in Sunderland, she trained at Newcastle-on-Tyne College of Art as an illustrator and industrial designer before attending Reading University in 1961 to study for an art teacher's diploma. Whilst at Reading, she worked on etching and printing, and became fascinated by the copper plates she was using. The decorative compositions she created with the copper plates led her to transform them into earrings and pendants. The non-conformist would wear the earrings in one ear rather than as a pair. Encouraged by friends and small commissions from the Craft Centre, London, she continued to experiment, whilst working as a textile designer, artist and teacher.

In 1964, with her husband, the well-known artist jeweller David Watkins, Ramshaw created brightly coloured fashion jewellery out of card. This artistic couple took the idea further by placing an adhesive on the back of each card jewel, so that they could be worn on clothing or directly on the skin. Notably, this innovative idea was taken up by JAR in 2013, at a lifetime retrospective of 'Jewels by JAR' at the Metropolitan Museum in New York.

Ring Sets

In 1969, Wendy Ramshaw decided to dedicate her time to design and jewellery making and became a professional jeweller. She started by redefining the ring, creating a series of thin multiple rings set with small cabochon moonstones to fulfil a request for one of her clients. These can be worn together on one finger creating a clustering effect, or in an infinity of

OPPOSITE PAGE: White Queen necklace, 1975 – amethyst. citrine, moonstone, sapphire, white enamel, gold
National Museum of Australia collection in Canberra. It was exhibited at the 'Jewellery in Europe' exhibition in 1975.
PHOTOGRAPH BY MIKE HALLSON; IMAGE COURTESY OF WENDY RAMSHAW

BELOW: Assymetrical earrings – amethyst, moonstone, peridot, topaz, yellow gold
PHOTOGRAPH BY BOB CRAMP; IMAGE COURTESY OF WENDY RAMSHAW

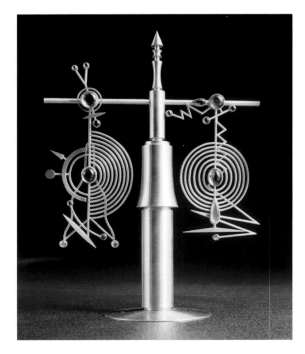

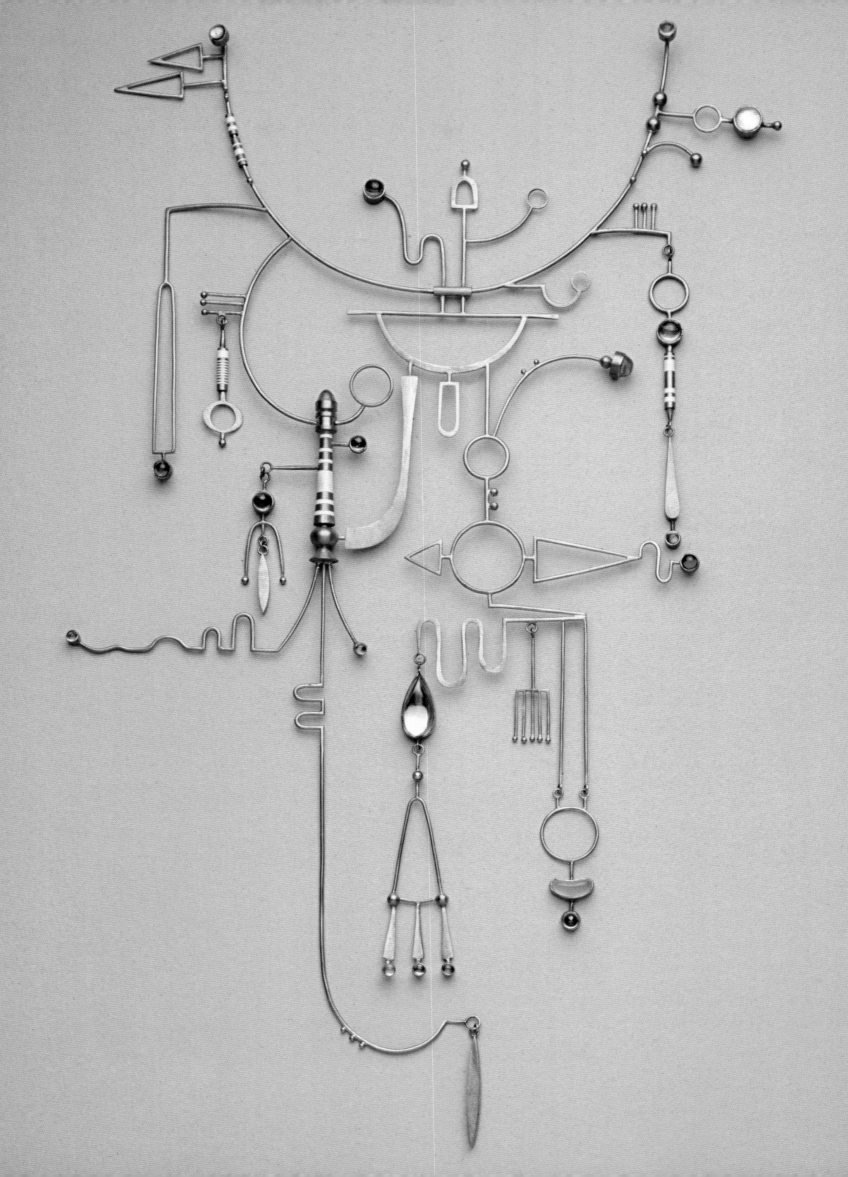

variations on different fingers at a time, bringing the wearer into the design process. Her first set led to many more, which have become Ramshaw's signature. These 'stacking' rings were to become fashionable in the 1990s and were adopted by many jewellery designers.

> "I aim for a kind of visual language to allow the eye to see a total piece, to read each separate part as well as the whole."

She explored her idea further, by giving the rings a stand so that they could be admired even when they were not being worn. At first she used cylindrical perspex stands, an idea taken from an earlier project. With time, the stands became more sophisticated, using such additional materials as enamel and acrylic inlays, ebony, brass and anodized aluminium. Ramshaw explains the importance of the stands:

> "I am concerned that these objects should be formally resolved when not being worn and have at times deliberately devised means by which they can be enjoyed out of context of the human form."

One particular style came to prominence early on in her career as seen in her Pillar Rings, with spire-like bezels in gold, gemstones and enamel bands, influenced by the architecture and city buildings of the late '60s and the space age trends following the moon landing and such cult films as Stanley Kubrick's *2001: A Space Odyssey* (1968) and *Clockwork Orange* (1971).

Exhibitions and awards

Her first solo exhibition was at the Pace Gallery, London, in 1970, confirming her place as a leading light on the arts scene in the late 1960s and '70s. This was quickly followed by the exhibition of 'British Design' at the Musée des Arts Décoratifs, Paris in 1971 and numerous exhibitions across Europe.

In 1975 Ramshaw created the White Queen series, of which two pieces were included in the 'Jewellery in Europe' exhibition at The Scottish Arts Council Gallery. Her inspiration came from the drawings of John Tenniel for *Alice Through the Looking Glass*. In the series, Ramshaw mixes pale blue sapphires with moonstones and agate.

That same year, she was named laureate of the De Beers Diamond International Awards for an amusing 18ct-gold and diamond necklace, reminiscent of Magritte.

Art as inspiration

Ramshaw's imagination has no bounds and inspiration is plucked from everywhere, just as an apple is picked off a tree. She has been particularly inspired by the forms and colours to be found in artists' work, such as that of Paul Klee, Wassily Kandinsky, Frida Kahlo, Henri Rousseau, and the sculptress Louise Nevelson.

Ramshaw worked for ten years (1989-1998) on the Picasso's Ladies Collection; it is an example of how she uses the canvas for inspiration, taking its colour, shape and poetry, to create a collection of stunning ring sets and jewels. Each piece is inspired by one of Picasso's sixty-six portraits of women. Taking the *Portrait of Dora Maar* (1936), as an example:

> *"I looked long and hard at this relatively conventional portrait before deciding to make a large linear brooch in platinum and gold wire for the left shoulder reinforcing the existing pictorial balance. The brooch does not exactly echo the cubist forms which will be seen through its open structure, however it repeats the hard triangular shapes. The addition of circular line and flowing wave add a sense of movement and openness."*
> Wendy Ramshaw - *Picasso's Ladies Catalogue*

ABOVE: Picasso's Ladies Collection, brooch for 'Portrait of Dora Maar', 1989 – platinum, yellow gold PHOTOGRAPH BY BOB CRAMP; COURTESY OF WENDY RAMSHAW

RIGHT: Necklace, 1975 — diamond, gold
Prize winner, Laureate of De Beers Diamonds International Awards.
PHOTOGRAPH BY DE BEERS; COURTESY OF WENDY RAMSHAW

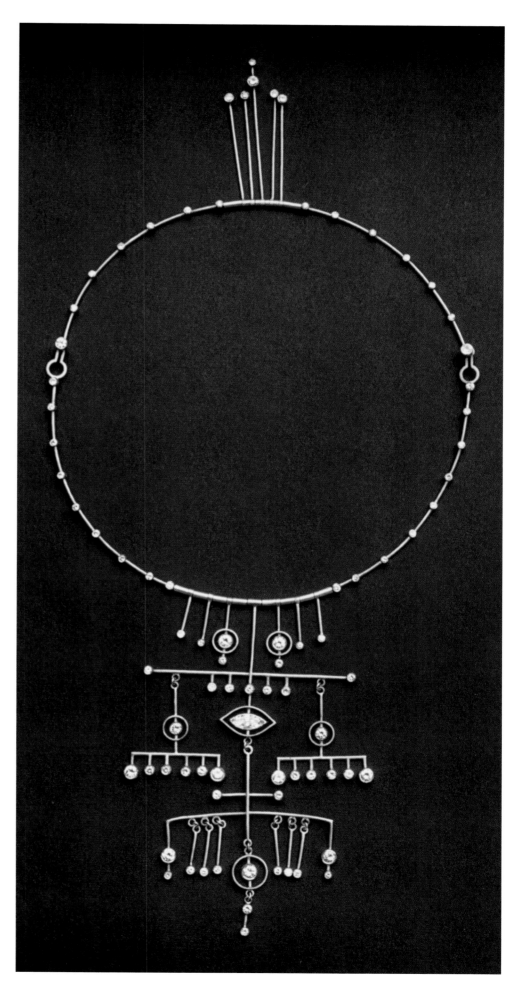

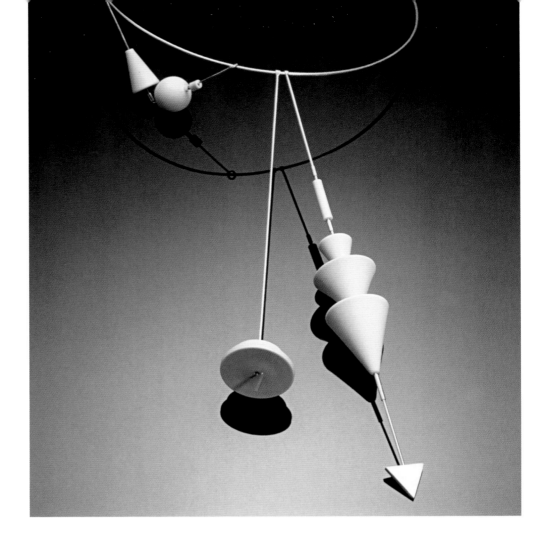

Collaborations

Remaining firmly within the realm of the artist, and through her many artist residencies, she has found inspiration and atypical materials in the most unusual places. Her first collaboration was with her husband, David Watkins, as artists in residence at the former Western Australian Institute of Technology, now the Curtin University, in 1978. She became fascinated with ceramics and aboriginal art, which led Ramshaw to use porcelain and ceramic forms, as well as emu feathers in many of her works. Blue and purple dyed feathers were a highlight in her work for the exhibition at the Victoria and Albert Museum, with the Wedgwood company in 1982.

Her work with Wedgwood was typical of many of her collaborations; she sought to use jasper beads and discs in differing nuances of colour, compiling arrangements of colour and shapes which could be 'analysed mathematically' starting with a simple form that would become more complex before returning to a simpler form. Wedgwood had a ready bank of such hues and beads for Ramshaw to work with. It is interesting to note that she took on the jeweller's mantle of playing with the lustres of the gemstones she chose, setting them with the matt muted light of the Wedgwood beads and discs.

The Barcelona Neckpiece was created later, in 1987, using dyed blue emu feathers and ornaments especially for the 'Prospectiva: Contemporary European Jewellery' exhibition in Barcelona. According to Ramshaw, it celebrates the exotic architecture of Antoni Gaudí without being influenced by it. It is also a celebration of the fusion of inspiration from different cultures, merging together to create a piece of art which is quite unique.

In 2006, Wendy Ramshaw took up two residencies: one at the Science Museum in Oxford, England and another at the Pilchuck Glass School in Washington, USA. The synergy of these two residencies gave birth to 'A Journey through Glass', an installation in Edinburgh in 2007, which consisted of glass forms, often taking the silhouettes of antique laboratory glass tubes, beakers and flasks, which were created with the collaboration of the Pilchuck Glass School.

ABOVE: Wedgwood Collection, Three Cone necklace, 1982
– white jasper, gold, hand-turned ceramic beads; suspended
from a nickel alloy neck wire
Victoria & Albert Museum collection
PHOTOGRAPH BY DAVID WATKINS;
IMAGE COURTESY OF WENDY RAMSHAW

OPPOSITE PAGE: Barcelona necklace, 1987 – dyed emu
feathers, green carnelian, Egyptian paste, vitreous enamel,
wood, gold leaf, silver gilt
*Provenance: 'Perspective: Contemporary European Jewellery'
exhibition, Barcelona. The neck piece celebrates the
architecture of Gaudí.*
PHOTOGRAPH BY BOB CRAMP; IMAGE COURTESY OF WENDY RAMSHAW

Materials for the Modern Age

Ramshaw was asked by Kenji Hashimoto to create a jewel that would celebrate the end of the 20th century. The result was the Calculator necklace, in which she decided to include many of the new materials that defined the age and the scientific world: silica glass, similar to that used for the windows of space craft; cubic zirconia, a synthetic stone that was specially cut into a bullet form; and acrylic, which was engraved with black inlaid lines.

Perhaps one of her most important pieces of jewellery came about as a consequence of a visit to the London Science Museum in 1999, where she was drawn to the possibilities of coloured nanocrystalline diamond. Originally developed by Professor Stanislaw Mitura in Poland for medical implants, they are produced in many colours, have a very bright adamantine lustre and they always give a bright patina. Ramshaw was to use this material for the Millennium Medal, commissioned to be presented to Queen Elizabeth II. It was a *tour de force*, taking the possibilities of jewellery to another level using the advances in technology to create a statement for the new Millennium.

Ramshaw also used nanocrystalline diamond for a series of rings for the 'Millennium' exhibition, taking its luminescence as the central theme in her work.

The material is seen again in Ramshaw's tiara for Queen Elizabeth II, created to celebrate the 50th anniversary of her coronation. The tiara was created in collaboration with the Calouste Gulbenkian Foundation Project, using medical steel, coated in nanocrystalline diamond.

Room of Dreams

Probably Ramshaw's most poetic and lyrical experience in the field of jewellery design, was her 'Room of Dreams' exhibition, which was to be such a draw in 2002 at the Scottish Gallery that it was revived in 2012 at Somerset House before touring the United Kingdom.

> "The dream is the room and every one of its individual contents is in some sense a part of a dream ...a series of stories and images waiting to be considered and discovered."

The jewels were inspired by various pieces of literature, such as *The Piano Player's Wife* and the children's tale, *The Twelve Dancing Princesses*.

The Red Queen ring set is influenced by *Alice in Wonderland*: Ramshaw has created an extraordinary symphony of gold and cabochon garnet rings, forming a finger covering of deep red clusters of light. The red is power, love, joy, ecstasy and, finally, blood, the very elements of life. Comprising 22 rings of different sizes and shapes of garnet, Ramshaw describes them as *"Soft voluptuous — sharp and pointy."*

Ramshaw has been honoured with countless awards and accolades throughout her career. She continues to experiment with new materials. Much of her later work has concentrated on large site-specific forms of art, from gates to public art commissions, many using her signature juxtapostion of geometrical shapes.

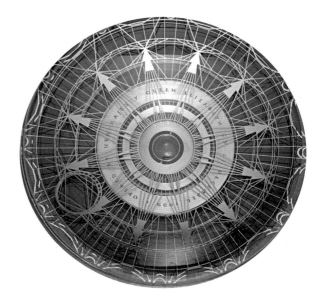

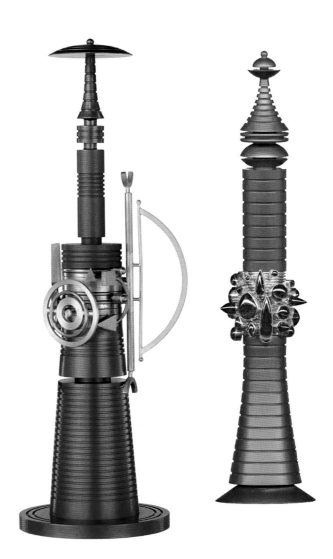

MARINA B
Engineering with Jewels

Splendid heavy gold jewellery set with intensely coloured gemstones… Jewellery that is of engineering precision and defined by the gemstones it uses… Triangles and elliptical shapes that create mosaics of form and opulence in colour… This is Marina B.

A brilliant mathematician and yachtswoman, Marina Bulgari Spaccarelli is part of the third generation of the Bulgari jewellery house, sharing her illustrious name with her sisters Anna and Xenia, and her cousins Paolo, Nicola, Gianni and Lia. On the death of her father Constantino in 1973, she took on a central role as a manager within the company until 1976. She felt compelled to make a change; leaving the family business, she set up her own company, Marina B., in 1978. Her first showroom was in Geneva on the Place du Molard. She exhibited in the top fashionable hotels of Monte Carlo, Gstaad and Saint Moritz, with stores following in London, Milan, Monte Carlo, Paris, and New York. During this time she never stopped travelling; not only did she visit her stores and her clients but she also went to Paris frequently to oversee her workshops. She would record all her ideas on the inside of blue Gitane cigarette packets. Noting the precise volumes she was looking for, she would then fax her sketches to her brilliant draughtsman, Jean-Pierre Varin to be correctly drawn.

It was Varin who introduced her to Jean-Pierre Brun, the owner of a highly skilled Parisian jewellery workshop, which in the past had specialised in the fabrication of jewelled boxes and mystery clocks. Although she used several jewellery workshops such as Duhem, Robert Sublon and Soubrenie & Bois; Brun was her principal workshop.

> *"Marina's creations were very structured, very architectural and constructed. She was someone who knew exactly what she wanted... nothing was left to chance. She was like Suzanne Belperron in this aspect. Very strict, if they didn't like the piece, they were capable of making you start over again. I don't know anyone like that in the business today."* Jean-Pierre Brun

Marina B gave all her jewels a name, be it a reference to her inspiration or the name of a client. Even a member of her family might be given place of honour; it was her way "*to give sense to the piece*".

The Marina B DNA
There are some very specific ideas that can be found in a Marina B jewel. As well as attention to detail, there are deliberate characteristics that can be found in most of her designs. Of these, the 'Chubby Chestnut' outline (a slightly flattened pear shape) and the Marina B cut (triangular cabochon) are the most renowned. The Marina B cut appears in many of her jewels, often used to set off the central stone. Its triangular shape was unusual for the time and became synonymous with Marina B.

ABOVE: Pivomab earrings, 1982 – citrine, onyx, diamond, yellow gold
The pendant gemstone is detachable and the surmount can be pivoted. Note the 'chubby chestnut' design. IMAGE COURTESY MARINA B

OPPOSITE PAGE:
FROM TOP TO BOTTOM:

Médiéval Arabesque choker, 1981 – mabé cultured pearl, mother-of-pearl, diamond, yellow gold; Lalli choker, 1982 – pink topaz, blue topaz, diamond, yellow gold; Huda choker – onyx, diamond, yellow gold; Oca choker, 1981 – rubellite, yellow gold; Lalli choker, 1982 – citrine, diamond, yellow gold

The chokers are mounted on springs for easy opening and closing.
IMAGE COURTESY MARINA B

Chokers

Chokers are an important part of Marina B's work. They are technically difficult to create without distorting the form. In particular, there is the issue of how to open the choker to get it on and off, whilst ensuring a snug fit when worn. The Brun workshop created a spring mechanism for the clasp similar to a crossbow: a leaf spring in the clasp retreats when the choker is open, and pushes the elements back together again when it is closed.

She created many necklaces using this clasp, including the Byzance (1978), Catherine (1979), and the Kashan series (1979). The Kashan series also had bracelets and cuffs and used the famous Marina B contour to create a series of links set alternately upright and upside down. The Selma Emerald choker is a spectacular example of ergonomic design, spring mounts, and stunning emeralds.

TOP: Kashan multi-gem choker, 1980 – green tourmaline, topaz, citrine, rubellite, amethyst, onyx, diamond, yellow gold *Mounted on springs* IMAGE COURTESY MARINA B

ABOVE: Selma choker, 1991 – emerald, diamond, yellow gold *Mounted on springs* IMAGE COURTESY MARINA B

ABOVE: Karen 4 Conique cuff, 1988 – steel, gold IMAGE COURTESY MARINA B

RIGHT: JP Pneu earrings, 1982 – triangular cabochon citrine, smoky quartz, onyx, diamond, yellow gold
The bead is interchangeable with other similarly cut semi-precious gemstones. IMAGE COURTESY MARINA B

RIGHT, BELOW: Pneu earrings, 1978 – citrine, onyx, diamond, yellow gold
One of Marina B's iconic designs; the bead is interchangeable with other similarly cut semi-precious gemstones.
IMAGE COURTESY MARINA B

Cuffs

Cuffs are another *tour de force*. Conical in shape to follow the silhouette of the wrist and lower arm, they pose a technical quandary. The cuffs are composed of links similar to her necklaces, but here the interlacing motifs have to move to allow the hand and lower arm to pass through; to counter this problem, the motifs on the inner part are shorter than those on the outside of the cuff. Her method was a meticulous attention to detail, including the dimensions for each jewel; with this professionalism she was able to patent all her designs and her inventive multifunctional mechanisms.

Linking it all together

The iconic Pneu earrings were a result of Marina B's search for a way to connect gemstones together without stringing or threading them, which she considered too mundane. A hole is created at the centre of the round colourful gemstones – which she describes as their *"belly button"* – and set with a cabochon gemstone attached to a 'bicycle guard', pavé-set with diamonds. The surmount is also set with a cabochon gemstone surrounded by pavé-set diamonds, creating an interesting juxtaposition of spheres, and a spade-like outline. Variations followed: Pneu perles in 1980 and Pneu 'JP', using the Marina B form as the surmount, in 1982.

Cardan (1987) – Marina B found a multitude of ways to set the rounded gemstone discs and created an interchangeable version of the Pneu earrings, christened Cardan. Next came the Cardan pearl and gemstone bead necklace using a unique system. Taking her inspiration from the joints of a gimbal compass from her sailing days, she rounded the 'mouth' of the joint so that it took on the form of punctuation-like commas. She used this link system again for her famous Fusilli parure in 1992, this time taking inspiration from pasta for the shape of the links. Square beads were to follow in 1996, using gold twists to disguise the threading of the beads.

Settings

Marina B was also not a fan of traditional claw settings. For her first pair of Pampilles pendant earrings in 1977, she disguised the four claws used to fix the rose diamonds by using a closed bezel. From this point on, she decided that if she were to use claw settings, then they must become a feature. In 1983, she created a distinctive style in turquoise for her friend's daughter, Gina. Other similar jewels followed, in pale and dark citrines, sapphires and topaz; earrings come in rubellite, emerald and sapphire. Derived from this collection came the Shirine ear pendants (1984), which rely heavily on claw settings and are very large, and have an extraordinary three-dimensional profile. Sophia Loren wore a pair of these dramatic ear pendants when she collected her Academy Award in 1991.

ABOVE: Pampilles pendant earrings – sapphire, diamond, white gold IMAGE COURTESY MARINA B

LEFT: Sophia Loren wearing Marina B's sapphire Shirine 4 ear pendants at the 1991 Acadamy Awards ceremony, at which she received an honorary 'Oscar' for her services to cinema. IMAGE © ZUMA PRESS, INC. / ALAMY STOCK PHOTO

OPPOSITE PAGE: Cardan pearl and bead necklace, 1988 – cultured pearl, citrine, onyx, yellow gold *Marina B disliked stringing pearls and beads, thus she developed a universal joint system by which to hold them.* IMAGE COURTESY MARINA B

ABOVE: Mitsouko earrings, 1986 – ruby, diamond, black rhodium-plated gold, yellow gold IMAGE COURTESY MARINA B

Fuji Yama 1986

Although Marina B has not visited Japan, she is a great admirer of their culture and traditions. The result is the Fuji Yama Collection, which echoes the Onda Collection, but with the motif spread over the entire jewel, like the spray from crashing waves. From her first Ecume models, dating from 1983, she went on to create large thick creole earrings (1986) and crescent earrings (1987), using blackened gold to highlight the gems. The ear pendant version, the Mitzouko earrings, resemble a cluster of chimes that peal as the wearer moves, reminding Marina B of Japanese bells.

In 1996 Marina B ceded the company to Ahmed Hassan Fitaihi. It was sold in 2010 to Paul Lubetsky, who appointed Giorgio Bulgari, Marina B's nephew, as creative director at the end of 2014. Marina Bulgari can look upon the future with the assurance that the Marina B brand will continue the adventure that she started back in 1978. A prolific designer, she has left over 10,000 drawings and more than 132 patents.

Marina B jewels are special; they are of the moment for women whose lifestyles and roles in the wider community have changed. She has created multifunctional jewels that can be worn during the day and dressed up for the evening. Earrings are reversible, gemstones are interchangeable, pendant earrings are detachable, leaving a discreet earring for the daytime…

ABOVE: Caty reversible earrings, 1983 – onyx, topaz, diamond, yellow gold IMAGE COURTESY MARINA B

LEFT: Fuji Yama Cuff earrings, 1990 – orange sapphire, diamond, black rhodium-plated gold IMAGE COURTESY MARINA B

OPPOSITE PAGE: A selection of Marina B's precise designs: Clockwise, from top left: Series of rings showing her use of baguette diamonds in her Alfa baguettes series; Design showing her 'Pivomab' earrings; Design for her 'Fuchxia' ear pendants, 1986 (note the chubby 'chestnut' outline); Variations of her Shirine 4 ear pendant designs, 1989; Design for Kashan manchette in yellow gold to be set with cabochon ruby, cabochon emerald, diamond and onyx, 1979, it was mounted on a spring and was limited to six versions of the cuff; Design for Kun bracelet in diamond and yellow gold to be mounted on a spring. COURTESY MARINA B

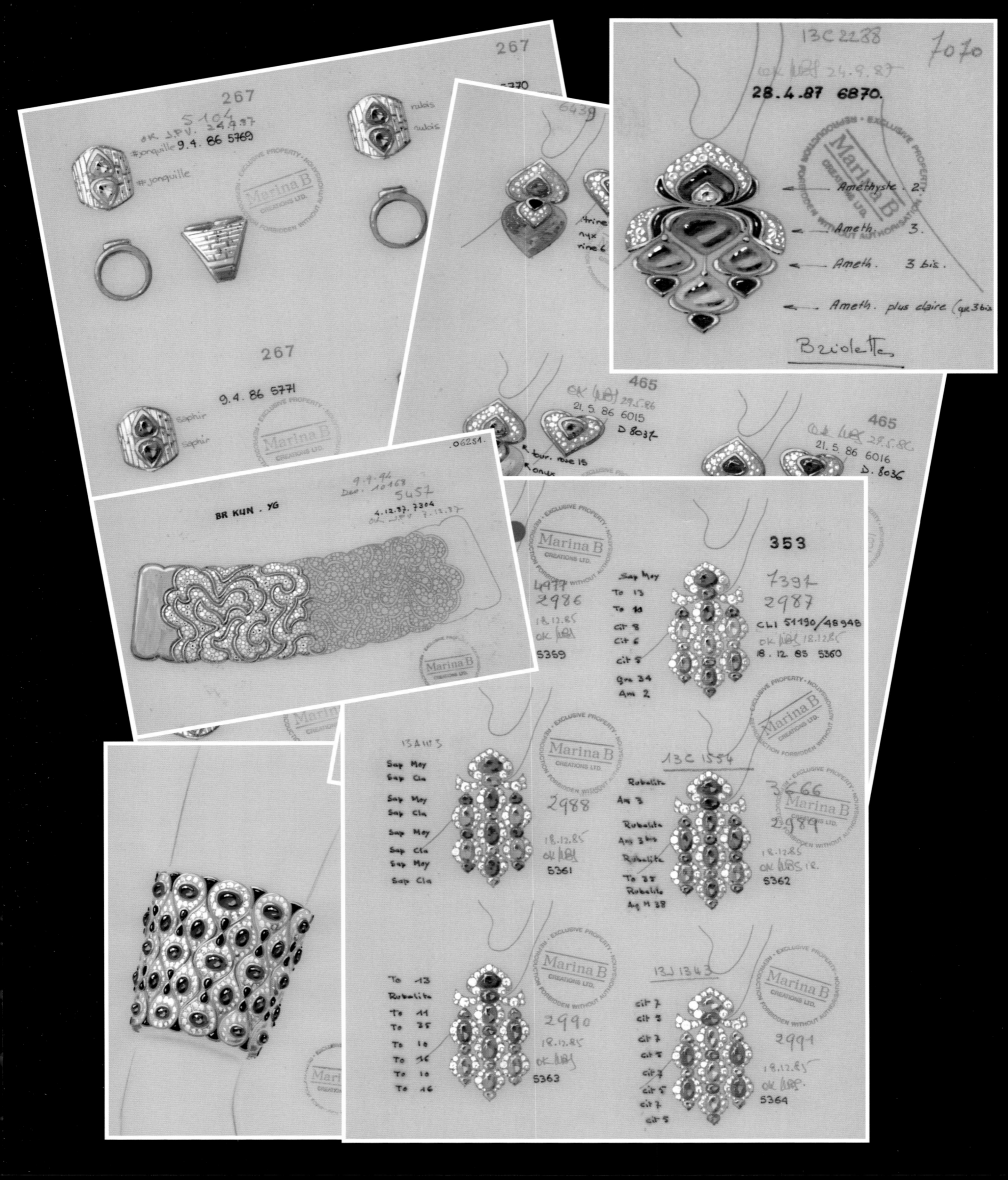

"I used wood because there was a decorative chalice between the windows at Boivin with small pieces of sandalwood. I loved the smell that came from the cup... At Boivin we only used ebony and sandalwood, later on my own, as MCB, I used many other woods."

MARIE-CAROLINE DE BROSSES
Sandalwood and Silver

Marie-Caroline de Brosses is the 'missing link' in the saga of the House of René Boivin. Though the *Atelier des dames* is well known for its immensely talented former creative designers, Suzanne Belperron and Juliette Moutard, little is known of de Brosses, who spent over 20 years designing for the company from 1970 until 1991.

She was just 22 years old when she was given the opportunity to meet Boivin boss, Louis Girard. Juliette Moutard was about to retire and the jewellery house needed someone to bring a fresh wave of ideas into the company. De Brosses had just graduated in Architecture from the Union des Arts Décoratifs and, by her own admission, knew very little about jewellery at the time; to this day she does not know who suggested her name for the post. Girard sent her to the Place Vendôme under instruction to sketch any pieces she saw in the show windows that inspired her. She returned with an empty sketchbook – nothing had excited her imagination. Girard was delighted and it was the start of a working relationship that lasted until Girard's death in 1986.

By 1981 Jacques Bernard had become the jewellery house's legal owner. Still answerable to Girard, de Brosses took on more responsibilities, negotiating the purchase of gemstones and gold as well as following their fabrication in the workshop. Though she spent a lot of time in the Far East due to her husband's job, she returned to Paris regularly and was very much a part of the design team. She also organised each of Boivin's big exhibitions: at the Biennale des Antiquaires in Paris, the French Embassy in Korea, and immediately afterwards at the French Embassy in Japan, 1990.

Extending the Boivin Legacy

De Brosses's designs, while fresh, continued in the tradition of the House of Boivin. She describes her own work as similar to that of Suzanne Belperron. Where her designs resembled those of Juliette Moutard, she made them more streamlined and pure, stripping away the decorative statements to bring back uncluttered strong lines. Moutard's Turban rings were transformed into easy-to-wear cabochon sapphire and diamond chokers. Boivin's tassel rings and link ring forms took on many different shapes and with de Brosses's touch, she gave them a new modernity. Boivin's drawers were full of broken carved rock crystal rings, in all probability left forgotten since the days before the Second World War; de Brosses gave them a new lease of life by hiding the flaws with gold and steel and setting them with gemstones depending on where the problem was.

ABOVE: De Brosses for René Boivin: Diamond ring – diamond, yellow gold
Note its bulging form, inspired by the shapes of televisions and refrigerators in the 1960s.
IMAGE COURTESY OF CHRISTIE'S INC.

OPPOSITE PAGE: De Brosses for René Boivin: Butterfly brooch, 1984 – yellow sapphire, peridot, citrine, cabochon sapphire, ruby, diamond, yellow gold IMAGE COURTESY OF RICHTERS' PALM BEACH, MIAMI

De Brosses didn't just continue the Boivin legacy, she added to it by introducing many iconic designs that were hers alone. Almost from the beginning, in 1972, she used pebbles (galet) that she found on the beach, which she would cut and polish and then set into rings. De Brosses has a definite preference for the colour blue, which is evident in her choice of sapphires and aquamarines in many of her pieces for both Boivin and MCB.

For the large heavy rings synonymous with the Boivin name, she refined the shank, making it more comfortable to wear and less cumbersome to the eye. De Brosses christened them her 'bagues décalés' (offset rings), which became a Boivin classic. Her first ring, which has been reproduced many times using different gemstones and metals, took a very feminine approach. The idea was to place the gemstone into a gently sloping 'dimple', creating a rounded bulging effect about the gemstone. The initial inspiration for the rounded-off square shape came from the televisions and refrigerators of the 1960s. De Brosses has adapted this form to numerous rings; it remains a part of her DNA with MCB.

The Boivin Menagerie

The classic animal-head pendants and brooches were a first in oxidised silver. It started with the panther's head in 1970, followed in quick succession with the heads of a lynx and a ram in 1971 and 1972; the lion was next, followed by the crab (with a witty secret compartment) and the elephant head (of which only three were made for a special commission), in 1973 and 1974 respectively. The oxidised silver jewels were de Brosses's way of opening the rarefied environment of high jewellery to people who could not or did not want to spend huge sums; it must not be forgotten that 1973 and '74 were the years of the first global petroleum crisis.

In contrast, richly jewelled fish held their mouths agape – they could have been a Moutard design but no, it was de Brosses. She gave them an amusing twist by threading a suede choker through the mouths of three fish.

De Brosses's jewels are light, articulated and ergonomic. She designed her delightfully articulated shrimp brooch after a lunch. Jewelled fruit and animals bedecked in multicoloured gemstones such as peridot, aquamarine and coloured diamond were all given the de Brosses treatment.

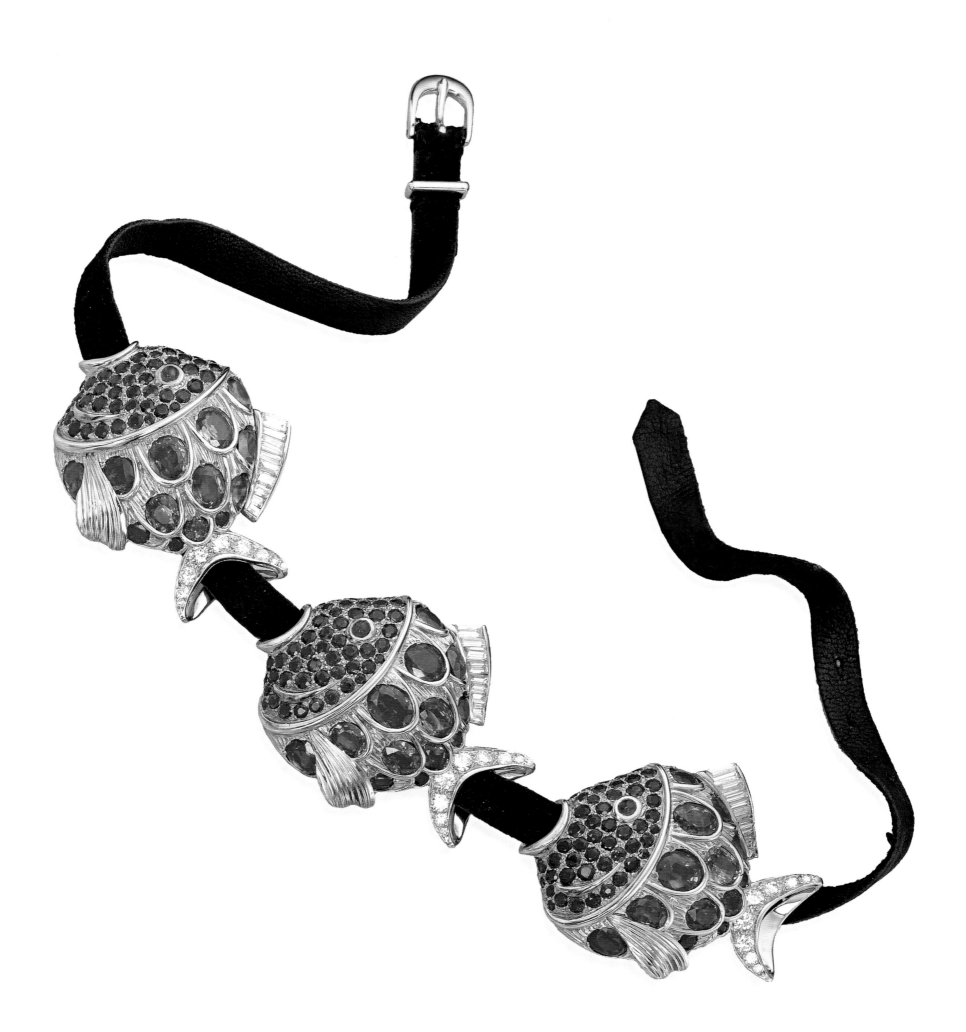

De Brosses for René Boivin: Necklace with changeable centrepiece – sapphire, diamond, yellow gold
The centrepiece pivots to give the necklace a different allure.
IMAGE COURTESY OF CHRISTIE'S INC.

Transformations

The informality of the 1970s and '80s gave de Brosses the opportunity to experiment. Boivin's workshop was known for its talent in creating mechanisms and de Brosses took full advantage of their prowess. Aware that she was designing for women whose roles in society were changing – they were working, juggling careers and family, and needed jewellery that was in step with their busy lives – she devised jewels that could be transformed from a casual sporty choice, into a more formal and glamorous statement for the evening.

One of her most iconic designs for Boivin was initiated by a request from Louis Girard for de Brosses to create an interesting design for a bracelet that could be made into a series of twenty for stock. (He promised the 20th bracelet to her, which she still owns to this day.) The result was her Bracelet à Cachette. The original design was a special commission for a gift for a horselover who didn't want anything too dressy. The result was a simple diamond-set bracelet that could be transformed by sliding a cover to hide the gems. The next two bracelets in the same style were each decorated with an elephant in diamonds. And then came the solution for Mr. Girard: a bracelet divided with four gold rounded bands that slide to reveal gem-set panels.

De Brosses for René Boivin: Bracelet 'á Cachette' (shown open and closed) – ruby, diamond, oxidised gold, yellow gold
The gold rings slide across to reveal/hide the gem-set segments.

De Brosses for René Boivin: Earrings, 1985 – diamond,
yellow gold
Inspired by the folds of a hanging towel.
IMAGE COURTESY OF CHRISTIE'S INC.

Inspiration

She describes how she came upon the idea for her bracelet of gold and wood stripes:

> "Monsieur Girard told me that I should take a stroll down rue Bonaparte, there
> was something there that would certainly catch my attention. I remember
> seeing a wallpaper pattern striped black and white which changed to white
> and black bands, by changing from thick bands at the beginning and shifting to
> narrower bands, until it just became a line before passing to white. I found this
> idea interesting and I decided to play with it further."

Later, when working under the brand name MCB, she experimented with tightening the gold
bindings, so that the ebony would be squeezed and would change form as it bulged out of
the openwork design of the gold cylinder-like strap.

De Brosses comes up with ideas from even the smallest details. One iconic form was inspired
by the manner in which a hand towel had been nonchalantly thrown over a hook:

> "I liked the way that the towel folded and the way it hung down."

MCB

The time De Brosses spent in Asia with her husband most certainly had an influence on her
work. This was particularly evident when she started working on her own under the brand
name MCB, in 1993.

The house of René Boivin had formed Brosses's eye and her style still retains some of that
DNA, though her work has progressed and taken on its own chic. Some enduring themes are
puzzles, knots, strings, links and, since 2005, squiggles.

> "I discovered a lot of rattan and cane work as well as braided straw, which
> were used to make entire houses; I loved this way of doing things and when I
> returned, I created many designs which were tied and knotted."

De Brosses for MCB: Tied Ebony pendant/brooch, 1995 –
ebony, diamond, yellow gold
Signed: 'MCB'
IMAGE COURTESY OF MARIE-CAROLINE DE BROSSES

For MCB, hearts in wood with gold studs that she had designed for Boivin were transformed
into hearts made of quartz, tied with gold thread; even pebbles were tied with gold.

Materials

De Brosses continued Boivin's original approach to materials, incorporating materials such as
ebony and sandalwood (which she liked for its aroma), pebbles, galuchat, silver and steel. She
was creating jewellery for the 1970s and the 1980s, which was not just about the weight of
gold and the size of the gemstone.

The catalyst was a client in 1971, who wanted a ring with a panther's head in black, for which
de Brosses suggested using ebony. Wood continues to be an important component in de
Brosses's work. She has introduced Ked wood to her repertoire for its aroma; amaranth
(purpleheart) for its glorious violet colour; sycamore, and, more recently, *Lignum vitae* wood,
which is greenish in colour and extremely hard.

FAR LEFT: De Brosses for René Boivin: Chaine marine (marine knot) ring, 1980s – sapphire, yellow gold
IMAGE COURTESY OF SOTHEBY'S INC.

LEFT: De Brosses for René Boivin: Rock crystal ring, 1991 – rock crystal, sugar loaf emerald, pear-shaped
cabochon sapphire, diamond, yellow gold   IMAGE COURTESY OF SOTHEBY'S INC.

Legacy

The backs of her jewels are important and they differ according to the price that her clients wish to invest; she regularly uses her initials in an openwork yellow gold scroll to create the back. In the Boivin spirit, she never signed her jewels; until, one day, a friend was admiring her work and her paintings and asked her why she signed her paintings but not her jewellery.

> "She insisted that I sign the bracelet that I had just made for her – that was the beginning."

A witness to Maison René Boivin's last twenty years, de Brosses has an innate sense of the Boivin style and is familiar with the designs and the jewels that passed through the iconic jewellery house. Going forward as MCB she has created her own style. Classic, built on simplicity and discretion, with forms that enhance, de Brosses's jewels glow rather than flash; they are instantly recognisable.

ABOVE: De Brosses for René Boivin: Ebony necklace – ebony, yellow gold IMAGE COURTESY OF CHRISTIE'S INC.

RIGHT: Design for MCB of an ebony and cabochon aquamarine parure consisting of a bracelet, necklace, ring and earpendants, 2008 – gouache on Canson paper
This was a private commission.
IMAGE COURTESY OF MARIE-CAROLINE DE BROSSES

"Tailored jewellery, not flashy jewellery."

MARILYN COOPERMAN
Stitching with Gems

Colour and composition are words that come to mind when viewing Cooperman's jewels, be they figurative pieces representing birds, insects and boteh-styled leaves or geometrical shapes defined in scrolls, gem-set slices, crescent and star outlines. Her gemstones are dollops of colour set in irregular patterns and underlined by a variations of cuts and sizes. She is a scrapbooker at heart, and her collages are the starting point for all her designs. Her style — revolutionary in the 1980s — has become a refined classic in 2017.

Having studied textiles and fashion at the Central Technical College in Toronto, Cooperman first went on to have a full and varied career in fashion, including: working on the *Auckland Star* in New Zealand; opening a small boutique called 'The Closet' to sell clothes she had designed; working with renowned designer David Smith, and then with Fred Leighton in Greenwich Village; forming her own clothing company, Max and Marilyn; being fashion director for *Seventeen* magazine; and working at Simplicity Patterns and then Vogue Patterns.

In 1987 she bumped into old friend Fred Leighton, who by now was Fred Leighton Estate Jewels on Madison Avenue and 66th Street. He hired her on the spot to come up with ideas for new jewellery designs. During the first week Cooperman designed an earring that found its way onto the front cover of the *New York* magazine being worn by Ivana Trump.

Whilst working with Leighton, Cooperman returned to college to learn about rendering. She attended FIT and was taught by the best. Next came wax carving, taught by Arthur Angelino; following a shaky start (she didn't believe she could do it), she now carves all her own waxes, and ensures that the proportions and sizes are absolutely perfect.

Cooperman liked to experiment, often reusing little discarded antique bits and pieces to create something new; sometimes she would take them apart to see for herself how they were made. After a tempestuous few years with Fred Leighton, Cooperman decided to set up her own jewellery design company with the help of Bernard Jacobs in 1994.

Cooperman has remained a close friend of Fred Leighton and continued as his guest designer at the International Art and Antique Fair in Palm Beach for many years. One of her most important collaborations with him was for the Chrysler Redux bracelet, which was set with baguette diamonds in oxidised silver with curvaceous yellow gold outlines, based on the architecture of the famous Chrysler Building in New York.

Many of Cooperman's jewels have been made to be worn together; her iconic slice brooches are intended to be worn in twos or threes:

> *"…wearing them together, they fit, it is like a song somehow…"*

OPPOSITE PAGE: Jody necklace with detachable pendant – multicoloured gemstones including sapphire, peridot, citrine, aquamarine, amethyst, yellow gold
PHOTOGRAPH BY CHRIS DAVIES;
IMAGE COURTESY OF MARILYN COOPERMAN

BELOW: The Chrysler Redux Bangle, 2000 – diamond, patinated silver, yellow gold
Special commission made in association with Fred Leighton
IMAGE COURTESY OF SOTHEBY'S INC.

The Jody Necklace

The Jody necklace was inspired by an 18th-century Georgian piece worn by her friend Jody Shields, novelist and one-time editor of *Vogue* and *House and Garden*,

"It stunned and captivated me! …I have rarely been influenced by a jewel, but I went ahead and carved the necessary moulds for the oval gem-set beads. I then created the layouts (a gem map) with my chosen and preferred stones."

These beads were to support a Maltese styled cross using similar gemstone settings. The effect is big and warm, yet it is also discreetly classic at the same time.

Indian influences

The sense of India is present in the rose-cut diamonds that Cooperman has used since her time with Fred Leighton. When Cooperman and Leighton visited India they bought many carved and sculpted emerald, ruby and sapphire beads, not necessarily with an idea in mind but just that one day they would come in useful. The textiles from India, the Paisley patterns and the boteh outlines are also there in her brooches, some set simply with emeralds, others using carved gemstones, one leaf married to another as brooches and also as earrings.

Natural themes

Though flowers rarely feature in Cooperman's repertoire – she finds them too sentimental – nature does provide Cooperman with many themes and shapes, including horns, shells, scrolls and snail-like ammonite swirls, as well as fish, sea creatures and starfish.

ABOVE: Snail swirl earclips – diamond, oxidised silver, yellow gold
IMAGE COURTESY OF MARILYN COOPERMAN

ABOVE: Phantasmagorical Sea Creature brooch – moonstone, patinated silver, yellow gold
IMAGE COURTESY OF MICHAEL KANNER, KANNERS JEWELRY

RIGHT: Boteh brooches – emerald, diamond, oxidised silver, yellow gold
PHOTOGRAPH BY CHRIS DAVIES; IMAGE COURTESY OF MARILYN COOPERMAN

OPPOSITE PAGE: Fish Lunching on a Pearl brooch, 1999 – emerald, pearl, sapphire, tsavorite garnet, spinel, diamond, patinated silver
The brooch was an anonymous gift to the Museum of Fine Art, Boston in honour of Susan B. Caplan. IMAGE COURTESY OF THE MUSEUM OF FINE ART, BOSTON

ABOVE: Mushroom bracelet – tsavorite garnet, opal, patinated silver, yellow gold
IMAGE COURTESY OF MICHAEL KANNER, KANNERS JEWELRY

LEFT: Apricot Slice brooches – citrine, topaz, patinated silver, yellow gold
PHOTOGRAPH BY CHRIS DAVIES; IMAGE COURTESY OF MARILYN COOPERMAN

BELOW: Portuguese earrings – diamond, oxidised silver, yellow gold
PHOTOGRAPH BY CHRIS DAVIES; IMAGE COURTESY OF MARILYN COOPERMAN

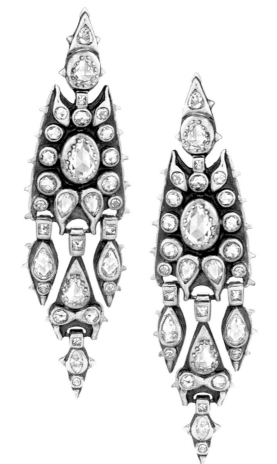

Cooperman also turns her gaze to the ground for inspiration, transforming mushrooms on the forest floor into a glistening opal bracelet.

The idea for her well-known tiger moth brooch came to Cooperman as she was rifling through interior design and architectural magazines. She happened upon a full-page advertisement for a curtain company and she was struck by the luscious quality of the beautiful curtains:

> "The whole page just struck me and in the fold of the drapery which came down the page, was a moth, I ripped it out and I went to the library on 42nd street and looked up moths and that's how I found the tiger moth."

Materials
Cooperman's gemstones find their home mostly in oxidised silver, which has a dark matt finish highlighting and contrasting with the bright lustres of the gemstones. It was a technique

revived from 18th-century jewellery and under Cooperman's flamboyant touch, she has given it a new life. Cooperman often associates this metal with rose-cut champagne and cognac-coloured diamonds. Her settings often imitate her beloved needlecraft, recalling her passion for sewing and different styles of stitching.

The warmth of wood has a place in many of Cooperman's designs. She first came upon the idea when she was visiting her old friend, the famous photographer George Kalinsky in Vermont. She had seen a small wren sculpted in wood in a shop, but hesitated about buying it and decided in the end that she had enough "stuff". At dinner that evening Kalinsky presented her with the little sculpture. The inspiration which came from the little wren caused her to make three similar brooches, which she sold immediately.

Cooperman's is a world of emotion, experiences and idiosyncrasies which she puts down to haphazard meetings and serendipity.

Tiger Moth brooch – Mississippi river pearl, cabochon ruby, yellow diamond, sherry-coloured diamond, patinated silver, yellow gold
IMAGE COURTESY OF MICHAEL KANNER, KANNERS JEWELRY

"My jewels express a joy for life and intemporal beauty"

PALOMA PICASSO
Statements of Style

The daughter of famed artists Pablo Picasso and Françoise Gilot, Paloma Picasso is instantly recognisable the world over. After attending the Université de Paris at Nanterre, Paloma started to make costume jewellery using rhinestones and strass crystals that she found on outfits at flea markets; it caught the eye of the press and soon she began to design for Yves Saint Laurent (a friend), followed by a stint with the Greek jewellery house Zolotas. On the death of her father, she took time away to help create a catalogue of his works and to help open the Musée de Picasso in Paris.

In 1979, Picasso was signed by John Loring, the new creative director for Tiffany & Co., marrying her talent and larger-than-life persona with one of the best-known jewellery brands. By 1980 she was designing her signature squiggles for the Graffiti Collection, inspired by her desire to make something positive out of New York City's urban street art, which at the time was considered vandalism, and her handwritten 'X' (kisses), given her love for jewellery with meaning, in silver and gold for Tiffany and Co. There followed large bold-coloured gemstones set within gold 'X's and heavy, rounded, yellow gold settings. The gemstones are bezel set, which adds to the heavy look that would later become part of her design DNA. Using simple, uncluttered lines that came to define jewellery in the 1980s, her designs have stood the test of time and become classics.

Picasso's personal style was as much a statement of the 1980s as her designs: with her glossy, jet black hairstyle and scarlet red lipstick, she used her unique patrician looks to market her

ABOVE: Picasso for Tiffany & Co.: Bezel-drop earrings – cabochon pink tourmaline, cabochon green tourmaline, citrine, amethyst, yellow gold
IMAGE COURTESY OF CHRISTIE'S INC.

RIGHT: Picasso for Tiffany & Co.: Graffiti Collection: 'X' and 'O' (love & kisses) cuff – yellow gold
IMAGE COURTESY OF CHRISTIE'S INC.

OPPOSITE PAGE: Picasso for Tiffany & Co.: Double bezel 'X' and 'O' statement necklace with coloured stones – cabochon amethyst, pink tourmaline, green tourmaline, aquamarine, citrine, gold
IMAGE COURTESY OF CHRISTIE'S INC.

CLOCKWISE FROM ABOVE:

Picasso for Tiffany & Co.: Venezia Collection, Luce pendant – yellow gold
IMAGE COURTESY OF TIFFANY & CO.

Picasso for Tiffany & Co.: Marrakesh bangle – yellow gold
IMAGE COURTESY OF TIFFANY & CO.

Picasso for Tiffany & Co.: Olive Leaf cuff – yellow gold
Inspired by the olive branch, a symbol of abundance and peace.
IMAGE COURTESY OF TIFFANY & CO.

jewellery designs alongside her own perfume and cosmetics. Her success brought more
success as she launched her own perfume in 1984 and a global brand.

Moroccan Influence

Picasso splits her time between Lac Léman in Switzerland and her home close to
Marrakesh in Morocco, an evident influence on her later gold jewellery collections for
Tiffany's. The Marrakesh Collection, for example, draws its inspiration from the intriguing
geometric patterns found in the architecture and artifacts of the town. She called on the
arabesques of the region's metalwork and the beautiful colours found in ceramic patterns.
For her Olive Leaf Collection, Picasso takes as her starting point the small delicate leaves

of the olive tree – her Moroccan home was built in an old olive grove. She has created a lightness that is the antithesis of her work in the 1980s while holding on to her distinct bold style.

Picasso's designs have taken on a softer, more curvaceous aspect; they are still big but now she also offers more delicate designs. They have an innate sense of peace and fulfilment, that was perhaps lacking in the 1980s – the decade of brash bling. As if to emphasise the difference between then and now, she no longer wears the red lipstick that made her an icon of the '80s. Paloma Picasso continues to work closely with Tiffany & Co., producing collections annually.

TOP LEFT: Picasso for Tiffany & Co.: Paloma's Charms bracelet: Sunglasses, Love, 'X', Paintbrush, Dove (the meaning of Paloma's name in English), Kiss, Lipstick – enamel, yellow gold
IMAGE COURTESY OF TIFFANY & CO.

TOP RIGHT: Picasso for Tiffany & Co.: Sugar Stack rings – pink sapphire, diamond, rounded square cabochon blue topaz, amethyst, yellow quartz, rose gold, yellow gold
IMAGE COURTESY OF TIFFANY & CO.

ABOVE: Picasso for Tiffany & Co.: Graffiti Collection, Love ring – diamond, rose gold
IMAGE COURTESY OF TIFFANY & CO.

PART THREE

What is Happening Now in
the Field of Jewellery Design

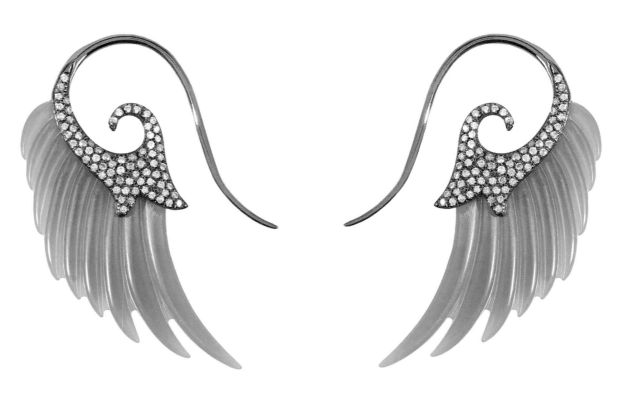

After the bold and ostentatious 1980s, the end of the 20th century brought restraint and a subtler brand image. People started to define themselves with their own style, looking for the unique and the original: a quieter, more refined chic, that was both elegant and understated. Running parallel to this tendency was an awareness of the body in street fashion: tattoos and body piercings took on a new meaning.

The 1990s was the beginning of a new era in jewellery design. Led by JAR and Chanel Inc., new designs and ideas were introduced; colour and unusual settings were accepted, such as the unconventional use – for the time – of setting gemstones upside down and mixing gemstones to create washes of colour. Long-forgotten techniques were reintroduced, oxidised silver and gold were revived. Jewellery was being defined by what the gemstone could do for the design; jewellery was once again about colour and light. So-called semi-precious stones were given their rightful place alongside the big five – spinels, opals and tourmalines of all colours became popular. With the new influx of young jewellery designer talent and the globalisation of communications, the ordinary person in the street was able to learn all about these 'new' gemstones.

It has been, and remains, an exciting period for jewellery designers and consumers alike. After 2010 there has been a coming together of ideas in the worlds of fashion and the arts, bringing a new dynamism to the whole sector. In Paris, couture fashion week coincides with shows for the jewellery houses, and galleries show jewellery alongside works of art.

The jewellery currents of the last 15 years included Pop Jewellery – a playful, colourful and surprising trend using a plethora of gemstones and noble metals – which translates into jewels that are more than a fleeting fashion. These are conversation pieces, made to make you smile. As younger people become aware that high jewellery can be inclusive, they are worn more as a statement than as decoration. A common feature of the new jewellery designers is their use of current technologies – CAD (computer-aided design), laser techniques – and new materials, such as ceramics, carbon fibre, zirconium and the increasingly popular titanium.

Holly Dyment's rings tell a story; she uses vivid colourful enamels to create images set with gemstones, which generate bright interludes as they catch the light and the eye.

Delfina Delettrez has been creating and nurturing a 'bad girl' image since 2007. The iconic surrealist pieces in her Anatomik Collection include enamel eyes peering out from beneath long gold mascara'd eyelashes. Her white gold, cabochon ruby and diamond hand bracelet is an exoskeleton of the human hand, and her famous pearl necklace and eyes in Murano glass were a first. Don't expect traditional styles with Delettrez's designs, they may be minimalist but they always surprise – either in the form they take or the way they decorate the entire finger, ear or hand.

Noor Fares uses simple designs with carved plumes to create accessible jewels. A multitude of coloured chalcedonies, agates and ebony wood create her Fly Me to the Moon Collection. Her Geometry 101 Collection includes a playful use of Rubik's cubes and cones with negative space.

Pascaline Janssens, formerly creative designer for Poiray in the '80s, has been quietly tracing a path for herself and her jewellery company, Arany, in Brussels. Her jewels are about a contemporary and timeless classicism.

LEFT: Holly Dyment: Vanitas ring – ruby, green garnet, enamel, diamond, yellow gold

These talents have come to the fore against a background of heightened awareness of sustainability and of a more ethical and ecological approach to conducting business. A restless global situation, from the wars in former Yugoslavia in the nineties to the increasing acts of terrorism from fundamentalist groups after the events of 9/11 in 2001 and the Arab Spring in 2011, have made it essential for jewellery designers today to think about their impact on communities around the world. Group consciousness brought about the Kimberley Process Certification scheme in 2003, which was conceived to prevent 'conflict diamonds' financing wars and human rights abuses. Similarly, gold is increasingly procured from ethical sources by this new group of jewellery designers.

The internet has become a compulsory conduit for modern designers; websites, blogs and vlogs are where most people will discover a jewellery designer's work for the first time. Bloggers and vloggers have a huge influence in this world, as they recount and give very opinionated advice on events such as exhibitions, auctions and the new designs and jewels making their 'stage' debut. Among the best are: *The Jewellery Editor*, founded by journalist Maria Doulton; *Jewels du Jour*, created by Natalie Bos; the French blog *Exclusive Bijoux* by Caroline Bigeard; and Katerina Perez's website.

The new generation of jewellery designers use social media – Facebook, Instagram and Twitter – to create and tell their story. Newsletters are essential; videos (the more inventive and artistic the better) are a backdrop to their creations. Galleries, such as the famous Colette in Paris, are a must to launch their edgy and fashion-conscious jewels. It is as much about being a part of the scene, as it is about being the person with the idea. To be a jewellery designer today means being always ahead of the game. Creativity never closes shop and it is an exhausting round of production, social media and shows – it is not for the faint of heart and the result is a group of passionate, creative and savvy women, who are pushing the boundaries just to be seen and heard above a sea of other brands.

ABOVE: Pascaline Janssens: Les Villes Collection, La New Yorkaise and La Parisienne rings – ruby, white gold, rose gold; amethyst, yellow gold
Inspired by the Chrysler Building and the Eiffel Tower. "We no longer live all our lives in the same city... but they always stay in our hearts."

RIGHT: Noor Fares: Geometry 101 Collection, Octahedron pendant – amethyst, diamond, oxidised gold, yellow gold

COLOUR AND LIGHT

Jewellery is all about colour and light. Colour surrounds us, creating shapes and forms, helping us to create a picture of what we are seeing. As light changes, so does our perception of those colours; it touches our visual sense. We unconsciously interpret distance, volume and texture, and we analyse the hue, saturation and the luminosity of the colours. So, when we describe a colour, we are actually describing how we *perceive* that colour.

The time of day will influence how certain colours are 'seen'; nuances and hues will vary from the early morning light to the evening. Gemstones will look different in bright sunshine than they will under a cloud-filled sky; the light of winter will differ to that of a summer's day. A jewel's appearance will not be the same in Mumbai as in Paris, say. Of course, for the wearer these concerns have been worked out by the jewellery designer.

Contrasts in colour temperatures (how 'cool' or 'warm' a colour is) create special spatial illusions: warm colours, such as orange, will appear closer and cool colours, such as blue, will seem further away. Also, areas of warm colours will seem larger than those of a colder colour. This effect is shown particularly well in the Butterfly Mobile earrings by French jewellery designer Sylvie Corbelin.

Above and Right: Sylvie Corbelin: Butterfly Mobile earrings – enamel, various coloured sapphires, moonstone, diamond, yellow gold

Opposite Page: Paula Crevoshay: Flora's Secret Lady's Slipper Orchid pendant – pink tourmaline, amethyst, green garnet, yellow gold
The scent glands of the lady's slipper orchid are represented by two cabochon amethysts, which make their own gentle play of light leading the eye to the centre of the flower before moving to the petals.
(Provenance: 'Garden of Light' exhibition, Carnegie Museum of Natural History, 2013)

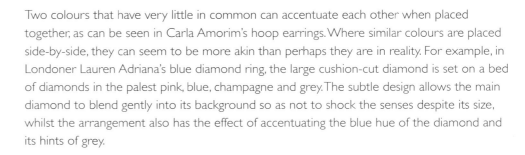

Two colours that have very little in common can accentuate each other when placed together, as can be seen in Carla Amorim's hoop earrings. Where similar colours are placed side-by-side, they can seem to be more akin than perhaps they are in reality. For example, in Londoner Lauren Adriana's blue diamond ring, the large cushion-cut diamond is set on a bed of diamonds in the palest pink, blue, champagne and grey. The subtle design allows the main diamond to blend gently into its background so as not to shock the senses despite its size, whilst the arrangement also has the effect of accentuating the blue hue of the diamond and its hints of grey.

The disposition of colours, and thus gemstones, has an influence on the whole look of the jewel; and jewellery designers exploit these properties to create their own bold and subtle combinations. Looking at Paula Crevoshay's use of opals and the colours that she marries with them, the difference in allure is immediately apparent.

The pavé settings popular during the last 25 years are a progression in colour tone that can create an impression of rhythmic light. The gradations of colour are created using different gems of similar hue, the designers exploiting the size and shape of the stones to create their own texture and story. Sylvie Corbelin uses gems of varying colours and cuts to stunning effect in her Minestrone rings.

Light is an extrapolation of colour in jewellery design. A jewellery designer will study how the light is reflected by, or refracted through gemstones and how it effects the gemstones in close vicinity. A real dynamic can be created, even in a rigid jewel, just by exploiting the single or double refraction of a gemstone and its lustre. Garnets and diamonds are brighter than a sapphire or a citrine say, which are in turn brighter than lapis lazuli and malachite. The monochroism, dichroism and pleochroism in gemstones (depending on the direction of the light, a gemstone may seem to change colour; this can be very slight or more pronounced as in tanzanite), creates an almost magical effect.

The level of a stone's transparency or opacity can be used to great effect. Lucia Silvestri for Bulgari, for example, creates wonderful statement jewels using contrasting lustres on opaque and translucent gemstones. They are all about theatrical opulence.

The beauty and value of an individual gemstone depends on its colour, clarity and lustre, but it is the designer's clever use of nuances and colour combinations that gives the final jewel its charm, energy and charisma.

LEFT, FROM TOP TO BOTTOM:

Carla Amorim: Hoop earrings – black tourmaline, yellow tourmaline, gold

Paula Crevoshay: Opal Plaque earrings – opal, pink tourmaline
(Provenance: Beyond Color Collection, Headley Whitney Museum; John Hendrickson Galleries Inaugural Exhibition, 2009)

Lauren Adriana: Shield ring – blue diamond, pink diamond, champagne diamond, grey diamond, platinum

RIGHT: Sylvie Corbelin: Minestrone ring – amethyst, turquoise, pink sapphire, sapphire, ruby, yellow gold

OPPOSITE PAGE: Lucia Silvestri for Bulgari: Odissi necklace – emerald, turquoise, red spinel, diamond, yellow gold IMAGE COURTESY OF BULGARI

"I try to never get bored with myself. My jewels must be striking and have a story to tell and they must be eye-catching, hence my jewellery design has always involved experimentation with colour and astonishing combinations. I never like to become stale."

VICTOIRE de CASTELLANE
Fun and Extravagant Chic

The Dior of old conjures up images of lily-of-the-valley, roses and wasp-like waists from the first collection in 1947. When Bernard Arnault took control of the company in 1984, he set about returning the house of couture to its former glory. In a brave and inspired move and with a view to the future, Arnault chose a jewellery designer from the hip Parisian nightclub scene. When Victoire de Castellane was engaged as artistic director for Dior Haute Joaillerie in 1998, she had already proven herself as creative director for costume jewellery at Chanel for 14 years under Karl Lagerfeld.

De Castellane's remit was to create a space and reputation for Dior in the high jewellery arena. Taking up the gauntlet, she burst onto the scene in 1999 with the stunning Milly-la-Forêt Collection, named after the gardens of the late Christian Dior.

> *"I wanted to play down jewellery, and strip it of the bourgeois stigma that is associated with it... It is perhaps a younger, more contemporary way of wearing jewellery."*

She created a pot-pourri of themes from Dior's DNA: ribbons and bows were given a new *élan*. From Dior's garden came rings covered in small daisy-like flowers, decorated with colourful lacquer and populated with small ladybirds and butterflies surrounding a large central gemstone. The Diorette rings were a huge success; they were an answer to the demand for something precious that remained young and wearable.

De Castellane had been looking to put fun into high jewellery and to create jewels that didn't take themselves too seriously. She turned to lacquer for inspiration and, working with three Parisian workshops, produced a palette of 89 different colours. (The range has since been reduced slightly, due to new regulations.) It was a brave move, as not many artisans at the time had experience with the use of lacquer, let alone with the variety of colours that de Castellane wanted. All the jewels were first crafted in yellow gold before being coated in a multitude of astonishing colours rarely associated with high jewellery. She used the three-dimensional effect of her sculpted flowers to add movement and flamboyancy, creating stunning bubble gum coloured jewels of real value and effervescence.

Dior: Diorette ring – aquamarine, amethyst, pink sapphire, yellow sapphire, tsavorite garnet, diamond, lacquer, white gold COURTESY OF DIOR FINE JEWELRY

OPPOSITE PAGE: Dior: Milly-la-Forêt necklace – emerald, jade, chrysoprase, onyx, pearl, red coral, ruby, amethyst, cultured pearl, diamond, yellow gold COURTESY OF DIOR FINE JEWELRY

TOP: Dior: La Fiancée du Vampire Collection, Noces de Sang
necklace – red spinel, diamond, white gold
COURTESY OF DIOR FINE JEWELRY

ABOVE: Dior: Egratigna Chipie ring – spinel, diamond, lacquer,
white gold COURTESY OF DIOR FINE JEWELRY

Colour

Colour and more colour are essential to Dior Haute Joaillerie. De Castellane would take a glass jar full of bright, garish, technicoloured sweets and, picking one out, say to Dior's gemstone dealers 'This is the colour I want!' This carefree attitude to the precious 'big five' gemstones meant that many other gemstones found their way into Dior pieces. Each gemstone came from a faraway place – to look at the gemstones was to travel, and to look at the design was to travel into another world. From this promising beginning came a sequence of collections: Diorette, Rose Dior, Mitza, My Dior, Belladona Island, Milly Carnavora, La Fiancée du Vampire, Le Coffret de Victoire, Les Précieuses, Le Bestiaire Fantastique, Reines et Rois, Le Bal des Roses, Dear Dior, Cher Dior, and Archi Dior.

La Fiancée du Vampire

De Castellane's La Fiancée du Vampire Collection celebrated Dior's arrival at the famous Place Vendôme, in November 2001. The collection took its inspiration from a Latin cross diamond pendant. The Noces de Sang (Blood Wedding) necklace features rosebuds and thorns; the red spinels and rubies allude directly to drops of blood, while de Castellane set the diamonds in such a way as to form thorns, spikes and barbs. Taking her inspiration from the Hollywood films of old, de Castellane explains:

"Drops of blood in technicolour are so red and so bold that they look almost painted. I have wanted to recreate this effect for such a long time."

Reines et Rois

Memento Mori are dressed with elaborate gem-set hair styles – 18th-century powdered 'Mesdames' are escorted by beguiling partners going to a ball; make-believe kings wear bejewelled headdresses. De Castellane seems to be saying: 'you may disguise yourself and have fun, but one day you will leave it all behind'.

Coffret de Victoire

In this collection – Victoire's Jewellery Box – huge gemstones take centre stage, dictating to de Castellane how they should be set. It is a collection without a theme; each gemstone is an individual, seeking to be dressed in its own particular way; cameos and intaglios vie for the best place. Rings show the 'skull and crossbones' of pirate ships; for de Castellane, they are stories of seduction, adventure and desire. De Castellane's skulls play dress-up: the skulls, made from a magnificent coral, mother-of-pearl, opal or turquoise, each 'wear' huge eccentric ear pendants of red spinel, iolite or opal and electric blue Paraiba tourmaline.

When de Castellane was putting this collection together, the ideas overflowed and inspiration came from travel, animals, figurines and people; even from old Bollywood and Hollywood films.

> *"With Coffret de Victoire I wanted to ... create an Aladdin's cave where you could stumble upon gold coins, skulls carved in jade or coral, and ancient jewels. The idea was to design a pastiche of cocktail rings that might have belonged to Napoleon III or could hail from Hollywood or 1950s Italy."*

ABOVE: Dior: Reines et Rois Collection, Roi d'Opalie pendant – pink opal, cultured pearl, diamond, platinum, white gold COURTESY OF DIOR FINE JEWELRY

LEFT: Dior: Coffret de Victoire Collection, earrings – shell cameo, spessartite garnet, pink tourmaline, fine pearl, andalousite, diamond, silver, pink gold
COURTESY OF DIOR FINE JEWELRY

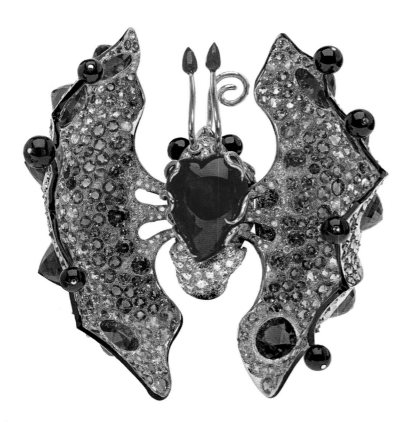

Belladone Island

Perhaps de Castellane's most important collection to date is Belladone Island, 2007, in which she imagines an island populated with carnivorous plants and butterflies. Jewellery historian Michèle Heuzé explains: *"It was this revolutionary collection that placed Dior Joaillerie as one of the elite."* De Castellane describes her inspiration:

> *"Belladonna is a toxic plant which Italian women in the Renaissance would put in their eyes to dilate their pupils; interpreted by men as a sexual signal... I love the idea that they were playing with fire and prepared to do anything to seduce."*

Certainly the jewels have a sinister quality to them, which is contradicted by the joyful display of brightly coloured lacquer and gemstones used to create them. They are colourful beautifully-made statements from a designer seeking to push the boundaries of what is permissible in the world of high jewellery. Each imaginary flower is given a witty, understandable, 'Latin'-inspired imaginary name, from the magnificent 'Reina Magnifica Sangria' to the 'Ancolia Veneinosa Pop'. The sinister element is accentuated by the sinuous play of each of the flower's stamens and by the hidden mechanisms with which the flower captures its prey. The Venus Fly Trap is an obvious inspiration for de Castellane's beautifully disturbing flowers, their petals closing to imitate a chrysalis and trap their victims.

> *"Carnivorous flowers morph into women trying to defend themselves in an aggressive society. I like to think that not only do I create jewellery, but I also give women something to cherish, something that gives them a sense of security and independence. Figuring out how to get the best out of life is my obsession and my guiding light."*

The rings in this collection are huge statement pieces; the petals of the Dracula Spinella Devorus flower have been tipped with diamonds and on the inside, each petal has been coated with glittering lacquer. As the petals open, there in the centre is a bright red spinel set with spindly claws, surrounded by diamonds.

De Castellane's mastery of colour is evident in the Grani Opalia Devorus ring, in which she uses an array of pale blue and pink sapphires, amethysts and garnets to complement or match the colours within the opal, so that the play of colour on the opal's surface seems to have been caught and devoured by the ring itself.

> *"I began with the idea of carnivorous female flowers, for which I created a place. The scenario was an island situated in the middle of nowhere, where the carnivorous flowers grew up completely alone, without a single male. This story made me think of B-movies involving Amazons, alone and captive on an island."*

Biennale des Antiquaires de Paris

The Biennale des Antiquaires show in Paris is the 'not to miss' show for all the great jewellery houses of the Place Vendôme. In 2012, de Castellane produced the Dear Dior Collection based on an exquisite array of Ethiopian opals and emeralds. These models veer away from her figurative collections, from her worlds of carnivorous jewels, to take their inspiration from the more grounded world of Christian Dior. However, de Castellane never being one to follow the well-trodden paths of her peers, has transformed classic themes into jewels that are feminine with a look to the past as well as to the present. Opals and emeralds are framed in lacework clusters of nuanced shades using differently shaped gemstones to create a stage for her symphony of colour. The effect is a sumptuous display of opaque and transparent forms, highlighted by diamonds and creating an intense femininity.

From Dear Dior, there was a natural progression to the Cher Dior Collection: a kaleidoscope of colour with claw settings that imitated stitch work and created the illusion of lace. Vibrant and alive, bright yellows clash with deep reds and oranges, with a touch of sobriety fashioned in pink. De Castellane describes them as coming between two Biennales (2012 and 2014), thus they are the 'babies' of Dear Dior. The original collection was composed of 21 jewels, from bracelets to rings and girandole ear pendants. The lightness of the pieces is due to their three-dimensional profile and the variety of cuts and colours of the gemstones; de Castellane explains: "*I suppose, they are the classic version of my idea of contemporary jewellery.*"

Archi Dior

The 2014 Biennale collection continued in this new direction, penetrating the secret world of *haute couture* – a world of silks, chiffons and brocades: exploring how they fell, their folds and pleats, as well as how a garment was structured using architectural outlines and forms. De Castellane took her inspiration from archival drawings sketched by Christian Dior years before and created an original and sophisticated series of delicate jewels, in which the emphasis was plainly on the properties of the textiles and their nuanced hues. One example was the Bar en Corolle Emeraude bracelet, which took its inspiration from the famous cinched-in waistline of Christian Dior's 'Bar jacket', in 1947.

The collection was christened for Christian Dior's passion for architecture, playing with the meaning of the word 'archi', which translates from French to mean 'extremely'.

ABOVE, FROM TOP TO BOTTOM:

Dior: Dear Dior earrings – black opal, emerald, amethyst, turquoise, demantoid garnet, sapphire, diamond, platinum, pink gold, yellow gold COURTESY OF DIOR FINE JEWELRY

Dior: Cher Dior earrings – emerald, yellow sapphires, pink sapphire, purple sapphire, sapphire, ruby, demantoid garnet, spessartite garnet, Paraiba tourmaline, diamond, yellow gold COURTESY OF DIOR FINE JEWELRY

LEFT:

Design sketch, Bar jacket, Christian Dior, 1947

Dior: Bar en Corolle Emeraude bracelet – emerald, pink sapphire, purple sapphire, demantoid garnet, tsavorite garnet, orange-pink spinel, diamond, white gold
COURTESY OF DIOR FINE JEWELRY

Gagosian Gallery

In March 2011 de Castellane displayed ten jewellery sculptures in silver and lacquer under her own name with the Gagosian Gallery in Paris for the 'Fleurs d'Exces' (Against Nature) Exhibition; the exhibition travelled on to New York. Each piece comes with its own pedestal or extraterrestrial world, a 'dwelling' for when they are not being worn. Using her famed lacquer work, de Castellane has created a phantasmagorical series of multicoloured pop art lacquer petal rings with fuschia-pink layered corollas, pockmarked with a multitude of cabochon emeralds, diamonds and tiny florets, creating an imaginative technicoloured 'anti-garden'.

> "De Castellane's intoxicating flowers personify the Romantic idea of women 'under the influence' of an opiate swoon, a psychedelic trip, an amphetamine high... They are dangerous because of the poisons that they secrete."
> Louise Neri, Gagosian Gallery

And yet her jewels are sugar-coated and sweet, of fairytales and fables.

De Castellane held her second exhibition, 'Animalvegetablemineral', at the Gagosian Gallery in London January 2014, which then moved to their New York gallery in March. This time she explored the serpent's hypnotic power in blue.

Imagination and inspiration

Her first foray into the domain of jewellery goes back to her childhood when she took the charm bracelet belonging to Sylvia Hennessy (de Castellane's maternal grandmother) and transformed it into a pair of earrings. She recalls how her grandmother, a friend of Barbara Hutton, had introduced her to the world of gemstones, little knowing where it would lead in later years.

> "I have loved jewels since I was a little girl. I was fascinated by the women around me who wore things that twinkled and made noise; I was especially attracted by the gestures that accompanied the jewel, the relationship between the jewels and the women who wore them. I was rather lonely and, as children do, I constructed an imaginary world, brightly coloured and artificial in contrast to the rather bourgeois milieu in which I was brought up... Later on I liked the idea that jewels possessed something precious; you could travel with them like little treasures. After that I became obsessed with scale, because the idea of disproportion, of wearing oversized jewels was very appealing. Undoubtedly this stems from my childhood memory of trying on rings belonging to adults."
> Victoire de Castellane, 'Fleurs d'excés', Gagosian Gallery

She is Victoire de Castellane, part of a team, a family of dedicated artisans who experiment, craft and transform her imagination into reality.

Lunae Lumen Satine Baby Blue ring, 2013 – sapphire, diamond, lacquer, white gold
(Provenance: 'Animalvegetablemineral' Exhibition, 2013)
Courtesy of the Gagosian Gallery

Opposite Page: Extasium Ethero Coitus, 2010 – diamond, lacquered silver, white gold; pedestal – nephrite jade
(Provenance: 'Against Nature' Exhibition, 2010)
Courtesy of the Gagosian Gallery

"Intimate surprises spun from thin air. Precious metals forged to last an eternity. Unwavering, uncompromising, unapologetically bold, unlike anything else… the incomparable thrill of one of a kind."

ALEXANDRA MOR
Cutting Edge

Alexandra Mor's office looks down upon the busy diamond district of Manhattan, New York. A hundred different languages are being spoken as people zig-zag between the yellow taxi cabs and honking cars as they go about their business. Yet there above the fray is an oasis of calm, a place where Alexandra Mor is creating and conceiving her purist and architecturally inspired jewels. Her fluid lines and simple blocks of colour merge into classic jewels, which, at first glance, are deceptively simple. The secret is in their proportions and in the clean outline that each jewel possesses.

Alexandra Mor grew up in Israel's multicultural melange. From a young age, she was exposed to handcrafted design by her French couturier mother, who made Mor's 'one of a kind' childhood clothes by hand. It was Mor's mother and aunt who taught her about the essence of detail, the hidden unseen features and the importance of the finish, which when brought together, create the essential style and chic of a piece of clothing. Mor would remember all these qualities when she started to grasp the exacting requirements of the jeweller's bench in 2004:

> *"Cutting, sawing, measuring, filing, burnishing, designing — I knew I had found my place."*

Working at the bench with master jewellers gave Mor an insight, which she capitalised upon before striking out on her own path. Even now, years later, when Mor sits down to design, the *"smell of burning yellow ochre"* transports her back to the *"unmistakable smell of [her mother's] ironing pad... the smell of the raw fabric"*; and she is reminded of the need for focus and for the attention to detail that brings authenticity and excellence.

LEFT: Curved dangling diamond earrings, Series 1/15 — diamond, platinum, yellow gold
These show Alexandra Mor's signature floating diamond melee and curved knife-edged wire detail.

OPPOSITE PAGE: Branch diamond and moonstone cuff — opal, diamond, platinum, yellow gold

ABOVE: Slanted cabochon emerald and diamond ring
(worn over two fingers) – cabochon emerald, diamond,
platinum, yellow gold
*"I love to combine old-world craftsmanship with contemporary
styles and techniques."*

BELOW: Peruvian green opal and diamond double ring –
cabochon green opal, diamond, platinum, yellow gold
*This ring shows Alexandra Mor's signature 'floating' diamond
melee and curved knife-edged wire detail.*

Mor's DNA

With her first collection, Mor introduced several signature themes that were to become a running thread throughout her work as an artist.

> *"My signature details are at the core of every piece, and they serve as both anchor and guide to my designs. Essentially, they're the building blocks of my creative DNA."*

She uses modern gemstone cuts, such as the scissors cut and the Asscher cut, embellished with knife-edge platinum lines, set in 'floating' diamond melee. She includes a layer of 18ct gold, almost hidden from view, another nod to the past and to add an extra warmth to the jewel.

The Emerald Cabochon

Mor's emerald cabochon ring was one of twelve original jewels in her first signature collection; it was like a magnet that drew the attention of many and it has become one of her most iconic designs. She was at the beginning of her career and at first was reluctant to buy the emerald: it was not a gemstone that you could traditionally call beautiful. And yet it played on her mind; it would pop into her consciousness at the most unexpected moments. She tried to ignore it, it was only when she awoke one morning having imagined exactly how she could set it, that she rushed out to buy it.

> *"Something about the various shades of green and internal textures made it even more interesting to me than a perfectly faceted stone."*

Mor's innate sense of proportion prevails in this surprising and most intriguing of rings. The design centres on the large cabochon emerald, with its unusual *jardin*. Aware that it was too big to be formed into a ring in the conventional sense, and taking a pragmatic view on the fragility of emeralds, Mor wanted to protect the gemstone at the same time. The upshot was a remarkably simple solution, creating a magnificent asymmetrical ring: a railing was placed around the lower half of the cabochon and the centre of the ring was moved so that the emerald would sit over two fingers rather than one, thus cushioning the emerald and preventing it from turning on the wearer's hand. The signature double claws creep up the sides of the gemstone, giving it yet more protection and lending a semblance of openness to the design. The single trapezoid white diamond underlines the movement of the ring and acts as a bracket to the emerald. A *tour-de-force*!

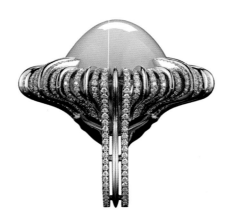

The Belt Buckle

When Mor was given five pieces of jade, she was asked by a collector to come up with a jewel that would use them all. Rather than taking the perhaps more traditional route of creating a necklace or a bracelet, she chose to create a belt buckle. It demonstrates the challenge and the creativity of a true artist. Using her signature knife-edge to frame the buckle, she had found a witty solution to an awkward conundrum. She used a textured white gold background in which to set the four jade discs and the antique jade plaque. The jade's gleam contrasts with the textured white gold and the scattered diamond melee.

The Personal Touch

Alexandra Mor recounts the story of her jewels from their beginning; each client is part of that journey. From the initial encounter with a client, there is a dialogue so that each may learn about the universe and the intentions of the other. The design and the selection of the gemstones is a process embarked on together and the outcome is always a jewel that possesses 'the heart of the collector' and the rich fabric of Mor's inspirations. Her collectors have a chance to work and watch alongside Mor and to witness their ideas become a reality. It is yet another nod to her past – that of the world of haute couture, which her mother and aunt once occupied – and to old world craftsmanship.

> *"When I design jewellery, I get to enhance human individuality. I'm also afforded the opportunity to inspire my collectors, who are able to take part in the creative process with me."*

Technology helps Mor at this vital stage; she creates an individual 'virtual jewellery box log-in page', where she uploads her ideas for her client to see, and then images of how the commission is progressing. It is a very personal involvement and the creation of a piece is always a special event. When the jewel is ready, her client receives a special personalised book that recounts the experiences that they have shared along the journey. From the ideas and designs, to the process of selecting the gemstones and the actual modelling and the fabrication of the jewel, these are all part of the story to tell to future generations.

ABOVE AND BELOW: Jade and diamond belt buckle – vintage Chinese engraved jade disks, black pearl, crocodile leather, white gold, yellow gold
The reverse shows Alexandra Mor's logo cage.

Many of Mor's pieces can be converted into more elaborate jewels for the evening or they can be 'dressed down' for daytime wear. One such example are the red coral and diamond chandelier ear pendants, which feature a long, single row of five drops gently graduating in size. From the small, almost heart-shaped coral, the drops flow from one to the next, trickling small diamonds between. The earrings can be 'dressed up' with a diamond half-moon arch, which supports two four-drop pendants. Deliberately playing with the size and number of the small diamonds, Mor creates a dynamic that is, above all, contemporary combined with a zest of ageless style.

A sense of proportion

There has been a progression since Mor started out; at first her designs had a strong angular presence but, with time, her jewels have become rounder and softer. Mor uses her knife-edge DNA to create open, curvaceous borders with which she frames her large gemstone centres. The pale green cabochon Peruvian opal ring is one such example, with its contour of elegance.

"As I seek to find my inspiration, I feel that I am exploring my own femininity and my role as a mother, a wife, as well as that of a jewellery designer. With this, has come softer lines, more curves and a better understanding of where I am going."

Inspiration

Mor finds inspiration in her personal history, of remembering where she came from. Often her inspiration comes from the simplest and most innocent of objects, a snowflake for instance. From this simple gift of nature, Mor has simplified it to create earrings and rings, and her doodling has taken the snowflake and transformed it into small bells, from which her elongated earrings emerge.

ABOVE: Intense Aquamarine ring – Asscher-cut aquamarine, diamond, platinum, yellow gold

BELOW LEFT: Detachable diamond Snowflake Drop earrings – diamond, platinum

BELOW RIGHT: Dramatic Chandelier earrings – 26 pear-shaped coral, diamond, white gold
The sides are detachable, transforming the pair into long drop earrings.

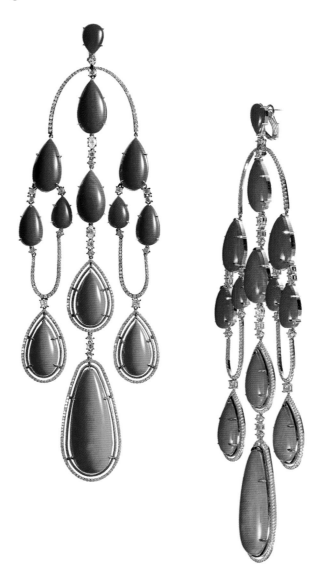

More recently, Mor has been trying out new ideas with a clientele who are looking for unique versatile jewels using gemstones that are themselves distinctive. Mor has created a succession of unusual earrings that can be dressed up or down by adding the pearls and rubies as drops to elaborate a pair of diamond ribbon bow earrings, again using her distinctive knife-edge settings. Mor's diamond ear studs with jade jackets are another style that can be transformed depending on the wearer's wish.

> "My goal is to design for the woman who is unwavering in her own authenticity; one who embraces femininity and makes bold statements, while exuding confidence without shame. For those who strive for the perfect balance between simplicity and extravagance."

Mor's jewels are young and of the moment. They are intensely personal. They carry into the twenty-first century the American ideal of jewels that can be transformed for different occasions. Simple earrings can be added to in order to create elaborate chandelier earrings, mixing and matching a variety of gemstone drops – an idea that has travelled across the Atlantic Ocean from 18th- and 19th-century Europe.

> "My intention is that it's created to remain, now and forever. A classic."

Detachable contemporary bow earrings – rose-cut ruby, ruby, pear-shaped rubellite, teardrop rubellite, natural pearl, diamond
Detachable components create several distinct pairs of earrings.

ORNELLA IANNUZZI
Mineral Treasures

The influence of Iannuzzi's childhood in the French Alps is evident to all who look upon her jewels. As a girl, she would find small mineral treasures on her hikes up mountain paths and from these beginnings she conceived her distinctive gritty settings.

As a student of Applied Arts, Iannuzzi became fascinated by the work of René Lalique, which was the catalyst for her interest in jewels and her use of unusual materials.

> *"He used all this material which was so unusual for jewellery at that time, I fell in love with the way he combined it all together."*

Iannuzzi creates unique settings for each of her treasures, be it a stone or a shell. Her deep interest in the geological formations of rocks and stones leads her to use their crystalline make up to create small jewels that hold the symbol of time. The strong colours of her minerals are set to enhance and emphasise the intensity of their colour and unique forms.

Background
A summer internship at Van Cleef & Arpels brought Iannuzzi into contact with the design process, techniques and control procedures of the great jewellery houses of the Place Vendôme. During that brief placement she learnt to appreciate the beauty of top-quality gemstones, the attention to detail and the House's immense respect for the handmade; it was a big change from her studies where she had used CAD and new technologies almost exclusively.

> *"The designs were in gouache, they were like masterpieces. I was really taken by this, the traditional French way of doing things."*

She continued her studies with the metalwork department under the aegis of the world-renowned jeweller David Watkins at the Royal College of Art in London, from which she graduated with a Master's Degree in 2007.

In 2008, Iannuzzi launched her first collection, Nature's Treasure; its central theme was pyrite mineral rock ('fool's gold') gathered from the Alps around Serre-Ponçon. Pyrite has an interesting crystal habit, forming cubes often inter-grown, stuck together and massive. They create many different shapes and their outlines inevitably point to how they should be set. Her cubic crystallization pyrite On the Rock ring is now part of the Alice Koch Collection, and gives a clear indication of Iannuzzi's design ethic, which is strong, bold and singular, enhancing the raw grit of nature. The pyrite is cradled within its sculpted parent rock and the ring's shank is carved to reflect the natural facets of that rock.

ABOVE: Nature's Treasure Collection, Cubic Crystallization Pyrite ring, 2008 – pyrite, black rhodium-plated silver, 24ct gold leaf

OPPOSITE PAGE: Les Exceptionnelles Collection, A l'Ère Glacière ring, 2012 – aquamarine on schorl, black rhodium-plated silver, silver

Iannuzzi makes no concessions to traditional styles in these rings, forged by Mother Nature. Her A L'Ere Glacière (The Ice Age) ring, takes its cue from the beautifully formed aquamarine crystal protected by a black tourmaline (schorl), which has been fissured to contrast the smooth facets of the crystal. The bezel has been scored to recall the fissures on the schorl, creating an interesting 'just dug up' mystic. Observe Iannuzzi's treatment of textures and thus the colour nuances of the tectonic metals such as the silver, bright shiny slate greys and the varied lustres of the black schorl: all have one job and that is to set off the intense blue of the aquamarine crystal. This is as powerful as you will get, it is surely a *'take no prisoners, make no concessions'* ring.

Blue is a constant colour in many of Iannuzzi's collections, for example, in the Les Exceptionnelles Collection, the Sur la Côte d'Azur ring is set with azurite from Morocco. The bezel takes on a similar texture to the crystal flakes of the azurite and the small sapphires highlight the blue. The natural and the faceted stones contrast one another, not only in form, but also in the matt of the crystal and the bright lustre of the sapphires.

Materials
Her second collection, Abyss, includes Ondine's Jewel ring. A friend had brought a shell back from Bali; enter Ornella Iannuzzi, who suggested making it into a ring. Utilising the sinuous shape of the shell as the bezel, Iannuzzi set about shadowing its soft lines. She chose rose vermeil to complement the chocolate and pink nuances of the shell. The creation is topped with a fresh-water pearl, chosen for its colour as well as its symbolic value of purity and truth. Artistic to the end, her rose vermeil imitates the outline of coral formations under the sea.

Fossilised coral also sees itself being given a new lease of life and from its white state it is given a regal Neptune-style treatment in which to flourish once again. The coral was found on a beach in Vanuatu.

Other than great artistry, one message comes through clearly: you do not need to include expensive materials to render a jewel a work of art. Exquisiteness is about design, detail and workmanship above all else. Iannuzzi's small works of art, or miniature sculptures, are made to be worn, to be seen and not left at home.

Iannuzzi became fascinated with opals whilst travelling and visiting the Welo mine in Ethiopia in 2010. Her Axum ring showcases a magnificent gemstone of opalescent caramel and orange colours shot with greens and blues and reds.

> *"I really went for bold colours like black, chemical green, orange and red."*

The angular form pays homage to the monolith stelae and the architecture of Axum, which dates back to the 4th century. The name for this collection, Lucy in Wonderland, combines the cultural references of Lewis Carroll's book *Alice in Wonderland* and 'Lucy', the pre-historic human fossil (*Australopithecus afarensis*) discovered in Ethiopia in 1974. Iannuzzi has conjured up images of bygone times when the markets were thriving, bustling with energy and the country was a powerful state welcoming traders and Pharaohs from afar.

ABOVE:

Les Exceptionnelles Collection, Sur la Côte d'Azur ring, 2012 – azurite crystal, sapphire, yellow gold, vermeil
The natural crystallisation of gemstones is the DNA of Iannuzzi's jewellery.

Abyss Collection, The Ondine's Jewel ring, 2011 – seashell, fresh-water pearl, 18ct rose vermeil

BELOW: Bespoke Collection, Souvenir des Mers du Sud ring, 2010 – Tahitian pearl, fossil coral, black rhodium-plated silver, green gold vermeil

OPPOSITE PAGE: Lucy in Wonderland Collection, Axum ring, 2010 – Welo opal, yellow gold
Inspired by the obelisks in Axum dating from the 4th century.

ABOVE LEFT: Les Exceptionnelles Collection, The Diamond Jubilee pendant mounted on a rough diamond necklace, 2012 – diamond crystal, diamond, 22ct gold vermeil

ABOVE RIGHT: Abyss Collection, The Uprising ring – baroque pearl, diamond, rose gold
Recipient of the Goldsmith's Company Award, 2015 and the International Jewellery London Precious Jewellery Award, 2015.

BELOW: Les Exceptionnelles Collection, L'Exceptionnelle Tanzanite pendant/sculpture mounted on a hematite necklace – tanzanite crystal, diamond, oxidised gold
Winner of the Gold Award at the Craft and Design Council Awards 2016.

Awards

In 2014 she collaborated with the well-known Parisian jewellery house, Capet, where she had been apprenticed during her studies in Paris before heading for London. Together, they created the retail collection Rock It, which won UK Jewellery Designer of the Year at the UK Jewellery Awards in 2015.

> *"My reason for using this particular shape is because I am fascinated by its mathematical complexity and all the theories that are related to the dodecahedron: it symbolises the quintessence of life, the ether according to the Alchemical approach."*

In 2015, her pearl ring, The Uprising, inspired by rolling waves, won both the Goldsmiths' Company Premier Award at the Goldsmiths' Craft & Design Council, London, UK and the Gold Award in Fine Jewellery in the IJL Precious Jewellery category.

2016 has seen Iannuzzi honoured with another Gold Award, this time in the Jeweller category, at the Goldsmiths' Craft & Design Council Awards, London for her intriguing tanzanite pendant, L'Exceptionnelle Tanzanite.

Ornella Iannuzzi is still only at the start of her career, and the future will surely be filled with many adventures and successes.

OPPOSITE PAGE: Cage Rock It! pendant, 2014 – opal bead, yellow gold
"An opal bead is 360 degrees of pleasure when you look at it. There is not a side which is not attractive... I wanted opal beads to roll around and display the rainbow of colours."

"I like to be subtle with my creations and that's probably the European influence."

NEHA DANI
Modern India

Based in Delhi, India, Neha Dani is one of a new generation of jewellery designers who are fusing Indian and European inspirations to create stunning, beautiful and wearable jewellery. As a child at home, Neha Dani learnt to study the minute details of nature and she has tried to capture this in her work. Travelling widely with her family, she visited many museums, which in turn helped hone her eye to the detail and the intricate workmanship of what was before her.

Naturally, Indian inspiration is evident in many of Dani's jewels; she cherishes her culture and is especially taken with the weave, both simple and complex, of Indian saris. The plethora of handicrafts from the different regions of India have also hugely influenced Dani's work.

Autumnal Leaves

Most of Dani's jewels are inspired by nature, but nature with a difference; her autumnal colours and shapes come from dried leaves on the ground and the simple pleasure of kicking those leaves. Listening to those crisp, rustling sounds inspired a series of pieces depicting curled dry leaves set with yellow, brown and champagne-coloured diamonds.

> *"We don't really see autumnal colours in India, only way up in the Himalayas. The trees' colour changes really fascinate me — it's very poetic!"*

The twisting and curling of the leaves create a multitude of whorls and waves that invite the eye to travel beyond the first shape to discover what is behind. There is an infinite number of shapes to explore.

The Feuille d'Or earrings have a special textural magnetism that draws the onlooker into their world: we want to touch and look closer. They are beautifully highlighted by using white rounded trillion diamonds, which create a soothing contrast to the irregular, almost angular outline of the leaf's curls.

In the same series, Dani has used round, faceted, cognac-coloured diamond beads of varying styles to trace a path of fallen acorns amongst the fallen leaves, set with a wash of small yellow and white diamonds piled on top of each other; note the clever use of champagne-coloured diamonds to suggest the shadowing of the leaf's curves.

OPPOSITE PAGE: Feuille d'Or earrings – canary yellow diamond, white diamond, yellow gold

LEFT: Autumn Feuille bracelet – yellow diamond, champagne- and cognac-coloured diamond beads, yellow gold

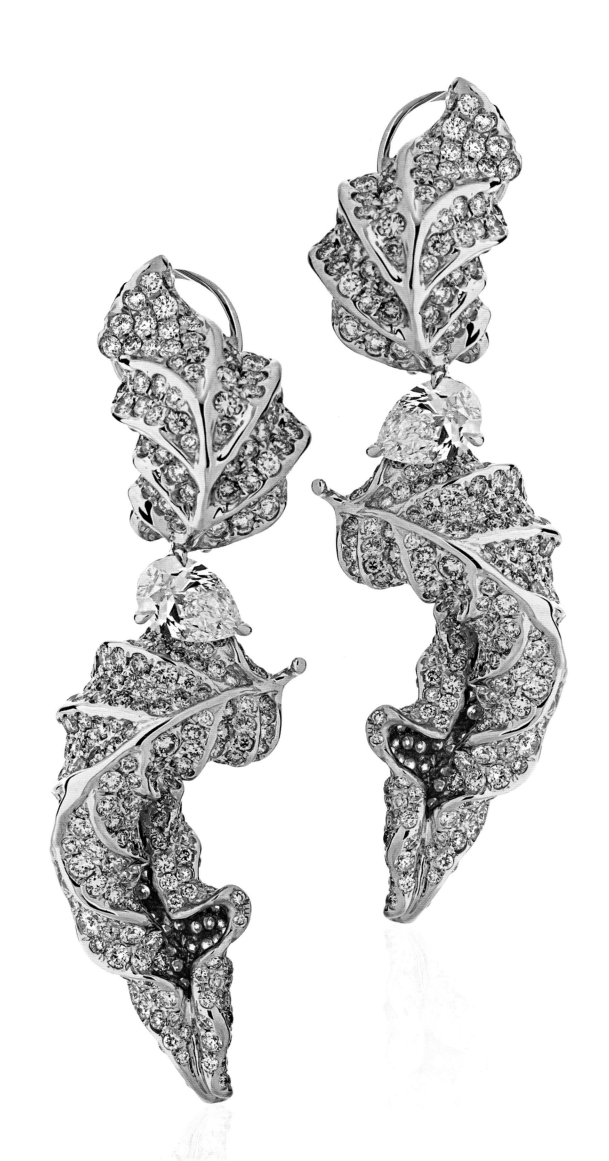

Dani studied at the Gemological Institute of America (GIA), first completing a design course and then studying wax carving; she became a Graduate Gemologist (GG) in 1997. She followed this by studying for the FGA (Fellow of the Gemmological Association of Great Britain) qualification in 2002. She says that the courses complemented each other – the GIA focused more on the grading systems of diamonds and coloured stones and the course at The Gemmological Association of Great Britain (Gem-A) was more concerned with the crystal structures and origins of the gemstones. Her career started in Mumbai, where she spent 10 years as a jewellery designer before moving to Delhi.

Flowers

Flowers have always been a large part of Dani's world. The Leela bracelet captures the essence of India – Leela is a sanctuary and a temple for contemplation. A faceted diamond bead is set at the centre of a double eight-petalled flower, its detailed outline achieved by using the time-old technique of filigree work (the twisting of gold and/or silver threads into jewellery). The diamond bead and the circular outline of the radiating petals represent universal harmony. The hexagonal outlines that link each flower, depict the energy and the strength of Leela.

The Pink Magnolia Ring sees Dani changing her palette to a gentle pink wash; the pink rose-cut diamonds trace the shapes of the intricate magnolia petals.

ABOVE: The Leela bracelet – white diamond, white gold

BELOW LEFT: Teal ring – sapphire, diamond, green rhodium-plated white gold, blue rhodium-plated white gold

BELOW RIGHT: The Pink Magnolia ring – pink diamond, white diamond, rose gold, white gold

OPPOSITE PAGE: Evita necklace – sapphire, diamond, blue rhodium-plated white gold

For Dani's Amarante bracelet, the florets are set with purple-pink fancy-coloured diamonds and tiny pink diamonds in a complex and sensuous waltz. From the carving of the wax and the transforming of the bracelet into metal, creating the skeleton of this wondrous piece, to setting the 11,000 pink diamonds has required 2,000 hours of workmanship. Dani's petal and leaf shapes are the result of her dexterity in sculpting and moulding the wax to create the shapes and outlines. This allows her to build up a jewel with multiple layers and patterns, giving each piece a certain complexity that will then be transformed in her workshops into her miniature interpretations of nature.

Neha Dani is a talent of the future, it will be interesting to see how her work progresses. At present, her designs appeal to both the Middle Eastern and Western worlds; India, her home, will be the next to discover her poetic jewels. She was included by the *JCK (Jewelers' Circular Keystone* magazine – the leading trade publication in the USA) in its 'Rising Stars Group', 2014.

Amarante bracelet, 2015 – purple-pink diamond, pink diamond, rose gold

"I paint with gemstones, not just with their myriad colours but with their light. Each gemstone has its own ability to transmit light inherent to that particular mineral. I call it 'tangible light'. It is truly the light of the earth."

PAULA CREVOSHAY
The Jeweller's Artist

Artist, painter and colourist; Paula Crevoshay has been guided on an instinctual path from childhood to become the extraordinary fine jewellery designer she is today. Her talent as an artist was recognised by the time she started at primary school; her early promise was realised when she completed a Masters in painting and print making at the University of Wisconsin, Madison in the USA.

Having audaciously secured herself a one-woman show at a New York gallery of some repute, she instead moved to Mumbai, India with her new husband. It was here, speaking with the local jewellers and metal workers, that she began the transition from painter to jeweller. Crevoshay started by making small pieces of jewellery with the finest tiny gemstones that she could find; small earrings and rings found their way into the jewellery boxes and onto the hands of her fans.

When the Crevoshays returned to the United States 3½ years later, they first earned a living buying and selling Tibetan carpets, until they realised that buying gemstones would be a lot easier and lighter to transport! From that moment Paula Crevoshay took up jewellery creation seriously.

She is renowned in the United States for using unusual gemstones, which she associates with other gems to create uniform, nuanced or contrasting and contradictory jewels. On her Galactic ear pendants she accentuates the deep green of the opal by using small points of green tsavorite garnets, the adamantine lustre of which also increases the perception of light.

LEFT: Galactic ear pendants – opal, tsavorite garnet, yellow gold

OPPOSITE PAGE: River Goddess pendant – chrysocolla, moonstone, opal, diamond, yellow gold
The chrysocolla was carved by Glenn Lehrer. The piece symbolises the life-giving force of water.
(Provenance: Beyond Color Collection at Headley-Whitney Museum in 2009; 'Garden of Light' Exhibition at the Carnegie Museum of Natural History in 2013)

A cuff bracelet set with a large green cabochon zircon uses its lustre to create a well of green light that is beautifully accentuated by small, faceted green tourmalines with the same colour tones. The facets give the tourmalines a contrasting character, which serves to highlight the luminosity of the central zircon. Subtle, discreet but definitely a statement.

Design

Crevoshay will usually take a gemstone and start by designing from the centre of the jewel outwards. She will have a clear idea in mind – she will know the shapes and the colours that she wants and when she picks up a pencil, the ideas flow on to the page.

> *"There is no brilliant inspiration for me as an artist, everything I ever do as a designer has a direct connection and reverence for nature itself."*

Where her famous pavé settings are concerned, her artistic talents are very much at the fore. She helps us see colour in shapes and forms, which combine to create an object. She helps to stimulate our senses, so that we see what is actually there and not what we think we see.

All Crevoshay's jewels are characterised by her use of yellow gold and the textures, matt finishes and volutes. She explains that yellow gold *"imbues the coloured stones with a warmth and a glow that you don't typically get with other metals."*

From early on, Crevoshay started to work with a small group of talented stone carvers. With stone intarsia master Nicolai Medvedev, she created special hardstone mosaics to include in her recent Zarina Series. These tiny stone inlays – *Pietra Dura* – can be seen in architecture all over Italy and Russia. Crevoshay adds her own vision to each of these special mosaics. She sets the intarsia (lapis lazuli, malachite, turquoise, opal and sugilite) in scallop shaped supports creating a contrast between the severe lines of the intarsia and the rounded curvaceous lines of the frame. She mixes ancient Egyptian shapes with those of the Italian style, bringing them together in her own contemporary interpretation.

Crevoshay's interest in ancient techniques and their contemporary descendants is derived from her studies in art history and anthropology at University and her need as an artist to preserve and encourage the techniques of the past so that they will not be forgotten. Another stone carver with whom she collaborates is Glenn Lehrer, who has carved the central torus that can be seen in many of Crevoshay's earrings.

TOP: Pietra Dura pendant – lapis lazuli, sugilite, opal, turquoise, malachite, amethyst, zircon, yellow gold

LEFT: Torus earrings – Oregon opal, blue zircon, yellow gold
The opal was carved by Glenn Lehrer.

OPPOSITE PAGE: Green cuff bracelet – green cabochon zircon (from Myanmar), green tourmaline, bright and satin finished yellow gold
(Provenance: 'Beyond Color' Collection, at Headley-Whitney Museum; John Hendrickson Galleries Inaugural Exhibition, 2009)

ABOVE: Poppy brooch – moonstone, fire opal, black diamond, diamond, yellow gold
(Provenance: 'Garden of Light' exhibition, Carnegie Museum of Natural History, 2013)

BELOW: Eternal Flame pendant – Brazilian opal, yellow gold
The opal was carved by Lawrence Stoller.
(Provenance: Beyond Color Collection, at Headley-Whitney Museum; 'Garden of Light' Exhibition, Carnegie Museum of Natural History, 2013)

She has worked with many of the talented stone carvers in contemporary America and created her Elements Collection around them to celebrate their prowess, taking Earth, Air, Fire, Water, and Ether as the central themes. As well as Medvedev and Lehrer, Crevoshay has collaborated with Sherris Cotter Shank, Thomas McPhee, Lawrence Stoller, Larry Winn and Larry Woods.

Exhibitions

Crevoshay has shown her work in many museums worldwide, from her first jewellery exhibition, 'Voices of the Earth' at the Carnegie Museum of Natural History and then at the GIA Museum in 2002, to 'Illuminations: de la Terre au Bijou' (From Earth to Jewel) at the Museum of Mineralogy, Paris in 2016-2017.

Crevoshay was asked to show at the Headley-Whitney Museum in 2009 to mark the opening of their new jewellery wing. She decided it should be an opportunity to go beyond what she was particularly known for – colour. Thus, the name for her exhibition: 'Beyond Color'. She wanted to show the outlines, shapes and forms that she saw recurring in her jewellery as well as being a platform for her distinctive colour combinations.

Her show, the 'Garden of Light' Exhibition at the Carnegie Museum of Natural History, was to pose a conundrum: how do you set up an art exhibition in a science museum? The answer was to create a theme around the garden and then to create bridges of understanding between the scientific stories of the gems, flora and fauna.

For instance, the Poppy brooch, with its exquisite display of reds and oranges, starts at the centre with a carved translucent moonstone beneath six radiating diamond-set arms. Note her characteristic use of large and small gemstones, which in this case creates three layers of sculptural petals, starting in the middle with the darkest hue; the second layer of petals are only a pinch lighter in nuance, before we reach the outer set of petals, which have a greater colour difference. This canny use of shading gives light to the whole flower, throwing back the emphasis to the centre of the poppy and the black diamond stamens. Poppies are a symbol of sleep, dreams and peace; they represent the wealth and extravagance of the flower kingdom.

Within the same exhibition, Crevoshay displayed a row of gem-encrusted orchids, each more opulent than the next. Alongside them were the pollinators, those created by Crevoshay and those from the depths of the museum's archive.

> *"The only missing element was man."*

Other mysterious creatures were to inhabit this garden of light, which mixed cultures and symbols to create exotic dream-like creatures in a Neverland of their own. The River Goddess – using a chrysocolla carved by Glenn Lehrer – is typical of this ethos; she expresses the essential nurturing nature water has for all living beings and the restless energy of water, sometimes tranquil, sometimes turbulent, in her everlasting dance of life.

Crevoshay's contribution as a jewellery designer is anchored in her colour combinations and her heavy gold settings, giving a richness and exotic quality to her jewels, which are principally about the gemstones – her choice of stone and the manner in which they have been carved, using the talents of stone-cutters in America. Her jewels have a touch of the Renaissance, the simplicity of the Arts & Crafts movement, and the gem savvy of the 21st century.

ABOVE: Orange Nectar Orchid brooch – fire opal, amethyst, diamond, yellow gold

RIGHT: Dawn's Early Light Butterfly brooch – opal, moonstone, zircon, yellow gold
(*Provenance: 'Garden of Light' Exhibition at the Carnegie Museum of Natural History, 2013*)

DESIGNING FOR THE BRANDS

Brand is everything. In order to create an ambience and a cohesive meaning for their collections, the main jewellery houses are all using inventive ways to put their message out into both the cyber and physical worlds. There has been a move away from the figurative mood of the 1990s and the early 2000s to more streamlined minimalist jewels that unite young street fashion with haute couture.

Take, for example, the new jewellery house Dauphin, founded in 2014, which is using its skill in marketing to be seen in important trendsetting galleries such as Colette in Paris and the Dover Street Market in London (DSML) and New York (DSMNY). It is also associating itself with fashion catwalks and contemporary art shows, such as those at the Serpentine galleries in London, as well as cleverly positioning itself on billboards at special events, such as the Cannes Film Festival. Lydia Courteille and Suzanne Syz have also done the same in the past.

The Creative Director

To tell the story of the brand requires someone dedicated to the creative vision. Enter the creative director. Dior Haute Joaillerie began the 21st century with Victoire de Castellane as Artistic Director. Other jewellery companies have followed suit: Boucheron brought in Solange Azagury-Partridge for three years. (She went on to create her own brand, to be found in her stores in New York, London and Paris.) She was followed by Claire Choisne. Bulgari appointed its own creative director, Lucia Silvestri in 2013. Silvestri's knowledge of gemstones and how to get the most charm from them was such that Bulgari turned a corner, albeit a gentle one, to bring their designs into the 21st century, and from the heavy gold settings of the '80s and the '90s, came exquisite blends of bold and nuanced colours from the finest gemstones.

LEFT: Lucia Silvestri for Bulgari: Aquamarine and diamond earrings – 2 pear-shaped aquamarines, buff-top sapphires, diamond, white gold

ABOVE: Dauphin, Paris: hair cuff, 2015 – diamond, pink gold

OPPOSITE PAGE: Victoire de Castellane for Dior Haute Joaillerie: Le Bal des Roses Collection, Bal de Paris ring – ruby, white quartz, diamond, white gold

One of the newest and most influential jewellery houses has to be Dior Haute Joaillerie, building on the iconic emblems of Dior and Christian Dior. Themes such as Milly-la-Forêt (where Christian Dior had a home), Mitzah Bricard (Christian Dior's muse) and roses (so beloved by Christian Dior, and used in the Le Bal des Roses Collection) were all part of constructing the brand image.

The Jewellery Designers

Some extremely talented designers, such as Nathalie Castro, decide to work under the hierarchy of the creative director for a Jewellery House; they help to transform an idea into a concrete proposition. They discuss their design choices with the creative director and then put their own creative talents to work, to incorporate the ideas of the team. Their drawings are a culmination of that understanding and collusion, which has been built with the creative director; they help to bring hundreds of ideas to life. It is an attractive option for a designer, allowing her to focus solely on creating beautiful jewellery without the distractions and stresses of running a company.

ABOVE: Nathalie Castro, De Beers: design for Serpent hand bracelet, 2008

OPPOSITE PAGE: Claire Choisne for Boucheron: Delilah mosaic sautoir – pink diamond, purple diamond, yellow fancy-coloured diamond, white diamond, pink sapphire, rose gold, white gold
(Provenance: shown at the Biennale des Antiquaires, Paris 2012)

"Engraving is really mind gymnastics, one needs to think in reverse and to master creating images backwards and dominate full and empty spaces."

NATHALIE CASTRO
Versatility

Imagination and ideas have never been a problem for Castro, her limits are only defined by what is physically possible and the style of the jewellery house for which she is designing at the time.

Nathalie Castro trained with the best. She graduated from the École Boulle – the famous college of fine arts and crafts and applied arts in Paris – in 1996 with a DMA (Diplôme des Métiers d'Art) in etching. She went on to work with the Opéra de Paris where she learnt to solder and to adjust to the large volumes required to make theatrical jewellery.

There followed a four-year collaboration with Victoire de Castellane at Dior Fine Jewelry, working with her on the Belladone Island Collection and the Bestiaire Fantastique Collection of 2004/2005. Ideas would bounce back and forth and the result was the amazing Reina Magnifica Sangria necklace. The details for the necklace were worked out in the traditional way by creating a 3-dimensional model in pink modelling wax, so that the balance, proportions and dimensions could be finely tuned. Castro also worked on the Méduse (jellyfish) ring in the Bestiaire Fantastique Collection; the challenge for this huge ring was to balance the ring between two fingers so that it did not tip to one side. For a similar ring in the same collection, the issue was to place the tentacles in such a way so as not to bother the hand. Each jewel had its own challenges.

When Castro left Dior after four years to seek out new challenges, she went on to develop ideas for a variety of famous brands, including De Beers, Piaget, Baccarat, Chopard and Chanel. The Medallion Collection that she has created for Roger Dubuis, for example, takes its inspiration from the game 'Player' and its choices of Truth and Action. The coloured enamel and diamond medallions express these themes.

TOP LEFT: Mahua ring – brown polished diamond crystal, pale yellow polished diamond crystal, diamond, white gold

LEFT: Charmer ring – brown polished diamond crystal, diamond, white gold

OPPOSITE PAGE: Designs for the Roger Dubuis project

Marguerite ring – garnet, white gold

Illusion and symbolism

Castro introduced holograms into some of her own jewellery pieces as long ago as 2006. They became the central jewels for her Prémonition Collection for the Joailliers Créateurs (Jewellery Creators) Exhibition, 2006, which travelled on to the International Jewellery Show in Japan. Her Petite Fille Amoureuse (Young Girl in Love) ring is made using an Ethiopian opal, under which is a hologram depicting a daisy, which comes in and out of view as the wearer moves her hand. Each petal is engraved with little messages: "Je t'aime" (I love you); "Un peu" (A little); "A la folie" (Madly); "Passionnément" (Passionately)… and so on.

Castro also uses engraving to convey her message on the Petite Fille Amoureuse ring. Hidden on the underside is a rebus: the eye of a manga character and the eye of the sun (the eyelashes are spread out, as in drawings of the sun at sunset) are next to each other. A flower opens in a burst of fireworks like a star; they are surrounded by a ribbon engraved with "petite fille amoureuse". This symbolises the awakening of young love as experienced by a young girl who is just discovering life.

The following year, Castro designed the highly original pendant La Piuta, which cleverly uses a hologram to create the illusion of being 3-dimensional. The piece was for a new exhibition by Joailliers Créateurs with the theme of 'Jungle Fever' and green gemstones. Castro took her inspiration from the legend of a flying city that shelters a huge crystal. The jungle-like lianas, using organic outlines resembling the alveoli of lungs, allegorically denote the trees as 'the lungs of the world'. The green canopy above forms a hollow heart – or perhaps a lung. The whole is set with emeralds, tsavorite and demantoid garnets. The round body of the pendant is a specially fabricated white sapphire (made by a specialist in sapphires for watches), under which there is a hologram, which draws the onlooker deeper and deeper into the centre, as if they are being sucked into a black hole.

Versatility is the requirement for jewellery designers such as Castro; there is a need to be completely adaptable to the style of the House with whom she is working and to understand what they are looking for. Castro's talent is matched with an imagination that effervesces in every direction.

ABOVE: Petite Fille Amoureuse ring – opal, hologram, yellow gold

OPPOSITE PAGE: La Piuta pendant – hologram, emerald, aquamarine, yellow gold

"When you are a jeweller, Boucheron represents something, when you conceive a jewel, you are accompanied by the finest professionals in jewellery making."

CLAIRE CHOISNE
Boucheron's Designer of Light

Claire Choisne came to Boucheron after a ten year stint across the Place Vendôme, in the ateliers of Lorenz Bäumer. She arrived in 2011 as creative director, just in time to take over the creation of Boucheron's jewellery collection for the prestigious Biennale des Antiquaires, Paris, 2012.

A New Beginning

A change in management brought with it the aim to give the Boucheron brand a sense of the contemporary, whilst staying loyal to the founder, Frédéric Boucheron's roots and ideas. As other jewellery houses have discovered, this is like walking on a knife edge – it is a precarious mix of looking forward but always being aware of where you are grounded.

Choisne regards creativity as a mental exercise: the more you do, the easier it becomes and the easier it is to develop those ideas. This experience and understanding of how a jewel is conceived – from the initial drawings, to the buying of the gemstones – gave her the prerequisites that Boucheron were looking for. Having trained as a jeweller at the BJOP (Bijouterie, Joaillerie, Orfèvrerie de Paris), Choisne brought to Boucheron a well-rounded inventiveness that took into consideration the bench jeweller's point of view.

Renaissance

Choisne's first act was to look through the archives, to discover for herself the design codes that defined Boucheron and to determine any forgotten or rarely used techniques, thereby getting an idea of Boucheron's aesthetic.

> *"Each collection starts with a word, for the Biennale in 2012 that word was 'Renaissance'."*

The serpent was a theme that appeared repeatedly in the archives. Choisne wanted to use it for one of her principle pieces of jewellery, but the question was how to create something new? Choisne's answer was to play with the concept of 'Renaissance': her creation depicted the snakeskin, which the snake had shed in its natural process of growth; she used white opal and rock crystal to represent the snake's scales. The inside of the snakeskin could be seen through the rock crystal scales and was entirely set with diamonds. This transparency created a technical challenge – how to keep the necklace flexible without it losing its shape and without showing the mechanisms, which are usually hidden within? The solution was to re-cut a certain number of diamonds to hide the system. Choisne's clever progression of light and transparency creates a dynamic sense of movement.

ABOVE: Boucheron: Carapace ring – sapphire, black gold

OPPOSITE PAGE: Boucheron: Metamorphosis Opalescent Serpent necklace – opal, pink opal, rock crystal, diamond, white gold
(Provenance: shown at the Biennale des Antiquaires, Paris 2012)
ALL IMAGES COURTESY OF BOUCHERON

From the same archive list, Choisne took another form sacred to Boucheron's DNA: the question mark. It flows gracefully around the wearer's neck, using no clasps; it is a masterful play of equilibrium and balance. She used this same shape both for the serpent necklace and the Bouquet d'Ailes necklace. For this second piece, she used it in conjunction with the *en tremblant* spring system, which had been in vogue during the 18th century. This technique creates a delicate scintillating aura to a jewel. Choisne creates a series of light, contemporary butterflies, with wings set *en tremblant* with green, yellow and pink tourmalines, using negative space to create a clever layered effect.

Having seen flowers and ivy designs, one after the other in the archives, Choisne started to think:

> *"Flowers, we see them everywhere in jewellery but we don't often see ivy as a theme. Ivy gives a strong image, I started thinking about ivy growing through the cobblestones of the Place Vendôme. I liked the contrast between nature and the town."*

Choisne's concept was to use rough diamonds, which had to be uniform in size and yet still look untouched; it was not easy to convince everyone involved as the craftsmen at Boucheron were only used to setting faceted diamonds. The framework of the necklace presented its own challenges: the metal scaffold holding the 'cobblestones' must be hidden. Eventually it was decided that each diamond would be held by a small hidden notch and prong, not dissimilar to the invisible settings from the 1930s. The concern was always to keep the cobbled effect as light as possible, both physically and aesthetically. Despite the initial lack of enthusiasm for the design amongst some, it was the first piece to sell, finding a new home across the English Channel. Choisne had made a successful debut.

TOP: Boucheron: Bouquet D'Ailes brooch – emerald, watermelon tourmaline, blue sapphire, purple sapphire, pink diamond, yellow diamond, diamond, yellow gold
(Provenance: shown at the Biennale des Antiquaires, Paris 2012)

LEFT: Boucheron: Bouquet D'Ailes necklace – emerald, watermelon tourmaline, blue sapphire, purple sapphire, pink diamond, yellow diamond, diamond, yellow gold
(Provenance: shown at the Biennale des Antiquaires, Paris 2012)

OPPOSITE PAGE: Boucheron: Ivy and Parisian Cobblestone necklace – rough diamond, diamond, white gold
(Provenance: shown at the Biennale des Antiquaires, Paris 2012)
ALL IMAGES COURTESY OF BOUCHERON

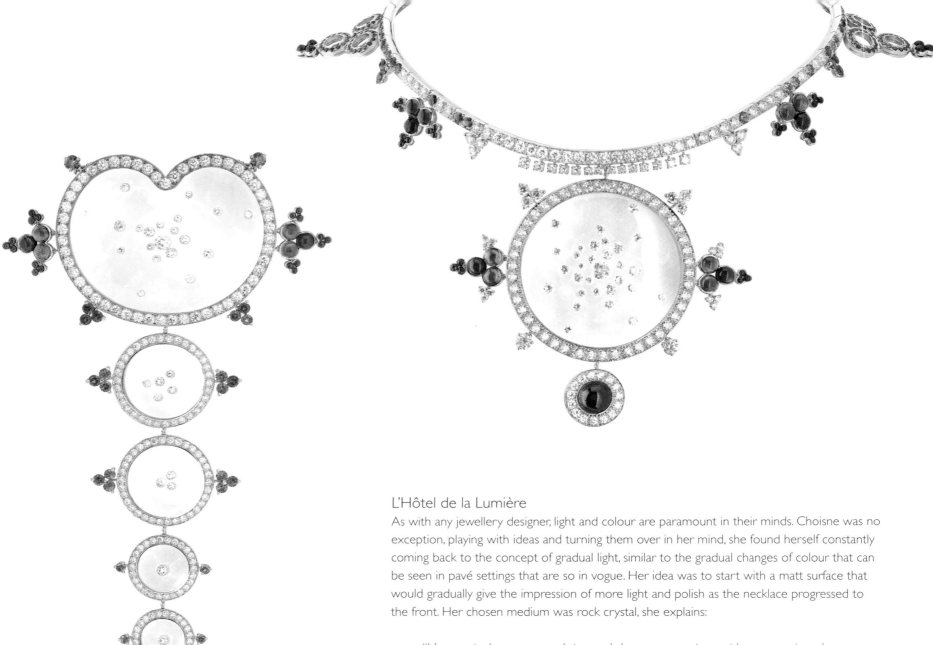

L'Hôtel de la Lumière

As with any jewellery designer, light and colour are paramount in their minds. Choisne was no exception, playing with ideas and turning them over in her mind, she found herself constantly coming back to the concept of gradual light, similar to the gradual changes of colour that can be seen in pavé settings that are so in vogue. Her idea was to start with a matt surface that would gradually give the impression of more light and polish as the necklace progressed to the front. Her chosen medium was rock crystal, she explains:

> "It's practical, you can work in much larger proportions without worrying about weight. It is transparent and can be sculpted into whatever shape you want."

This is not a new technique, but a medium that revisits jewellery designers from time to time; think 1930s Boivin, Cartier and Belperron… Gemstones are easily set in rock crystal and Choisne has taken advantage of this to create a series of unusual pieces, which were shown at the 2014 Biennale des Antiquaires, in Paris. She incorporates Boucheron's signature cornflower-blue cabochon sapphires with aplomb, creating necklaces and rings as original as they are embedded in Boucheron's DNA.

The theme for the 2014 Biennale was 'Le Voyage' (Travel), or, more the idea of dreams of elsewhere. The stunning Ricochet necklace comes from a visit of the mind to Japan and its gardens, where water is so present; the shape of the necklace evokes the idea of skimming a stone on the water and the ripples radiating out as it bounces.

She also took her inspiration from a classic form typical to Boucheron, the Ava, in which a gemstone is set surrounded by negative space giving it the illusion of floating. She set the diamonds in the rock crystal so that they too gave the illusion of floating. She placed her three

---

ABOVE AND LEFT: Boucheron: Ricochet necklace (front and back) – rock crystal, sapphire, diamond, white gold
Inspired by skimming stones on the surface of the water.
(Provenance: shown at the Biennale des Antiquaires, Paris 2012)
ALL IMAGES COURTESY OF BOUCHERON

blue sapphire punctuations periodically, 'à la JAR', to embellish the jewel and to increase the intensity of blue as the eye travels from the white centre to the blue-tinged contours of the jewel. The necklace has been conceived so as to flow down the wearer's back. The whole necklace can also be detached and worn as a simple choker with a brooch of 'buttons'.

The Jewellery designer

The job of the designer in a Jewellery House is to perpetuate the essence and the DNA of the House, as well as to keep the designs contemporary and relevant to the present day. They work with an experienced and knowledgeable team of highly dedicated and skilled jewellers and setters.

> *"Everything is a team effort, many of the jewels that we create require 3,000 hours of work to make in the workshop. You don't just need to have ideas, you need to have patience and an ability to communicate."*

From the major designs, smaller equally exquisite pieces are created, so that more people have an opportunity to be part of the Boucheron dream. Thus diamond-studded ivy pendants and rings became part of the Lierre de Paris Collection, for example.

Choisne gives a light, unusual take to classic ideas. She designs jewels that are clearly Boucheron and proudly proclaim its well-known aesthetics, whilst giving the collections a youthful spring in their step as they advance into the 21st century.

TOP: Boucheron: Ivy ring – diamond, white gold

RIGHT: Boucheron: Rêves d'Ailleurs Collection, Trésor de Perse necklace – cabochon sapphire, rock crystal, blue chalcedony, diamond, white gold
(Provenance: shown at the Biennale des Antiquaires, Paris 2014)
ALL IMAGES COURTESY OF BOUCHERON

A SENSE OF PLACE

The histories and cultures of countries have a huge influence on jewellery designers from across the world.

The wonderful opulence of Bina Goenka's work strikes at the heart of what is important in India: colour and the wedding ceremony. Carla Amorim's Rio Collection transforms the architecture of the modern capital city, Brasília (designed by Lúcio Costa and Oscar Niemeyer) into colourful jewelled effigies.

For each of Monique Péan's collections, she takes care to use the inspiration of the country that she has visited and to employ the artisans of that country to help create her jewels. Thus for her Ahe Collection – which takes its name from the word for 'evening star' in the many French Polynesian dialects – she explores the way that light plays with the water in the Tuamotus archipelago lagoons.

Michelle Ong uses her cross-cultural roots in Hong Kong to bridge the history and symbols of China with those of Europe, to weave a universe of light, inventive jewels that invite the wearer to touch gently, as they would the finest silks.

Other jewellers start with the origins of the gemstones – where they were discovered or mined – to conceive their own interpretation of the country.

TOP LEFT: Monique Péan: Lahnse Collection, Scrimshaw Geometric Signature ring – fossilised mammoth bone with hand-carved blueprint scrimshaw, diamond, recycled oxidised white gold

BOTTOM LEFT: Bina Goenka: 'Richard' (The Gecko) brooch – Zambian emerald, tanzanite, Vietnamese ruby, coral, pink sapphire, yellow sapphire, orange sapphire, yellow diamond, pink diamond, black diamond, white diamond, gold

OPPOSITE PAGE: Michelle Ong: Meander bracelet, 2000 – hauynite, ruby, pink sapphire, blue sapphire, garnet, emerald, diamond, silver, platinum

"Handcrafted jewellery is a dying art and over the years, I've realised that the single most important thing I can do to nurture this art is to support my artisans."

BINA GOENKA
Explosion of Colour

Bina Goenka is known for the opulence of her hugely colourful jewels, which are anchored in Indian traditions. She launched her jewellery line in October 2007 and soon after created her first bridal collection. She admits this was probably a little ambitious so early on; yet, with hindsight, she feels it was a crucial step towards getting herself on the right track.

"It slowed me down in my ambitions to expand and put me firmly on the manufacturing floor, mastering creativity to an international level."

Her focus is on getting the artisans (*kaarigars*) on board with her ideas, to persuade them to experiment, to try new techniques, such as beating gold into the thinnest of wires and to create gold mesh that can withstand weight. Each of her skilled workers has a special technique and she only needs to look at a jewel to know who the craftsman was. Each year, Goenka's team creates about 100 one-of-a-kind pieces.

Background
Self-taught, the first significant jewel was for a friend over twenty years ago, when she was just starting out.

"The way I thought then was completely out of the box — and I still think the same way. People don't change their style; it only gets sharper and more focused over time."

From the poorest to the wealthiest, all Indians wear jewellery. Growing up in India meant that she was constantly aware of jewellery and its importance in Indian culture, yet her ideas on jewellery design were different. Her design ethic comes from within, from her experiences and from forms found in nature, which she combines with geometric shapes.

Gold
She works with raw gold and uses its natural matt finish to create part of the dialogue between her ideas and the jewel.

"I have experimented time and time again with only one metal, the most precious to all Indians — gold. I like to explore how many faces gold can show the world and how many looks one can craft from the same metal."

LEFT AND OPPOSITE PAGE: Gaia necklace/bib — South Sea pearls, small natural pearls, diamond, white gold, yellow gold

Ganesha

Each year, Goenka creates a new Ganesha in clay (the elephant-headed deity in the Hindu religion who brings knowledge and tears down obstacles), which she decorates with the jewels from each of her new collections. Many companies in India have a Ganesha deity. Goenka is no different, she observes the culture of her country whilst moving forward, reconciling old traditions with a new future. It is this sensitivity that Goenka brings to her jewels.

Collaborations

Goenka's jewellery is about colour, so the ethical gem producer Gemfields – with its Zambian emeralds and amethysts, and rubies from Mozambique – was the obvious choice. Goenka dedicated 12 months (2012-2013) to working with Gemfields and produced a number of startling designs, such as her now famous bell-shaped vanity case/evening bag.

The idea behind the vanity case was to find a shape that had a uniform surface, uninterrupted by edges, to represent the "colourful explosion of the Big Bang", the sun and its planets.

"The seamlessness of the universe could not be executed in any geometric form."

Goenka uses a series of circles and circles within circles, set with amethyst, emerald, ruby and white and yellow diamond. The gemstones embody the earth's crust; they start at the top of the bell, where our galaxy is positioned, and then widen towards the bottom, where they symbolise the infinity of the universe and serve to express its huge expanse. It is an extraordinary work of art, which highlights Goenka's Indian Hindu roots.

"The resonance of the bell as chimed during prayer invokes the gods, and its fundamental sound is said to be the sound of the universe, which is the resounding 'OM' that originates and vanishes into eternity. It reminds us of the meaning of creation, preservation and destruction."

The vanity case is in fact made of a gold mesh, which acts as the framework on which to set her gemstones.

Gaia

Another collaboration was with the first International Indian Jewellery Week (IIJW), in 2010; Goenka had been asked to create an exceptional jewel for the show, with very little time in which to conceive and execute the piece. Goenka christened it 'Gaia', after the Greek goddess who was born out of chaos. The jewel symbolises the Tree of Life and encapsulates the themes of growth, prosperity and the future. The huge, yet delicate, branch-like jewel is a bib covering the front of the wearer as a breast plate. The narrow gold branches are decorated with diamond florets and leaves.

ABOVE: Lord Ganesha pendant – emerald (from Zambia), pearl, yellow diamond, white diamond, fur, white gold, yellow gold

LEFT: Finger Foliage ring – certified natural seed pearls, emerald, diamond, white gold, yellow gold

OPPOSITE PAGE: Theia vanity case – amethyst, pearl, emerald (from Zambia), ruby, pink tourmaline, silver, gold

The Bridal Collection

The bridal jewellery trousseau is an essential asset, which is invested in and collected from the day a daughter is born; it is part of a bride's dowry. For the most part, these jewels are in gold, but for those who can afford to try something slightly different, the jewels are set with magnificent gemstones. These collections, or parures, include a ring, a bracelet, a choker and a chain – in that order.

"The entire parure should have similar elements yet be different in design so that one can always make the most of all the pieces independently."

Goenka creates two collections of wedding jewellery every year: the Shiv Parvati – Varmala Collection is her most sophisticated bridal collection to date. Created in 2015, it is based on her use of rubies from Mozambique and emeralds from Zambia through her collaboration with Gemfields, as well as including many diamonds and pearls. A collection of 36 pieces, it is important as it replaces the traditional *Varmala* (floral garland) that is placed around the neck of the bride by the groom.

Goenka's collection of jewels caters for each ceremony in the wedding, from the *Roka* (the betrothal), the *Grih Shanti* (the prayer ceremony for peace in the home and during the wedding) and the *Mandap Mahurat* (the blessing of the wedding), to the *Mehendi* (the henna painting ceremony for good luck, for the bride and her close friends and family); the *Sangeet* (a celebration between the two families before the wedding itself) and, finally, the *Pheras* (the wedding).

Many traditional jewels worn with the bridal ensemble find their place in the collection: the *Maang tikka* or *Mathapatti* to adorn the head; the braid for the hair; the earrings, earcuffs and earchains; the *Nathni* (nose ring); the necklaces or *Har*; the *Baajuband* (armband), bracelets, bangles; the *Haathphool* (a handpiece), rings, and midi rings; as well as the *minaudière*. At the waist, a cummerbund (a jewelled belt) is worn and, finally, on the feet and ankles, *Payals* (ankle bracelets) and toe rings are worn.

The bridegroom is also decked out with a *Har* (necklace) and an ornate jewelled dagger, a *Kalgi* (jewelled turban pin) as well as jewelled buttons and cufflinks.

Varmala Collection

Goenka is trying to introduce a new concept with this collection, which takes into consideration the garments and headdress that the bride wears and removes the risk that the *Varmala* garlands will not match the colours of the bride's regalia.

"The Bina Goenka bride is adorned with a Varmala that follows the same style as her headpiece and the other jewellery that she is wearing, with the option of attaching fresh flowers to the piece."

Goenka's vision for the future of jewellery design is interesting:

"We have no distinctive styles now, unlike Elizabethan, Victorian, Mughal or other periods; I am aiming to set a standard and style that can be the benchmark for identifying the jewellery of the present in future years."

ABOVE: Varmala Collection, Maanga tikka (headdress that is worn falling over the forehead) – ruby, emerald, briolette diamond, diamond, white gold, yellow gold

BELOW: Varmala Collection, Sarpesh Kalgi (jewelled turban pin/brooch) – emerald bead, emerald, ruby, orange sapphire, spinel, brown rose-cut diamond, yellow rose-cut diamond, faceted diamond discs, red rhodium-plated gold, white gold, yellow gold

OPPOSITE PAGE: Varmala Collection, garland/pendant – ruby, coral, natural purple pearl, briolette diamond, faceted diamond beads, marquise diamond, diamond, yellow gold, white gold

"My gift is to create and I thank God for this gift."

CARLA AMORIM
Ora et Labora – Pray and Work

Stretched elongated drops, long oval loops and hoops, circles, collages of beads and open circles – Carla Amorim's jewels are hugely colourful and above all they have a serious sense of place. A Hollywood red carpet favourite, at the Oscars and the most prestigious music award ceremonies in the United States, Amorim's jewels and her accomplishments are the pride of Brazil. Her pieces have adorned actresses and singers from all backgrounds, including Jennifer Lopez, Hilary Swank, Marion Cotillard, Gwyneth Paltrow and Mary J. Blige at the BET Honors ceremony, 2015.

Born in Brasília – a city that first came into existence in 1960 – to a family from the famous and mystical Minas Gerais region of Brazil, Amorim was surrounded by gemstones growing up. Emeralds, aquamarines, morganite, tourmaline, topaz and diamonds are but a few of the treasures to be found in this landlocked region of Brazil.

Amorim started as many jewellery designers have done before her: unable to find jewellery that she enjoyed wearing, she started to make her own. Friends admired her style and began to order similar pieces for themselves. After two years of receiving clients in her home and at her friends' homes, she opened her first store with her sister Kelly, at the Kubitschek Plaza Hotel in Brasília. Since these simple beginnings in 1993, Amorim has been prolific in the number of collections that she has designed and the number of stores that she has opened. Her ideas come from three important pillars: Brasília, nature and religion.

"These are simply the DNA of my creative spirit. I observe, sometimes it is a small ray of light or a texture that will be the trigger to the design for a new jewel."

Architecture
Brasília's modernist architecture has been an important influence on Amorim.

"The city is similar to my temperament, I like the city, it is beautiful and inspiring. I don't need to leave my city to be inspired, I have Brasília's sky and its horizon."

Amorim's jewellery takes Oscar Niemeyer's fluid lines and transforms them into settings and jewels that have surprising solid forms. Her Brasília ring, for example, took as its inspiration Oscar Niemeyer's National Congress building.

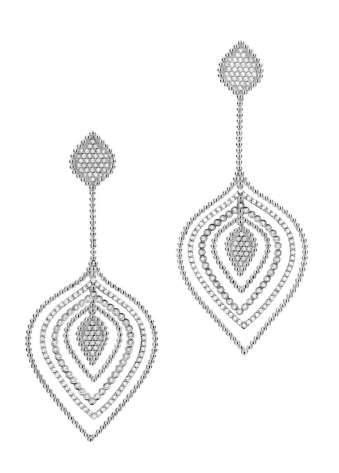

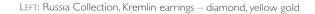

LEFT: Russia Collection, Kremlin earrings – diamond, yellow gold

OPPOSITE PAGE: Brasília Collection, ring – diamond, rose gold

RIGHT: Terra da Garoa ear pendants – diamond, rose gold

BELOW: Russia Collection, St. Basil earrings – ruby, tsavorite garnet, rose gold

BOTTOM: Russia Collection, Ballet earrings – nude quartz, black diamond, black rhodium-plated gold

Many of Amorim's collections make reference to other architectural landmarks in São Paulo and Rio de Janeiro. Early on in her career, Amorim would regularly visit São Paulo to see her sister, who lived there at the time, to show her and her friends her latest jewels. The sisters opened a store in Belo Horizonte, the capital of the Minas Gerais region, followed by two stores in São Paulo.

The São Paulo Collection is inspired by a walk through the city: the colours in the street, the Garden district, the Ibirapuera Park and the Copan building – a masterly symphony of curvaceous façades. The Martinelli building and the Municipal Theatre are represented with different coloured golds: pink, yellow and white. Amorim describes the streets of São Paulo as "coloured and bleached". Her Terra da Garoa earrings are called after the city's colloquial name, which translates as 'Land of Drizzle', referring to the constant light rain that is a feature of São Paulo.

The Russia Collection pays homage to the architecture of Russia as well as shapes and outlines that have had an impact on Amorim's imagination. Her Kremlin earrings and Ballet earrings are light, lace-like jewels that dance beside the cheek. They evoke her Renda Sé Collection, created with negative space and patterns, which Amorim says remind her of lace with their transparency and exquisite detail. This style is the antithesis of her architectural inspiration. Instead, they suggest and trace the outlines of shadows and movement.

Tradition

Brazil's musical heritage is evident in the Repertorio Collection inspired by the great songs that have been immortalised in the Brazilian psyche, such as *Canto da Sereia* (a Siren's Song); *Marinheiró So*, a traditional seafaring ballad; and *Luz do Sol* by Caetano Veloso. As a conductor directs her orchestra, so Amorim creates jewels to represent this popular music using the colours of local gemstones, such as chrysoprase, dumortierite, fluorite and quartz.

Nature

Nature is a constant inspiration for Amorim:

> *"Its colours, shapes and movements are simply incredible, whether fruit, flowers, waterfalls, sand dunes or the sea."*

It has been the origin of many of her signature jewels, such as her Sea Foam ring.

> *"The texture reminds you of the bubbles formed by the waves as they hit the beach and return to the sea."*

It is a texture that has crept into all her collections and is constantly present. Her Nacional Collection includes many features of Brazil's countryside and natural wonders; moments that have been frozen in time with her beautiful fluid shapes; they come from rivers, caverns and waterfalls. Her magnificent Araguaia earrings literally fall from the wearer's ears, simple but so evocative, using her 'sea foam' as the thread.

Colour

The luxuriant foliage of the great tropical forests, cleaved by the flowing strength of the Amazon, have also had an impact on Amorim's designs. She talks of her fondness for green colours in the form of pistachio nuts, herbs and in gemstones such as jade, emeralds, green opal and Paraiba tourmalines:

> *"I'm in love with all stones but the colours of the Paraiba tourmaline and emerald remind me of the sea."*

ABOVE LEFT: Nacional Collection, Jalapão ring – yellow gold

ABOVE RIGHT: Classicos Collection, Sea Foam Composition ring – yellow gold

LEFT: Meu Caminho Collection, Folhagem ring – tsavorite garnet, black diamond, rhodium-plated gold

OPPOSITE PAGE: Nacional Collection, Araguaia earrings – diamond, white gold

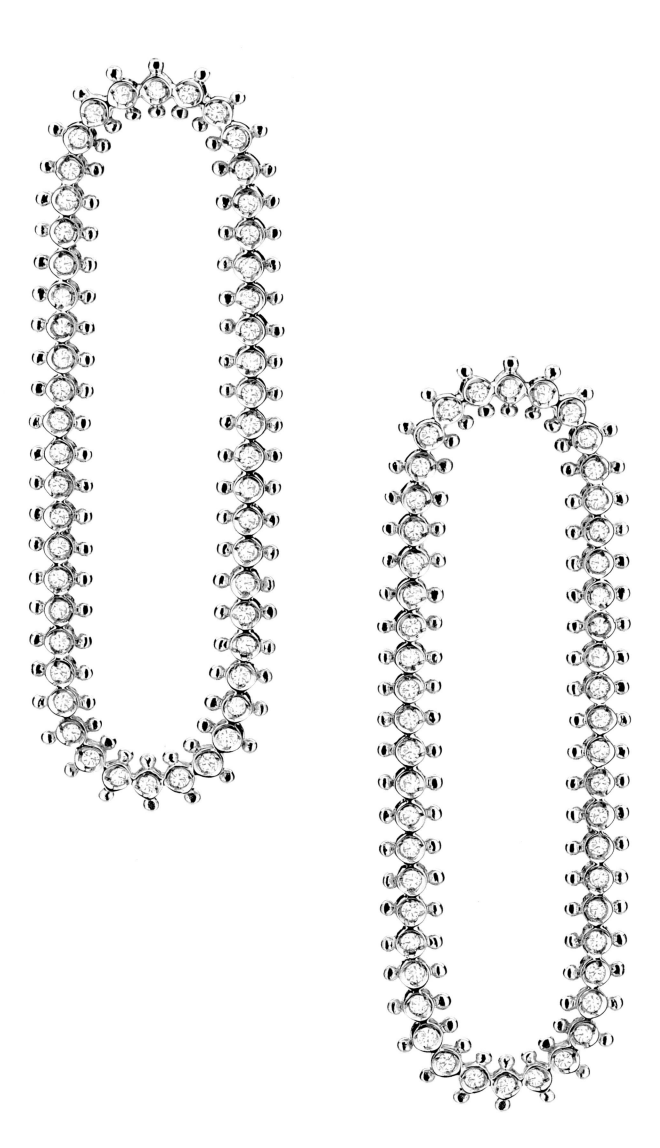

"I use fair trade and conflict and devastation free stones to promote fair business practices and sustainability."

MONIQUE PÉAN
The Ethical Jeweller

To plunge into Monique Péan's jewellery world is to take an explorer's path to communities living in far-flung spots across the globe. Her jewels are inspired by the places she visits on her travels and by her interaction with small villages and their artisans. The upshot is a highly unusual style, based on the environmentally responsible sourcing of materials.

Péan, a graduate of the University of Pennsylvania, had been working in the world of finance when her younger sister, Vanessa was tragically killed in a car accident. Péan found working with her hands therapeutic and took a design course. Monique Péan's own jewellery line was the result, launched in 2006.

All her pieces are designed using conflict-free gemstones set in recycled gold and recycled platinum. Conscious that gold is usually extracted using an extremely destructive process that releases cyanide, lead and mercury into the environment, Péan chooses not to add to that environmental destruction. In line with this ethos, a proportion of Monique Péan's profits go to financing sustainability projects each year to provide wells and basic sanitation in small villages throughout the developing world.

Unusual materials
One of Péan's first trips was to Shishmaref, a small Alaskan village on an island close to the Bering Straits, just south of the Arctic Circle. Whilst visiting the community, she became aware of fossilised woolly mammoth bone and fossilised walrus ivory that was appearing in abundance as newly melted glacial areas revealed their secrets. Péan created the Bering Collection to reflect the material that she had gathered and used local artisans to carve asymmetrical 'iceberg' forms to create a permanent link with the terrain and the people, from which she had found this precious fossilised material.

Fossilised dinosaur bone found on the Colorado Plateau ranging from 146 to 156 million years old, has been agatised over time and is found in stunning lavenders, yellows, browns and blues, as well as black with hints of red. The cells of the bone have been preserved due to the crystallisation that occurred as the bone petrified; their colours come from the minerals in the sedimentary rock dating back to the late Jurassic Age, which have seeped through the petrified bone structure. Péan was first attracted to the material because of the intricate patterns, which remind her of abstract art. It complements her minimalist and graphic style.

ABOVE: Bering Collection, Black Sunburst ring – fossilised walrus ivory, white diamond, recycled white gold

OPPOSITE PAGE LEFT: Sut'ane bracelet – natural brown agate, blue sapphire, mocha and vivid sunburst fossilised walrus ivory, white diamond, recycled rose gold

OPPOSITE PAGE RIGHT: Atelier Collection, Dinosaur Bone bracelet – sapphire, fossilised dinosaur bone, diamond, recycled yellow gold

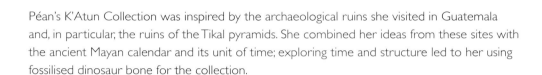

Péan's K'Atun Collection was inspired by the archaeological ruins she visited in Guatemala and, in particular, the ruins of the Tikal pyramids. She combined her ideas from these sites with the ancient Mayan calendar and its unit of time; exploring time and structure led to her using fossilised dinosaur bone for the collection.

Architecture

Péan's interest in architecture and hence architectural lines was inspired by her admiration for architect Richard Neutra's Case Study Houses and Philip Johnson's Glass House blueprints. Work by the sculptor Richard Serra is another well of ideas:

> *"I was inspired by Serra's ability to master the manipulation and control of industrial materials into unconventional shapes that draw attention to the unique materials used."*

On a smaller scale, this could be a definition for Monique Péan's jewellery. Exploring this concept in her Tu'Til Collection, she conjures up images of the Tikal pyramids in Guatemala, swathed in the lush greenery from the surrounding rainforest.

Péan also admires the sculptor Mark di Suvero, and the way that his work uses negative space, drawing attention to the resulting shapes that are indirectly formed. Péan's jewellery plays with these ideas of texture, negative space and symmetry — exploring their infinite possibilities. She uses a dictionary of contrasts: ancient and modern, natural and manmade, legend and reality. Her thoughtfully-created jewels are highlighted by tiny diamonds and in particular, old rose-cut diamonds with their gentle lustre. Interestingly, she also uses rose cuts for their triangular facets, which subtly underline her geometrical shapes.

Her use of flat gemstones allows for design intricacies in the setting, which is as important to the overall design as the materials she uses:

> *"I personally find the way that flat stones appear to be floating, very elegant."*

Péan has the stones cut to create unique outlines, which in most cases are gently traced on the outer edge by tiny diamonds, giving light to the whole piece.

Her choice of materials is a combination of personal preference and finding those which tell a story. For instance, the extraordinary meteorite earrings, which epitomise Péan's design DNA of natural angular lines, unusual material, negative space to create an abstract ideal.

Unusual fine stones abound in Péan's Lahnse Collection, inspired by her travels to Norway. She uses stones such as gilalite, lepidolite and spectrolite, as well as the better known labradorite, for its lovely steely blue iridescence, and dendritic agate, with its landscape-style patterns. The construction blueprints of modernist architects, alongside the distinct design aesthetics found in Norway, have also had a huge influence on this collection. 'Lahnse' comes

ABOVE: Lahnse Collection, Pentagonal necklace — blue sunburst fossilised walrus ivory, white diamond, recycled oxidised white gold

TOP RIGHT: Tu'Til necklace — fossilised dinosaur bone, vivid grey fossilised walrus ivory, straw-coloured topaz, white diamond, recycled rose gold

BELOW: K'Atun 2 ring — fossilised dinosaur bone, white diamond, recycled yellow gold

OPPOSITE PAGE: Lahnse necklace — black tourmaline crystal, blue tourmaline, moonstone, dendritic agate, spectrolite, cream fossilised walrus ivory, white diamond, recycled white gold

from the Norwegian word for balance and Péan plays with the "juxtaposition of negative space and layered textures", which are so much a part of the Norwegian landscape. The Oslo Opera House's undulating wall had a considerable impact on her ideas. Péan creates structural shapes; in her pendulum earrings, for example, she juxtaposes Guatemalan jade – which signified life, fertility and power to the Ancient Mayans – with fossilised woolly mammoth bone, millions of years old, to powerful effect.

The Renhet Collection took its inspiration from contrast between Norway's modern architecture and the country's natural formations such as the fjords gouged out by glaciers, frozen waterfalls and rugged terrain; 'renhet' is the Norwegian word for 'purity'. The Aurland lookout point had a major influence on her work, resulting in her use of negative space and the construction of geometrical shapes seen in this collection.

Péan has been awarded many honours, including the CFDA/Vogue Fashion Fund award in 2009 and, in 2015, the *Wallpaper* magazine honoured her with their 'Best Jewellery' design award. She has brought a new and exciting facet to the world of high jewellery, providing a fresh consciousness of our imprint on the world. Her sustainable ethos of sharing will surely grow in popularity as we advance further into the 21st century.

ABOVE: Renhet ring – grey sunburst fossilised walrus ivory, fossilised dinosaur bone, black Guatemalan jade, white diamond, recycled white gold

TOP LEFT: Lahnse Collection, Pendulum earrings – black Guatemalan jade, fossilised woolly mammoth bone, white diamond, recycled white gold

LEFT: Renhet Collection, Scandinavian meteorite earrings – meteorite, white diamond, recycled rose gold

OPPOSITE PAGE: Renhet Collection, Collar necklace – fossilised woolly mammoth bone, fossilised woolly mammoth tooth root, grey fossilised dinosaur bone, white diamond, recycled white gold

"The key to a great jewel is to create an illusion through movement and space"

MICHELLE ONG – CARNET
East meets West

Hong Kong is a city of towering skyscrapers casting their shadows over Harbour Bay; huge ocean liners and cargo ships plough through the deep straits of the bay, dwarfing the small ferries scurrying back and forth to Kowloon and Central. The vitality and industrious energy of this bay could easily define Michelle Ong, as she looks down upon this scene from her studio above. Totally committed to detail and the hard work that this entails, Ong creates extraordinary jewels that epitomise Hong Kong's reputation as the point where East meets West. The result is a mix of Chinese symbolism – porcelain, clouds, dragons and peonies – alongside more Western themes. This can be seen in her Azure Lattice bracelet and earrings, which marry the Greek meander pattern with references to blue and white porcelain and Chinese screens.

Ong met her business partner Avi Nagar at a diamond importers' dinner in the '70s and they have worked together ever since. Their first company was set up in 1985 and the Carnet brand was born in 1998. From making jewellery for herself and then progressing to making jewellery for her friends, Ong has built up an almost cult following. Her clients delight in wearing her light playful earrings and her huge floral works of art, which are light enough to wear on the most delicate of fabrics.

Textiles
Textiles are her passion and in Hong Kong, where temperatures rarely dip below 10°C in winter, wearing beautiful jewellery on light materials is the norm at any time of the day. Ong magically manages to imitate that light fluidity so characteristic of fragile fabrics. Her lace-like necklaces imitate crochet needlework, in which her threads are of gold and diamond. A technical *tour de force* of patience, each link is individually finished so that the necklace will react like the silks and chiffons that Ong so admires. The use of white, brown and champagne rose-cut diamonds, along with her signature oxidised silver, weave a lyrical quality to her jewels of nuanced russets, browns and beiges.

From the very beginning, Michelle Ong has had her own workshop. Her bench jewellers are among the best and she has been able to develop a rapport with them, which means that they know exactly what she is looking for. The Glowing Jade and Gems necklace took two painstaking years to complete – each jade gourd was individually set in titanium and gold, held together by using the tiniest of screws. Its inspiration came from the Sancai porcelain of the Tang dynasty, a period also known for its hairpins and neck collars, and from designs in the West.

LEFT: Organdie necklace – brown diamond, white diamond, white gold

OPPOSITE PAGE: Azure Lattice bracelet – blue sapphire, white diamond, titanium, platinum
Inspired by blue and white porcelain and Chinese screens.

OVERLEAF: Glowing Jade and Gems necklace – jade, emerald, purple sapphire, garnet, brown diamond, white diamond, titanium, white gold
In Chinese culture, a gourd acts as a charm, which is believed to protect the wearer from illness and bad spirits.

Inspiration

Michelle Ong takes her inspiration from all around her: the small ordinary things in life, those that are hidden in plain sight, from clouds forming in the sky above, a musical note or the jagged edge of a leaf, they all get processed in this artist's mind. Her Emerald Garden ring is inspired by nature and more specifically by chicory!

Gemstones

Rose-cut diamonds, in particular, have been part of her repertoire from very early on, long before they were rediscovered by other jewellery designers. They are a constant in her designs:

> "They have a purity of form and light that fascinates me – a beautiful glow-like light diffusing through the clearest of water."

When Ong saw a cat's-eye cabochon aquamarine for the first time, she was captivated by its unique qualities:

> "When I saw it, I was taken by its presence and size, but also by how feminine and wearer-friendly it was. I wanted to emphasise the beauty of the stone without overpowering it."

She decided to surround it with delicate diamonds, sapphires and Paraiba tourmalines; the result was the striking Luminous Spring brooch. Ong came across a pair of unusually cut

TOP: Emerald Garden ring – emerald, green garnet, diamond, white gold

ABOVE: Renaissance Rose ring – very pale pink rose-cut diamond, white diamond, rose gold, white gold

RIGHT: Luminous Spring brooch – cat's-eye aquamarine, pink sapphire, Paraiba tourmaline, white diamond, platinum

FAR RIGHT: Sea Sparkle brooch – Paraiba tourmaline, sapphire, pink sapphire, purple sapphire, titanium, white gold

emeralds, with their wide drop-like outline in an old setting. Attracted to the deep rich quality of the emeralds, she was reminded of a peacock's display and it was from this idea that she built her own interpretation of a peacock feather. The earrings are as light as... yes... a feather, and have been made so that each barb gives the whole earring flexibility and movement as the wearer moves. Its lightness is helped by the open space around the intensely green emeralds themselves.

From as early as 2005, the Carnet repertoire has been using cabochon diamonds, which have a wonderful liquid quality and look like raindrops or dew. In Ong's Sparkling Lotus bangle she mixes and contrasts tsavorite garnets and emeralds with brilliant diamonds and cabochon diamonds, using a stylised diamond asymmetric vein structure to contrast with the rounder outline of the lotus leaf itself. As in nature, the leaves capture the rainfall and dew at its centre.

Paraiba tourmaline is another favourite and has appeared many times in Ong's jewellery. She dilutes the vibrant, almost fluorescent, turquoise colour of the tourmaline by complementing them with grey diamonds or pale pink or blue gemstones. The Sea Sparkle brooch demonstrates this perfectly, with its gentle hues giving the impression of a sea becalmed; what genius made her use the form of a mussel to create such an understated and telling jewel?

Perpetually active, Ong's spare time is taken up by her philanthropic work as chair of the First Initiative Foundation, which encourages students in the domains of art, design and music.

ABOVE: Radiant Peacock earrings – emerald, grey diamond, brown diamond, white diamond, white gold

LEFT: Sparkling Lotus bangle – tsavorite garnet, emerald, white diamond, platinum
Note the cabochon diamonds – a first!

STORIES TO TELL

The magic of jewellery design is such that culture and symbolism from different countries can be told in an infinite number of ways from gemstones found in iconic mines, such as turquoise from the Sleeping Beauty mine in Arizona, USA, or opal from the Welo mines of Ethiopia, to the legends hidden in the lines and shapes of each jewel.

Kara Ross uses her Pangea Collection to recount the legend of 'Mother Earth'. Ross places carved gemstone symbols around the bezel to denote the diversity of the cultures and religions that exist on this wonderful Earth.

Lydia Courteille mixes history and symbols to create small jewels of conjecture, to marvel at over time. Her Animal Farm Collection brings together George Orwell's famed tale and Marie Antoinette's farm at Versailles. More recently, the Scarlet Empress and the Queen of Sheba Collections are wonderful examples of history and legend coming together in such different worlds as Catherine the Great's Russia and the 20th century Soviet Union.

Sylvie Corbelin uses France's history and lets us gaze through the looking glass at the small pleasures of rural life in a Europe of another time. Further afield, her images of Japan take us to the foothills of Mount Fuji and the breathtaking silk kimonos of a Japan steeped in tradition.

Other designers create their own stories and references to the history of a place and they juxtapose ideas that can be woven together to create a piece of jewellery, which opens the way to conversations with those who look upon the jewel.

ABOVE: Kara Ross: Pangea Collection, pendant – green beryl crystal, blue topaz, diamond, yellow gold

RIGHT: Suzanne Syz: Coast to Coast earrings – diamond, titanium, white gold

FAR RIGHT: Lydia Courteille: Animal Farm Collection, Pig's Head ring, 2012 – pink sapphire, diamond, enamel, white gold, rose gold *After George Orwell's* Animal Farm. *The pig is crowned in honour of Marie-Antoinette's Hameau at the Château de Versailles.*

OPPOSITE PAGE: Sylvie Corbelin: Geisha earrings – cabochon pink sapphire, tsavorite garnet, turquoise, emerald, ruby, moonstone, translucent green enamel, cabochon pink spinel, cabochon peridot, cabochon aquamarine, champagne-coloured diamond, white diamond, white gold, yellow gold

"We tend not to make little tiny jewels because quite honestly why bother to wear them if no one can see and appreciate them."

KARA ROSS
The Jewellery Geologist

Natural beauty and big bold statements from the Earth's crust are signature themes in Kara Ross' jewellery. Starting well before the crop of new jewellery designers using untouched minerals, Ross began her story slowly but surely at the beginning of the 1990s.

She recalls how, at the age of 14, on a family trip to Kenya, her mother, an amateur jeweller, allowed her and her sister to choose two gemstones each. On their return to home, they took their stones to a shop on Jeweller's Row (the Philadelphian equivalent to New York's Diamond District). It was to be an eye opener for Ross to see the jeweller translate an idea from a poorly drawn design into a beautiful jewel – two fluted, emerald-cut green tourmalines set with small diamonds to a gold shank.

> *"When you see the green wax, you think that it is so ugly and then when you see it cast and you see the diamonds and the finished piece… That was very special, to have been able to see how the ring was made at such a young age."*

Background
Ross graduated from Georgetown University in 1988 before going on to do a stint at the GIA in New York:

> *"The GIA education is worth so much, you learn so much about stones you have never even heard about; to differentiate one from the other and their quality. I can grade diamonds in my sleep and tell the difference between a synthetic ruby or a fracture filled emerald. This knowledge is the basis from which to grow a business."*

For Ross, the gemmologist, jewellery design is about highlighting the beauty of the mineral; they just need an appropriate setting. She uses unusual materials, such as volcanic lava, rock crystal, and different woods such as ebony and maple. Her Petra Collection (Latin for 'stone') features gemstones in their pure and raw form. Some have been set beside polished versions of the same stone, creating an interesting contrast of texture and light.

Dimensions
Size and proportions are central to her designs. She likes the power and 'wow' factor of the larger-than-life jewels, insisting that to wear one piece is enough.

Youth's ring – tourmaline, diamond, yellow gold.
This is the ring that Ross designed when she was 14 years old

OPPOSITE PAGE: Aquamarine crystal necklace, 2006 – aquamarine crystal, diamond, yellow gold

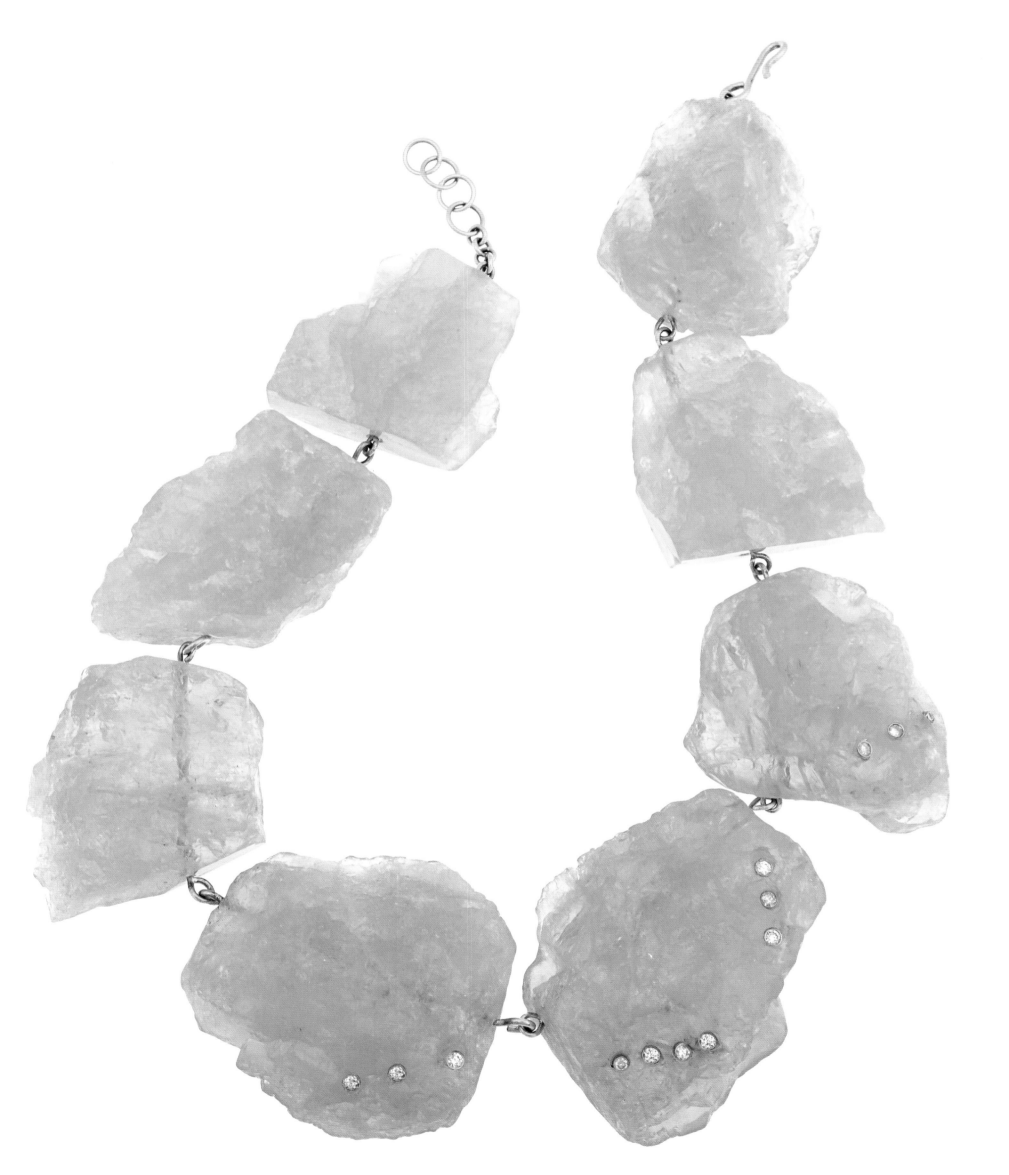

CLOCKWISE FROM TOP LEFT:

Split Series, Petra ring, 2014 – crystal uvarovite, polished chrysocolla drusy, diamond, yellow gold

Pangea Stacking Band rings, 2013 – diamond, yellow gold

Pangea ring (top and side view), 2012 – cabochon blue topaz, peridot, opal, diamond, yellow gold
Pangea refers to the supercontinent – the single land mass – that existed hundreds of millions of years ago, before it broke up into the seven separate continents of today.

Quartz Crystal ring, 2004 – quartz crystal, yellow gold

From creating unique pieces, Ross began to understand that the requirements of the retail jeweller are different to the artist's vision; they struggle with the big daring art piece. Retailers are looking for a 'ringleader' from which a series of smaller designs can be created and which will attract a wider audience. To help bridge this gap, Kara Ross created the Pangea series ('pan' from ancient Greek for 'entire' + 'Gaia', Mother Earth). Taking her inspiration from the time that the world was only one landmass, Ross created a ring using one large blue topaz cabochon that spins on its axis, representing the Earth spinning on its own axis. She then placed a series of diamond zigzags to represent the continents, these have been set so that they can open and close, indicating the continental drift that occurred all those millions of years ago. Around the bezel and on the sides of the ring, mosaics of small hand-carved gemstones recount the story of mankind, representing the diversity of religions, cultures and ethnicities in the world. From this ring have come an endless mine of ideas for earrings, bracelets and necklaces – all featuring the signature zigzag.

OPPOSITE PAGE: Petra earrings, 2014 – malachite/azurite matrix, chrysoprase, peach drusy, diamond, yellow gold

Special commissions

In 2005, Ross discovered how light jet (fossilised wood) could be and this was the catalyst for a series of cuffs made in jet and in other materials such as ebony, maple and zebra wood.

Her use of wood led to an important commission from the White House for President Obama and the first Lady. Using wood from a magnolia tree that had grown on the White House lawn, Ross was asked to create a number of pieces, which would be gifts for visiting heads of state. The collaboration continued, with Ross creating special gifts for special visitors and employees at the White House.

Experimentation

Experimentation is a word that Ross never tires of, she is constantly looking for new possibilities. In 2013 she created the Transformation necklace, which uses concrete debris from a building formally located in the Hudson Yards, on the West Side of Manhattan. Interestingly, she also added to the mix black and white photographs, showing the rail yards as they had originally existed. Set in sterling silver, the concrete debris was polished, carved into geometric pieces and highlighted with black and white sapphires. A highly original piece, it plays with the ochre, cream and grey colourings found in this common material, which has been transformed into a contemporary and surprisingly classical piece.

Branding

2013 saw Kara Ross establish a boutique on the upper East Side:

> "It's a jewel box but it's beautiful, it's mine, it's a wonderful freedom to have."

It is here that she tests her ideas on the public, listening to their ideas and comments and creating brand awareness. She highlights her unique concept, transforming nature's beauty in its crystal form into jewels that enhance the beauty of the wearer. Her pieces can be found in many museum collections around the United States, including the San Diego Natural History Museum, as well as the GIA museum in Carlsbad. Ross is part of a group of women jewellers not afraid to experiment, with a similar audacious spirit and an innate sense of style, which includes such greats as Jeanne Toussaint, Renée Puissant and Suzanne Belperron.

TOP LEFT: Jet cuff, 2005 – jet, mother-of-pearl, diamond, yellow gold

LEFT: Puzzle Piece Series, necklace, 2010 – zebra wood, diamond, yellow gold
(Provenance: permanent collection of the Museum of Fine Arts, Boston.)

OPPOSITE PAGE: Transformation necklace, 2014 – concrete debris, photographs, black sapphire, white sapphire, sterling silver
(Provenance: 'Multiple Exposures' exhibition, Museum of Arts and Design, New York.)

"To start creating you have to be rebellious — courageous enough to refuse what has already been established. Art doesn't exist without provocation."

LYDIA COURTEILLE
Fantasy and Dreams

Lydia Courteille crafts jewels filled with dreams, tales and history. From her jungle of Amazonia crafted in superbly sculpted green turquoise and vines of diamonds descending into tangled hanging lianas surrounding mottled turquoise matrixes, to carved sugelite orchids inhabited by orange sapphire beetles; hers is a world of fantasy and castles in the air. The fascinating sculpture of a beetle in blue turquoise echoed by a bejewelled pink sapphire, black rhodium-plated beetle is a testimony to Courteille's witty use of colour, form and their opposites.

Courteille, an acknowledged expert of 18th and 19th century jewellery with a specialist knowledge of parures and cameos, started out as an antiquarian before deciding to create her fabled jewels in the early '90s. Cameo brooches popular in the 19th century and glyptics were transformed into large rings, creating conversation jewels. Ancient Egyptian artefacts have been brought back to life to live another day.

The vitrines in her tiny Majorelle-blue boudoir beside the Place Vendôme, are a window into her magical microcosms. In the theatrical window displays, one is just as likely to meet a red parakeet perched on the shoulder of a gibbon, as a *Memento Mori*, a reminder of our earthly mortality, a theme that runs through her collections. These scenes, alongside her images of porcelain doll-like figurines on her website, transport us into her imagination and allow us to journey into her world. It is a style that has been admired and copied by many a jewellery designer today, yet she was at its beginning.

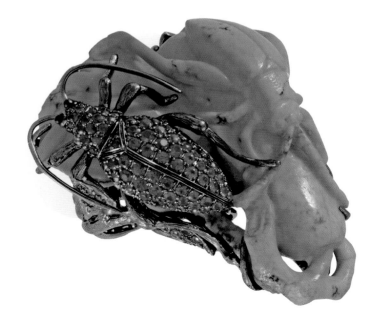

LEFT: Bestiare Collection, Beetle ring, 2011 – ancient turquoise glyptic, ruby, green garnet, rhodium-plated black gold

OPPOSITE PAGE: *Illustration for the Topkapi Collection, 2016, showing Courteille's jewels — an arm bracelet, pendant earrings, diadem, double ring and pendant; all set with ruby, rubellite, sapphire, green garnet, white opal and black rhodium-plated gold.* DIGITAL IMAGE BY NATALIE SHAU

ABOVE: Vendange Tardive Collection, Vine earrings, 2013 – amethyst, tsavorite garnet, garnet, rhodium-plated black gold

RIGHT: Homage to Surrealism Collection, Harem ring, 2012 – enamel, diamond, rhodium-plated black gold

BELOW: Serpent pendant earrings – yellow sapphire, yellow tourmaline, green tourmaline, tsavorite garnet, peridot drops, white diamond, rhodium-plated black gold

Colour

Colour is an important feature in all Courteille's collections: deep purple amethysts alluding to the rich wines of the Vendange Tardive Collection; bubblegum pink of the phosphosiderite mined in Chile in her Sweet and Sour Collection – the bright yellow veins running through the stone underline the bright yellow sapphires and topazes that she uses in the creation of her long-legged bugs and beetles; deep blues and ochre colours of the boulder opals in the Abysse Collection...

The cultural influences of Ethiopia's ancient Christian orthodox traditions, processional crosses, the lost tribe of Israel, the Ark of the Covenant, the famous architecture of the rock hewn churches of Lalibela and the 1000-year old frescos in the cave churches of the Gheralta Mountains are all brought together in Courteille's Queen of Sheba Collection, set with large acid green peridots and yellow tourmalines, echoing the colours of Ethiopia's green countryside and the yellows of the sulphurous Danakil Desert.

"I have collected stones and fossils since I was eight years old, so my initial idea of jewellery was to reconcile nature with human creativity."

Mexican fire opal with its kaleidoscopic plays of colour and its wealth of shapes and outlines provide Courteille with the ideal backdrop to create her exotic creatures – salamanders and turtles mix with monkeys and scorpions. We discover the stories of another time and another culture – her Santa Meurta pendant is a gentle recognition of the special cultural practices of some communities in Mexico.

Art and Literature

Courteille's inspiration can also come from works of art and literature; in her Homage to Surrealism Collection, she references such masters as Salvador Dalí and René Magritte. Courteille's inspiration is eclectic, she is moved by the art of Frida Kahlo and the writings of the French 20th-century writer and politician Simone Veil, as well as the works of authors such as Paul Éluard, Colette, Pierre de Ronsard and Victor Hugo. Hieronymus Bosch's *The Garden of Earthly Delights* and paintings by Gustav Klimt, Francis Picabia and Van Gogh have had an important influence on Courteille, as have the sculptures of Janine Janet. Courteille is inspired by all that surrounds her, from the past and the present, using historical references for jewels with meaning.

'Sweet & Sour' collection, orchid ring, 2013 – phosphosiderite, yellow tourmaline, yellow sapphire, diamond, yellow gold

Memento Mori and Vanitas

Courteille is perhaps best known for her vanities and *Memento Mori*, a theme that has fascinated her since her time as an antiquarian. They are a reminder of the brevity of human life, ambition and the futility of greed. Courteille's skulls take many forms, from rings enveloped in the American, British or French flag representing the blind futility of nationalism to a *Memento Mori* skeleton walking across a lapis lazuli globe of the world. Skulls sculpted in coral, rock crystal and set with diamonds are transformed into reminders of our own mortality.

"I want to share my culture and my emotions through my jewellery. I want my jewellery to initiate and provoke amazement, there should be discovery."

LEFT: Memento Mori pendant – lapis lazuli, white diamond, white gold

ABOVE: Stars and Stripes Vanitas ring – blue sapphire, ruby, white diamond, rhodium-plated black gold, white gold

OPPOSITE PAGE: Pirate Skull and Crossbone Vanitas chain – champagne-coloured diamond, rhodium-plated black gold

"Titanium allows me to work on a bigger scale with no weight and moreover titanium can be used in many different colours, and you know, I love colour!"

SUZANNE SYZ
Contemporary Fun

On the third floor of an early 20th-century building on rue Céard, just metres away from Lac Leman, there is an extraordinary showroom dedicated to contemporary art jewellery with a mission – to put fun and a light touch back into perfectly made high jewellery, using only the most poetically evocative and whimsical of jewels.

Bruno Bischofberger, an art gallery owner from Switzerland, introduced Suzanne Syz and her husband Eric to the 1980s Bohemian art world of New York. When Syz and her husband moved to New York, Syz helped out at Annina Nosei's gallery from time to time, hanging pictures for exhibitions; it was here that she met the up-and-coming artist Jean-Michel Basquiat. Bischofberger's introductions meant that she mixed and mingled with such illustrious art figures as Francesco Clemente, Andy Warhol and Julian Schnabel. From these beginnings, Syz and her husband created an important collection of contemporary artworks.

It was during this period in New York that Suzanne Syz's inspiration and ideas began to take form in her jewellery. Her Pop Art Collection reflects this exciting phase of discovery: for example, the Life Saver earrings, in a panoply of different eye-catching colours, all touched with diamond letters, spelling messages such as 'Me 4 U', 'Love Me', and 'Kiss Me'.

> *"I always felt that it's important to embrace contemporary artists who represent what's happening now. That's what's interesting."*

It is evident that Syz is of the 21st century. She experiments, using alternative metals such as titanium and zirconium to create jewels with a difference. Titanium is twisted into spirals and coils, creating original bracelets set with diamonds; she uses a memory titanium wire for her micro pearl jewels, threaded to create light floating pieces, such as her emerald ring and her earrings suspending Burmese blue sapphire drops. It is a true contemporary technique and touch to create a strong classical design.

LEFT: La Colombiana Perfetta ring, 2011 – emerald, micro pearls, diamond, titanium, white gold

OPPOSITE PAGE: Life Saver earrings – multi-coloured agate, diamond, yellow gold

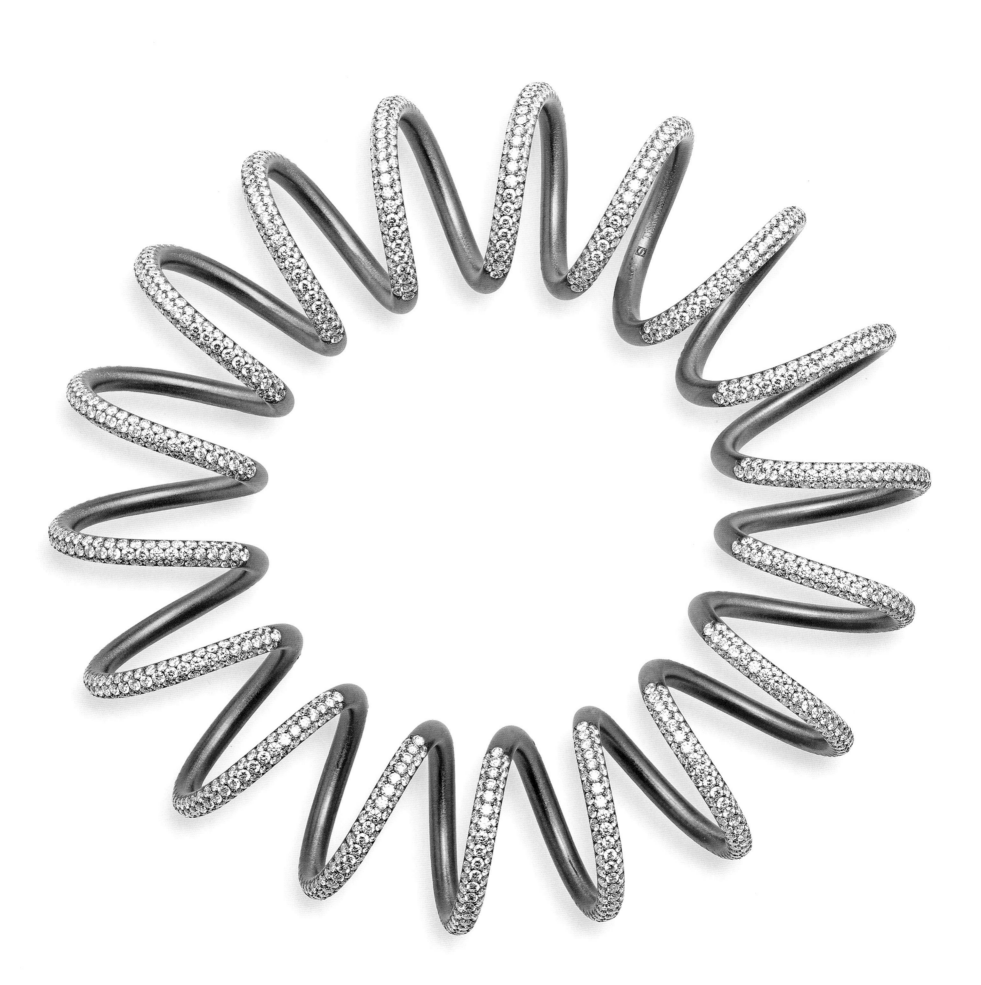

OPPOSITE PAGE: Drive Me around the Bend bracelet – diamond, titanium

RIGHT: Ali Baba's Trove ring – Paraiba tourmaline, 'domed crown' diamond, titanium

BELOW: Tie that Knot earrings – briolette beryl, diamond, titanium

Syz takes rough and semi-rough gemstones, using their contours and polished surfaces to show and enhance their natural beauty. One of her favourite gemstones is the electric blue Paraiba tourmaline; she loves their brilliance and the intensity of their colour. For her ring and ear pendants she has set the tourmaline within a bed of upside-down diamonds, which have been specifically cut for the crown on wristwatches.

Background

Each piece is one of a kind; she produces about seventy unique jewels each year using the highly experienced craftsmen who have followed Syz on her journey from the beginning. These are artisans who thrive on finding a solution; they start with an attitude of *"Let's see…"*, rather than *"No, this is impossible"*.

Having decided to set up her own jewellery business, Syz took four years to learn the art and craftsmanship of *haute joaillerie* from the workshops. It took time to convince them that she meant business and that she wasn't there on a whim.

For Syz, the joy of designing, of creating and of overcoming the technical obstacles are all part of being an artist. Ideas come from everywhere: Lifesaver sweets during a snowstorm at Newark airport; medical pills transformed into amazing hardstone and enamel earring clusters, as well as more naturalistic and figurative sources, such as mushrooms, frogs and leaves.

> *"A few years ago, I saw some barbed wire and thought it looked like an interesting material, I loved its contemporary look, I made earrings in coloured titanium. Another time I saw a collection of seventeenth-century wood spheres at the Biennale des Antiquaires in Paris, that looked just like some that I had seen in Hong Kong by the artist Ai Weiwei. I took the idea and transformed it into earrings in the shape of blue spheres."*

ABOVE: Take It or Leave It earrings – enamel, rose-cut diamond, diamond, yellow gold

BELOW: Rough Love ear pendants – dendritic diamond slices, rough red spinel, rose-cut diamond, diamond, titanium, white gold

BELOW RIGHT: Shanghai Lily earrings – lavender jade, purple sapphire, diamond

OPPOSITE PAGE: Atomic and Barbarella Robot earrings – ruby, sapphire, enamel (blue, pink, red and yellow), yellow diamond, black diamond, white diamond, yellow gold

Syz's amusing and witty ideas continue after the jewel has been finished; she uses the modern medium of video to create entertaining backdrops to her jewels, allowing us to take part in her ideas. A collaboration with Swiss artist, Philippe Fragnière showed her jewels mixed amongst sweets with a joyful nonchalance.

> *"A serious stone is more wearable and young, if it's set with some humour."*

In 2016, Syz collaborated with the Swiss glass sculptor John Armleder to create an environment in which to display her tiny treasures. The sculptures are composed of a base of broken glass, named after the Japanese pastry *Dorayaki*, onto which an iridescent glass bell is placed. Syz intends to cooperate with a new artist each year following her instinctual passion for contemporary art.

Syz's design ethos is "the unique, the fun and the playful"; components which she pours into each of her jewels and which will stand the test of time and become part of jewellery history.

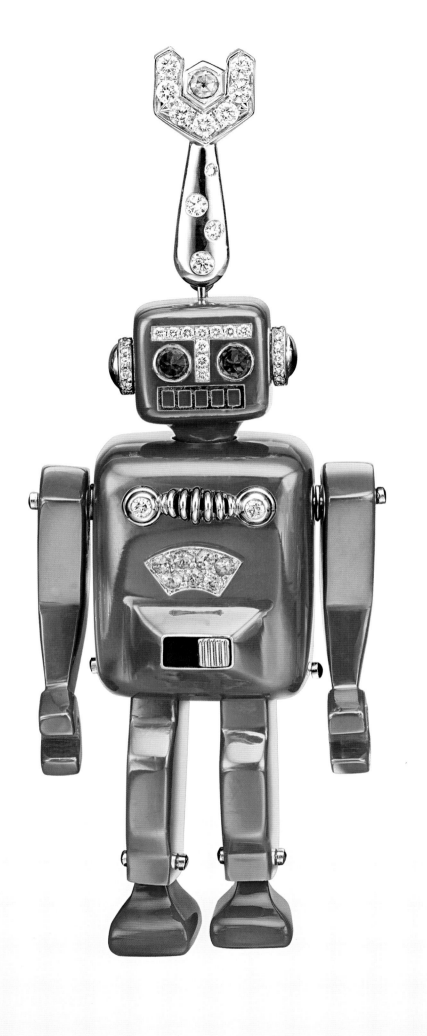
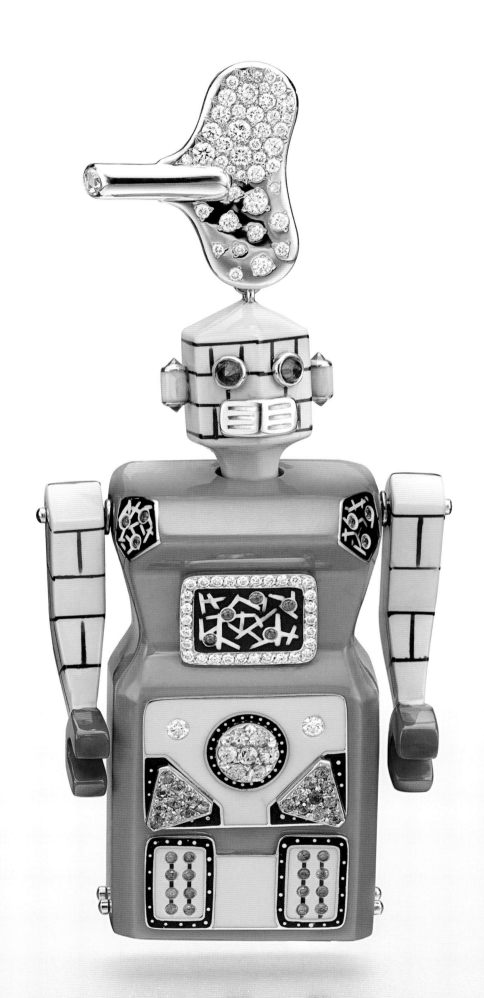

"The senses are wide awake when you create, be it cooking or designing. I quite often compare what I do to cooking. It's the visual aspect, certainly there is no smell in what I do but there is the sense of touch, it is very sensual."

SYLVIE CORBELIN
A Creative and Literary Spirit

Ever since her childhood in the countryside, Sylvie Corbelin has been a voracious reader. The poetic ambience created by French authors, such as François Rabelais, Baudelaire, Chateaubriand, Flaubert and Balzac have had an immense influence on her work. She also visited many museums as a child, though, as she freely admits, this was not necessarily out of choice. It was from this foundation that Corbelin built up an awareness of small objects and realised how interesting they could be; it helped define her taste, her likes and dislikes.

"I have a love for objects and my jewels before all else are objects."

Later, it was renowned antique dealers who directed her to what was truly beautiful. Her friend, jewellery dealer and great Art Deco expert, Michel Perinet, had a huge influence, as did Pierre Staudenmeyer of the Galerie Neotu.

Whilst a Law student in Lyon, Corbelin also took up gemmology at the National Institute of Gemmology, which had just opened its doors in Lyon under the aegis of Hubert Lagache. Having completed her studies, with some antique dealing on the side, Corbelin soon started to be attracted to ancient cameos and other old gemstones, and from there, to antique jewellery.

The next, natural step, was to create her own jewellery. Her very first collection was the Initées (The Initiated), the snake. Snakes have always held a fascination for Corbelin:

"When a snake crosses your path you are terrified, it is a vision of fear, it stops you, paralyses you."

Corbelin has transformed this vision into a smooth gentle creature that wraps around and hugs the skin:

"A snake with no aggression, it is smooth and like all my animals it has beautiful eyes. It has a gentle smile – like the Mona Lisa."

Elle Obtient Tout Ce Qu'elle Désire – Solstice (She gets all that she desires – Solstice) ring – ruby, amethyst, yellow beryl, tsavorite garnet, pearl, rose-cut diamond, champagne-coloured diamond, diamond, white gold, oxidised gold

OPPOSITE PAGE: Jardin necklace – abalone pearl, cabochon ruby, rhodolite, opal, amethyst, tanzanite, blue sapphire, diamond, black rhodium-plated gold, yellow gold

Snake ring – ruby, rose-cut diamond, champagne-coloured diamond, black rhodium-plated gold

Théléme ring – black opal, white opal, emerald, kunzite, amethyst, diamond, black rhodium-plated gold, yellow gold

OPPOSITE PAGE: Pectoral torque – abalone pearl, blue sapphire, orange sapphire, tsavorite garnet, ruby, rhodolite garnet, diamond, yellow gold

Snakes represent a link, a connection with someone, someplace, or a concept:

> "For me it is a silent creature and perhaps most importantly it is an animal which sheds something in order to grow, thus one must shed our baggage to grow within."

To bring variation to her collection, she uses the claws from the gemstone settings to create an illusion of reptile scales.

Scales, spiders, insects and birds… they all have a special place in Sylvie Corbelin's garden. To wander into this garden is to take a moment from one's busy life to ponder on these small creatures and objects. She takes us to faraway places, to mixes of culture and traditions, touching a potpourri of colour and light; we can almost smell the spices and perfumes lingering in the air.

Her extraordinary ring Théléme (made from 100 grams of 22ct gold) represents Rabelais' imaginary garden, a cottage garden. Inspired by the craft of *pique-assiette*, in which broken shards of crockery are used to create mosaic decoration, Corbelin has arranged richly luminous opal slices mixed with gemstones bought from the famous Louart workshop in Paris. Her deliberate choice of 22ct gold was to create orange gold sun-like reflections as the light shone off the ring.

In other jewels, Corbelin threads in dreams of faraway cultures, such as Japan or North Africa, and throws an inquisitive eye on the significance of such diverse subjects as the Eye of Horus and Calder's mobiles. Not a fan of fairytales, Corbelin is attracted to what is beautiful and fragile, and textural contrasts, such as rough with smooth. This is clearly seen in her Ramdam signature rings:

> "I like metal, metal allows you to see a design in three dimensions. If you cover it completely in gemstones, the design becomes flat; too much pavé kills the energy in the sculpture."

Corbelin mixes square cuts with ovals and pears and long narrow cuts in every colour, to create even more contrast:

> "My pavé settings are all about the gemstones, I call it my 'minestrone'. I mix them all together just as you would do for a soup with pasta and beans. The result is an edgy contour."

Playing with Light

Light is a vital quality in Corbelin's designs, creating contrasts, nuances of colour from reflections and refractions, it breathes life into her jewels, giving them presence. The light at night is a favourite theme: she refers to Van Gogh's *The Starry Night* as having more yellow than black; even dusk and dawn have an abstract magic that she dreams of catching and placing into a jewel that she can wear. This dream led her to create her extraordinary pectoral torque, which takes its cue from her love of night's gentle, mysterious glow. Using abalone mother-of-pearl for its slate greys and iridescent greens and blues, she created her own 'Starry Night'.

> "I love the reflections of the mother-of-pearl on the gold and the violet flashes in daylight which recall the night's shimmering aura."

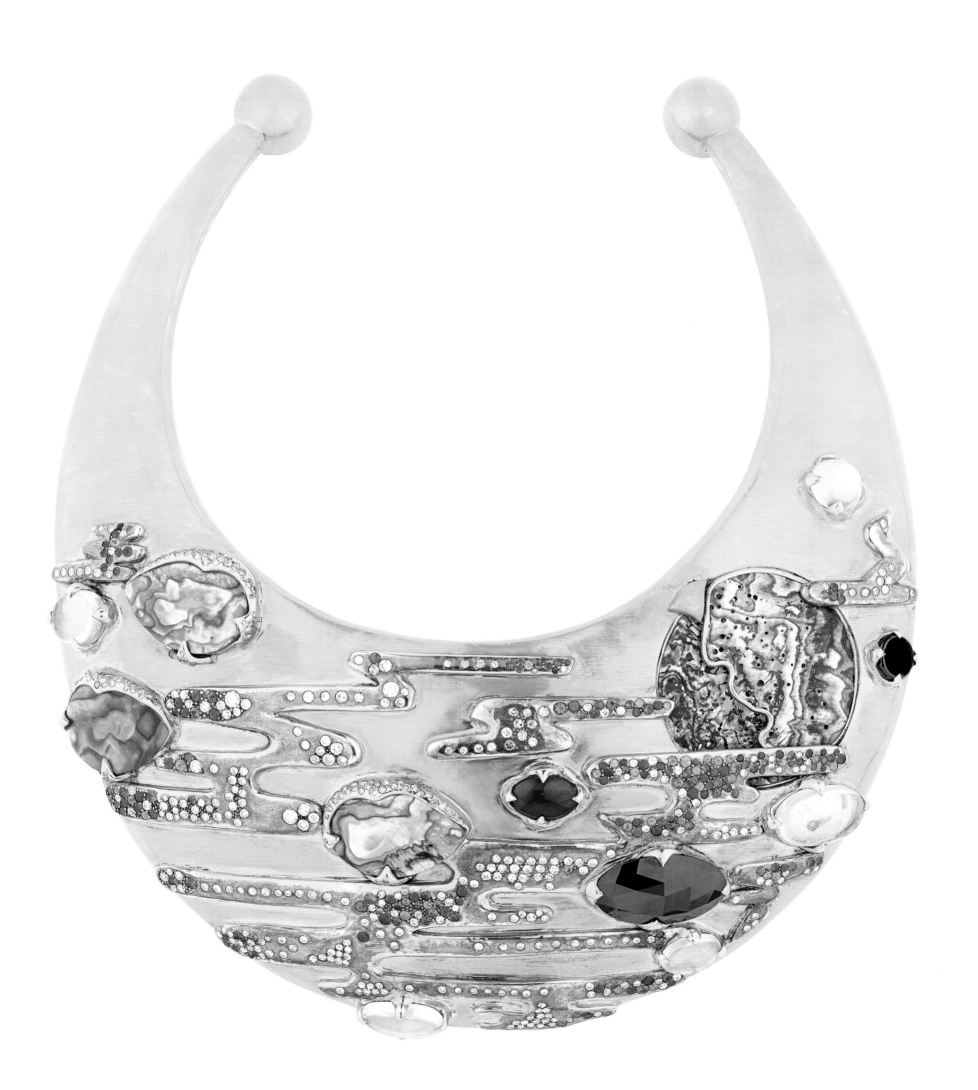

ABOVE: Butterfly brooch – resin, butterfly wings, tourmaline, sapphire, emerald, diamond, yellow gold

LEFT: Butterfly brooch – resin, butterfly wings, amethyst, purple sapphire, pink sapphire, aquamarine, tsavorite garnet, textured yellow gold

RIGHT: Mt Fuji. Mobile earrings (front and reverse) – ruby, diamond, white gold, oxidised yellow gold

BELOW: Marquise Palace Collection, Chandelier earrings – pink sapphire, pink diamond, rhodolite, ruby, pink spinel, diamond, yellow gold

Butterflies and Mobiles

The butterflies' ephemeral beauty is caught between Corbelin's fingers, seizing an instant in their short lives and rendering them immortal. Real butterfly wings are saved in resin and cradle the large gemstone that becomes the creature's body.

In the Far East, butterflies are a symbol of young love and revered for their fragile beauty. Corbelin has used this motif to create her famous mobile earrings, which are all about balance and precision, so that they move effortlessly when worn. As with Calder's mobiles, the most important element is balance – to create an equilibrium between each butterfly.

The inspiration for Corbelin's mobiles came from an unusual source: happening upon a painting by Utagawa Hiroshige, known for his paintings of Mt. Fuji.

> "When you look at all the great masters, Mt. Fuji always seems to be painted under the rain, or covered in snow or clouds."

She started to wonder how she could make rain or snow fall in her jewellery designs. Clouds were the next step and thus clouds and Calder became her next thought. If she could make a mobile, she could make clouds float… She chose Chinese and Japanese shapes for her clouds (ruyi) and on the backs she showed, using gold outlines, a bridge and a path under cherry blossom (in ruby), which led up to Mt. Fuji under the rain (in diamonds).

The Marquise Palace Collection brings us back to Corbelin's European roots; taking a model from the 18th century, she recreated a series of chandelier earrings with matching rings. To give them a modern touch she used colour, as though 'dipping' them into a pot of paint, to get the required gradient. To achieve this effect, she used very pale pink sapphire and then pink garnet and, finally, the intense pink of tourmaline. She created similar series in different colours from blues and greens, to oranges and yellows.

The figurative creativity of Corbelin's world is a refreshing use of her French roots and her literary background, which has led to collections that are as original as they are familiar. She creates a comforting universe of reverie, which acknowledges the past, and cleverly uses cultural allusions to give a modern interpretation.

THE NATURAL WORLD

Nature has had an enduring influence on every artist since the beginning of time; and this is as true for jewellery designers as it is for painters and sculptors. They use Mother Nature as a potpourri of inspiration, picking out small facets to mix and match. Cindy Chao's tattered butterfies, Katey Brunini's antennae-decked butterflies, and Sylvie Corbelin's resin-set winged butterflies may have a common starting point, but they are all so different. Aida Bergsen twists gold into a sinuous floral brooch and her snake rings slither around the wearer's finger, while Luz Camino seeks inspiration from flowers, the stars and the constellations in the night sky.

Even the planet's most unloved creatures, such as spiders have been given a second chance with Kaoru Kay Akihara's tiny, delicate interpretations. The sea's contribution is notable: shells, sea urchins and lobsters populate this glittering wonderworld: Juliette Moutard's starfish brooches are iconic; saltwater alligators catch piranha fish as they coil around Lydia Courteille's Paraiba tourmalines; Cindy Chao's emerald-cheeked pufferfish shimmer through the water; and Paula Crevoshay's sculpted seahorses seem to float on by. The watery theme continues with Anna Hu's Celestial Lotus necklace and her Monet's Water Lilies necklace.

Though the inspiration of nature is universal, each jewellery designer has their own interpretation and style, and this is what makes their jewellery so exciting.

LEFT: Aida Bergsen: Flora brooch – ruby, diamond, oxidised silver, palladium, rose gold

OPPOSITE PAGE: Cindy Chao: Pufferfish brooch (Black Label Masterpiece no. 8) – emerald, sapphire, conch pearl, triangular diamond, diamond, titanium, white gold
Made to celebrate Cindy Chao's 10th anniversary in 2013.

"What has been lost and what will be lost, the circle of life. This beautiful and irreplaceable nature expressed in jewellery. That is Gimel."

KAORU KAY AKIHARA – GIMEL
Nature's Poet

The simple beauty of nature is the essence of Akihara's delightfully witty jewellery. The words of Abe Warburg (1866-1929), "God is in the details" are constant in Akihara's mind as she creates her pieces: small, quiet reflections of the world about her.

Hidden on the slopes of the red mountains overlooking Kobé, she has built a haven of calm and industry, bringing together craftsmen who share her understanding of the universe and of Japanese traditions to create her brand, Gimel. From here, they can witness the flowering of the cherry blossom, and the changing colours of the maple trees and the zelkova trees, transforming from the greens of summer to the reds, rusts and burnt oranges of autumn.

Flower brooches catch an instant in the life of the flowers, immortalising them for future generations. Invisible to the admirer, tiny insects peer out from under the leaves and petals. These silent inhabitants were inspired by traditional kimonos: the exquisite silk patterns of the public face, *tatemae,* are always accompanied by a small secret expression that represents what is private. This inner self, *honne,* is guarded from public scrutiny. The *honne/tatemae* divide is extremely important in Japanese culture; one's private feelings are just that – private. Akihara's little insects are the wearer's secret.

Kimonos are covered in social symbolism, stating the rank and position of the wearer. The most beautiful kimonos were decorated with silk-embroidered flowers and creatures – peonies, chrysanthemums and maple leaves mixed with cranes, butterflies and dragonflies. The decoration is heavily symbolic: the plum tree, for example, represents winter and yet it is full of promise that spring is not far away, while the dragonfly signifies late summer and early autumn. Akihara's jewels tell us similar stories, they also depict the seasons, and her dragonflies and turtles are crafted with the same grace as these kimonos.

Gemstones

Akihara loves to use garnets with diamonds, she finds that the single refraction and the high adamantine lustre of both families complement each other. She admires the frankness of their light, she says that they give a *"clearer brighter brilliance"*. Tourmalines are another favourite, the electric turquoise blue of the Paraiba tourmaline and the deep yellow colours with hints of grey are another.

Pink diamonds are sourced at the Argyle mines in Australia and find a home in her singular Cosmos and Chamomile brooches, which conjure up thoughts of chabana flower arrangements from the ancient tea ceremony rituals of traditional Japan.

ABOVE: Sunflower brooch
Close-up of the back showing Kaoru Kay Akihara's signature hidden secret, in this case a tiny ant.

OPPOSITE PAGE: Sunflower brooch – yellow tourmaline, demantoid garnet, yellow diamond, diamond, sapphire, platinum, yellow gold

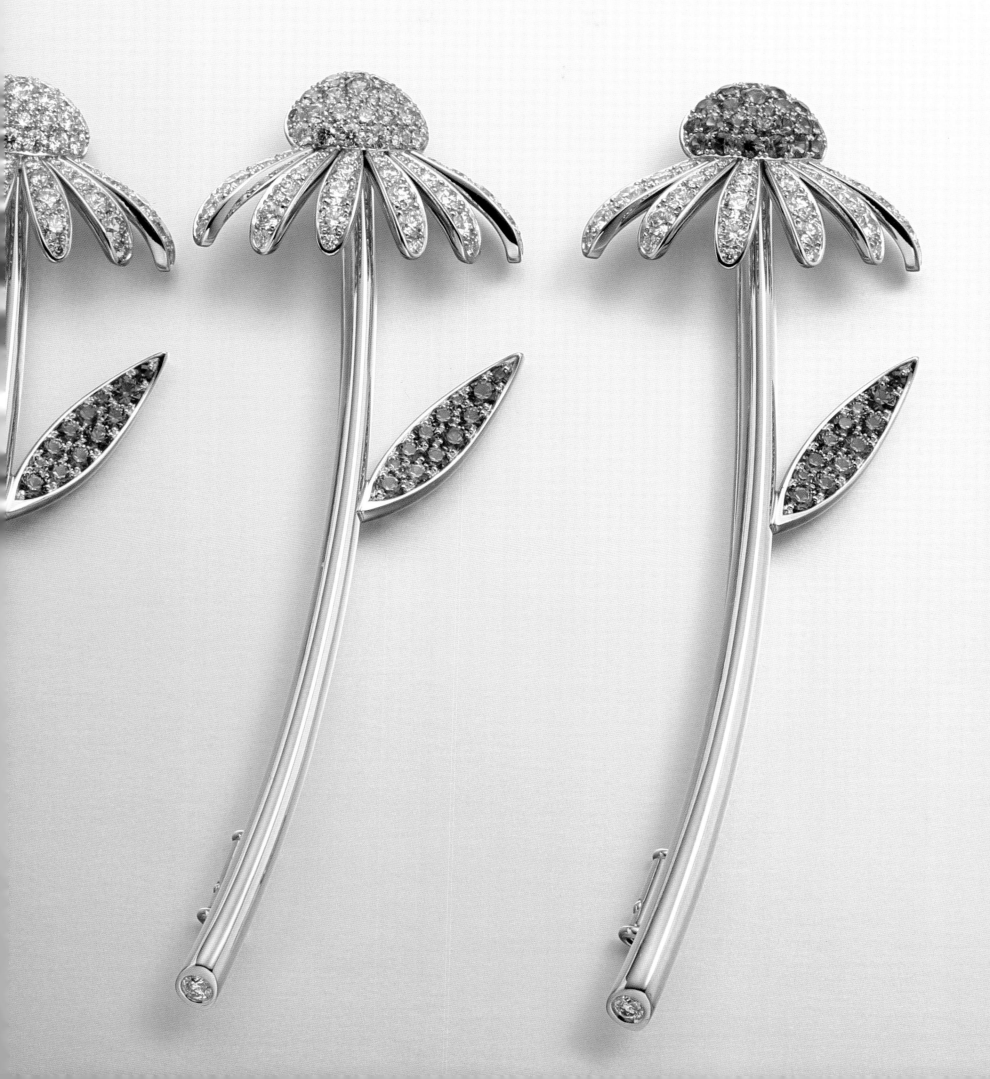

Pink sapphire, demantoid garnet, diamond, platinum

Pink diamond, demantoid garnet, diamond, platinum

Yellow diamond, demantoid garnet, diamond, platinum, yellow gold

Yellow diamond, demantoid garnet, diamond, platinum, yellow gold

Purple sapphire, demantoid garnet, diamond, platinum, yellow gold

Spider pin – mandarin garnet (spessartite), demantoid garnet, spinel, diamond, platinum

Her large pink diamond floral brooch was commissioned to celebrate the Argyle mine's 25th anniversary 'Beyond Rare' campaign. The deep pink colour of the central diamond was imitated as the tints of pink fanned out over the petals reaching the tips in pure white.

Akihara likes to include opals in the Gimel colour palette. In one piece, an opal with an extraordinary, almost harlequin, play of colour is transformed into a ginkgo leaf. Revered in Japan for their longevity and fortitude, ginkgos are the bearer of hope and love.

The bean is another Japanese symbol for good luck. In her Bean brooch, Akihara sets it with a milky white opal from Ethiopia, which has a gentle, very subtle red and green flame play of colour. The skin is decorated with tiny demantoid garnets and black diamond.

Akihara introduces a more architectural touch to her colourful garden spiders. The long, spindly, diamond-clad legs create their own contemporary design. The duality of the soft, faceted curves of the upside-down gemstones and the 8-legged angular design, create an interesting dialogue. The watery transparency of the gemstones and the smooth culets give the jewel a light touch.

Background

Born in 1944, Kaoru Kay Akihara studied economics before going on to study Jewellery Appraisal and Design at the GIA in Carlsbad, California. In 1974 she became a diamond trader after seeing the new modern cut, which at the time was not widely available in her home country. During the '80s Japanese boom, she designed one-off pieces for a select group of clients. Then, with the recession looming and a mounting awareness of man's effect on the environment, Akihara moved to understated design and found her true calling; in 1991 she set up her company, Gimel.

Acutely aware of the necessity to maintain the delicate balance between industry and nature, and deeply concerned about the consequences of climate change, Akihara has made it her mission to encapsulate the fragile beauty of nature and to transmit it to future generations.

RIGHT: Cherry Blossom brooch – demantoid garnet, sapphire, pink diamond, platinum, yellow gold

OPPOSITE PAGE: Ginkgo brooch – opal (from Ethiopia), diamond, yellow gold

"I am that strange adventurer in another era, fascinated by societies, culture, politics and religion from all periods."

KATEY BRUNINI
Magical Realist

Individually minded, with travel and curiosity at the centre of her ethos, Brunini has lived and experienced the diverse cultures of the North African continent as well as those of Sardinia and Sicily. With a degree in History and Art History under her belt as well as a qualification in Design and Gemmology, Brunini decided on jewellery design as her career after a visit to the jewellery department of the Cairo Museum in 1992.

> *"A jewel is not only a beautiful object, it is an immortal object with the sensibility that it is crafted from natural resources inspired by art, design, politics, trade, finance, society and culture. I mean you name it and it's going to outlast any chronicle of a certain era… It's a witness to what is actually going on at a specific point in time."*

Returning to the United States in 1992, Brunini took up an apprenticeship in San Diego at Jessops, a family-owned jewellers, as a custom designer working with early CAD software. Her apprenticeship with Jessops was vital to her progression: she learnt how metals worked and how much pressure and heat could be applied to different gemstones before they fissured or broke. At the end of the four years with Jessops, Brunini went 'walkabout', starting her travels again and spending an unplanned two-and-a-half years abroad, ending up in Sardinia and then Sicily. Her design aesthetic is a combination of traditional training, Italian craftsmanship and lyrical chiaroscuro in metal.

Her first five jewellery collections (which remain in production today), were influenced by this period. The first pieces from her iconic Twig Collection were completed when high polished gold was popular, so her jewels stood out because of their natural and textured aspect.

> *"I don't believe in trend jewellery, a jewel is for longevity, it is legacy."*

Ethos
Brunini believes that jewellery should be strong enough in its design to last from generation to generation, and well made enough to stand the wear and tear of time. The ancient Egyptian jewellery of Cleopatra's time looks as good today as it did all those years ago, that is the magic of jewellery.

LEFT: Body Armour earrings – buffalo horn, moonstone, diamond, yellow gold
The buffalo horn is carved with Maori symbols.

OPPOSITE PAGE: Medium Twig necklace – opal matrix, irradiated blue diamond, sterling silver

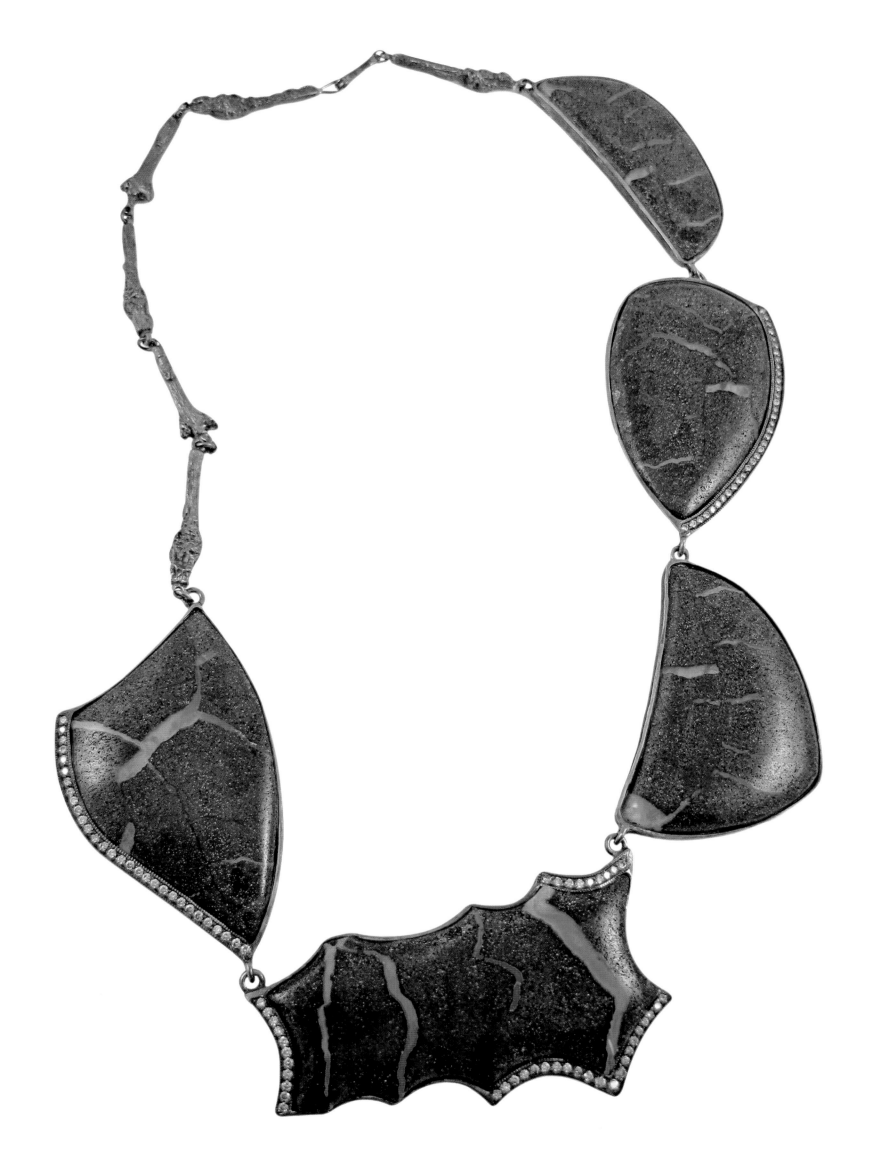

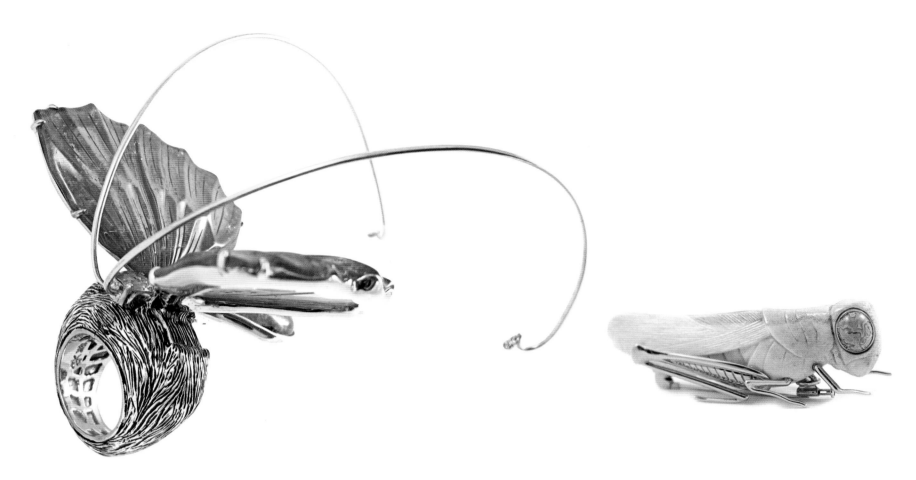

Brunini's jewels all have that magic. Mundane materials, such as cow bone and moose and elk antlers, are brought together with opal, coloured diamonds and brightly coloured cabochon gemstones in her strong signature gold structures and shapes, which can be found in her first DNA, Vertebrae and Twig Collections, which together make up her 'Shapes of Strength' signature collection.

In her Vertebrae Collection, the shapes are modelled on a rattlesnake spine. She calls it *"metallic Kundalini"*, an Eastern form of yoga, from the idea that the spine is the centre of energy in the human body.

> *"Jewellery with a backbone – stand up for your beliefs and for yourself."*

The Collection is tactile and the articulated pieces work closely with the contours of the body, while the gold gives the pieces weight and presence.

Symbolism

Anthropology has always been an interest for Brunini; she studied Egyptian history and became fascinated by the significance of the Mountains of the Moon, whence, it was believed, the Nile was born. Like cartographers before her, she was constantly surprised that on an otherwise uncharted map of Africa, the Mountains of the Moon would consistently be marked.

Since that fateful day when she stepped into the Cairo Museum, Brunini's interest in ancient cultures has never abated. She uses their symbols to pass on messages to her modern-day enthusiasts. The animal totems in her Spirit Animals Collection are derived from native traditions and folk art:

> *"They are messengers, teaching us, and protecting us through spiritual challenges."*

Her twig motif, which is a running theme throughout her work, captures the strength of nature and transposes this strength onto the wearer. They are a reminder that we all hit bumps in the road, but we carry on.

TOP LEFT: Spirit Animal Collection, Butterfly ring – watermelon tourmaline, opal, sterling silver, yellow gold

TOP RIGHT: Spirit Animal Collection, Grasshopper pendant – cow bone, agate, yellow gold

CENTRE LEFT: Vertebrae Toi et Moi ring – emerald, diamond, yellow gold

BOTTOM LEFT: DNA ring – zircon, green diamond, white diamond, yellow gold

Opal

Opal is particularly important in Brunini's one-of-a-kind pieces. From petrified opalised wood, to the colour combinations and the organic and geometric shapes, through to the light that draws the wearer into the stone, for Brunini, designing with opals is "like painting with stones".

Her twig cuff is set with a large lizard skin-like opal matrix, similar to petrified wood in appearance; she uses lavender pink diamonds to trace the opal's form and to underline the pink opal filled fissures, which give this matrix its extraordinary character. Rather than encircling the whole stone, the diamonds are set on one side of the opal matrix, suggesting its form as an artist might do and creating a subtle and fascinating jewel. The rose gold twigs and the sterling silver wood-like engravings, all serve to emphasise the petrified wood patterns in the opal matrix itself.

The Twig necklace with its five opals, uses a similar technique with blue diamonds to create the effect.

Brunini also uses cocobolo wood. She explains:

> "You see it in wood carving furniture inlay; in jewellery dating back
> 500–600 years. I find wood and bone as important as diamond."

In the Skipping Stones Collection, she delves into childhood memories, bringing to the fore stones skipping over the surface of the water creating small ever-growing ripples, until they are no more. She calls this life's 'ripple effect': nature has a continuity, and although it is ever changing, it passes seamlessly to the next generation.

Inspiration

The sources of Brunini's inspiration are endless: science; simple family memories; Native American 'dreamcatchers'; the Yucatan; and even Mayan offerings from her many travels… but also from 'flashes', her own 'Eureka' moments, when she might be looking at a valley in the mountains above Telluride (USA), for example, and suddenly be inspired to create a series of jewels that encapsulates feminine strength:

> "…melting Renaissance sundials and compasses with futuristic Mad Max and
> a dose of Metallica."

Historical references come high on Brunini's list. For example, Thomas Jefferson and the Declaration of Independence inspired a new collection around chains:

> "How does one translate the symbols of history into veritable art? It is
> the relationship between Thomas Jefferson and Sally Hemings that inspired
> this collection."

Colour

Stunning colours are a hallmark of Katey Brunini's work; she is attracted to big bold colours and shapes, to inclusions within the gemstone with which to tell a story. Colour has to be strong and the opaque stones, which have a special place in many of her jewels, are about the absence of light, which is so central to many of her designs.

Katey Brunini creates a place where her passion for science and history can co-exist within her unusual creations. Hers is a world of adventure and culture, in which the only restraint is what is technically possible.

ABOVE: Large Twig cuff — opal matrix, diamond gold, rose gold
Brunini's choice of rose gold is governed by the pink opalescence in the opal itself, which creates a gentle calming allure to the large bracelet.

BELOW: Skipping Stones Chandelier earrings — opal, ruby, black oxidised sterling silver

Petrified opalised wood bracelet – petrified
wood with opal, sterling silver, yellow gold

"I like to use materials of absolutely no value to create something of great value. I think like Dalí, who wanted to protest about the importance given to price of the materials in jewellery. I believe that the art of the design and the art of the craftsmanship should be valued above the material worth of the gemstones."

LUZ CAMINO
The Stargazer

The queen of plique-à-jour enamelling, Luz Camino has been creating her interpretation of the natural world from Madrid since 1977. Through her endeavours, she has kept alive a skill that was falling into decline and is now beginning to reappear in jewellery around the world. Plique-à-jour enamel attracted Camino because of its stained glass-like appearance. Using pale and dark, transparent and translucent, it lends a delicate fragile beauty to her jewels, echoing the fragility of nature; and it is light, light to wear.

Nature
Nature is Camino's primary source of inspiration:

> *"I lived for 22 years in a house in Navarra and spent a lot of time gardening. It was there, in the garden, that I decided that all the beauty of the flowers should be transformed into jewels."*

Camino's flowers include red poppies (made from resin in her kitchen); lavender, using amethyst and purple sapphires; and ears of wheat, using citrines. These flowers – with their simplicity and ethereal quality – can be found in museum collections around the world, including the V&A in London and the Museum of Arts and Design in New York, as well as the Musée des Arts Décoratifs in Paris.

LEFT: Peony Leaves in Winter brooch, 2015 – plique-à-jour enamel, diamond, silver, gold

OPPOSITE PAGE: Butterfly Nebula brooch – plique-à-jour enamel, labradorite, sapphire, pink sapphire, amethyst, ruby, tanzanite, diamond, platinum, silver, gold
Camino was inspired by a photograph taken by the Hubble telescope of a galaxy.

ALL IMAGES, PHOTOGRAPHY BY FERNANDO RAMAJO

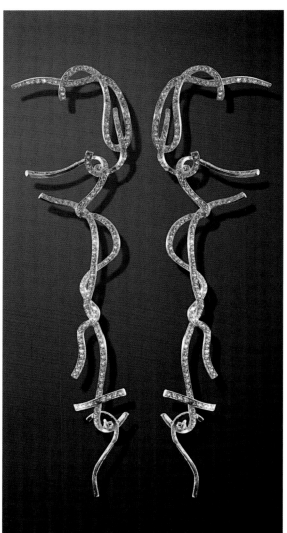

ABOVE LEFT: Wisteria brooch, 2008 – amethyst, enamel, diamond, yellow gold

ABOVE RIGHT: Mimosa brooch, 2000 – citrine, diamond, silver, bronze, gold

LEFT: Shoestring Potato ear pendants, 2014 – yellow sapphire, yellow gold

OPPOSITE PAGE: Stars necklace, 2000 – diamond, white gold

ALL IMAGES, PHOTOGRAPHY BY FERNANDO RAMAJO

In Camino's manicured garden, mimosa brooches have been set with citrines and diamonds; they grow alongside wisteria in sculpted amethyst and gold. Each jewel is a flash of colour and a lesson in sculptural prowess.

"Spring and autumn flowers are so beautiful that I wanted to wear them."

The Stars

In the garden, Camino's eyes look up to the skies above, fascinated by astronomy; she is not interested in the poetic descriptions of the stars and the moon, but the real 'nuts and bolts' of the topic. Thus her 'cosmic' jewels all have a gritty reality about them, of which her star necklace is an excellent example; the stars are set in clusters as might be seen through a telescope.

Everyday Treasures

Even small common items can find themselves transformed into jewellery, from pencils to potatoes; eating hamburger and chips with her son, she picked up some chips in her hand and they came up as a chain, and she exclaimed: "Look! A pair of ear pendants!" She creates sculptural jewels that represent her universe of everyday treasures; the hidden and the ordinary, which go unnoticed by the man in the street. It is in the shadows that she finds beauty.

Materials

An interesting aspect of Camino's jewels, is the multitude of stones she uses to create each of her sculptural pieces. She brings a potpourri of unusual gems, such as barita, kyanite and sun stone into the arena of high jewellery. She chooses her stones for their colours and their shades and her gemstones come from every corner of the world to find themselves set side-by-side. Her Sweetgum brooch for example, is not only decorated with plique-à-jour enamel, it has fire opals from Mexico, Padparadscha sapphire from Vietnam; yellow tourmaline from Nigeria; hessonite garnet from Sri Lanka and peridot from Pakistan.

Background

Camino came to Paris as a student to learn French. Fascinated by the world of couture, she went on to study fashion and textiles at the Chambre Syndicale de la Haute Couture for several months and completed her dissertation on the relationship of fashion with the great jewellery houses of the Place Vendôme, the centre of high jewellery. Several years later, in 1973, she enrolled herself in the Escuela Sindical de Joyeria de Madrid and spent her time learning the wide range of techniques of the bench jeweller. Not only did she use these skills to create her first jewels, she also met many of the artisans who would later become a part of her world, including the workshop that now does her enamel work. Although Camino is no longer a bench jeweller, she uses her experience to communicate and discuss with her artisans. Very early on in her training, she recognised that for her, the big challenge was to become a designer. Encouraged by Joel Arthur Rosenthal to do what she felt was right, to have courage in her convictions, she moved away from worrying about cost and let herself 'fly':

> "With jewellery you always feel constrained because of the price, but once you let that go and do what you like, it really changes everything."

Her Violet diadem is such a piece; who else would take the bane of a gardener's existence and transform it into an exquisite diadem? The white violet is an offering of small tantalising white trumpet flowers in white enamel with tiny pavé diamond centres.

Camino's Tulip necklace is carved with great attention to detail: the rock crystal flowers are translucent with jagged edges; transparent cinnamon enamel striations, lit with tiny red spinels and diamonds, dress the petals; the contrasting heavy bronze stems and leaves create a splendid natural effect that serves to emphasise the delicateness of the tulip flower. Looking carefully you can also see the gold back to the necklace, which not only touches the skin but also shows the extent of Camino's attention to detail.

> "Because I don't like to see much metal, I love to use enamel in all its forms and colours."

Camino does all her metal finishes and patinas herself. Silver takes a black or brown patina, whilst green patinas are used on bronze, a combination which she frequently uses in her floral compositions.

> "I often use bronze with a green patina as I have done in the tulip necklace and the violet diadem."

ABOVE: Tulip necklace, 2006 – rock crystal, red spinel, diamond, bronze, yellow gold
The two lower tulips are detachable and can be worn separately as a brooch, creating a simpler tulip choker.

OPPOSITE PAGE: Violet diadem, 2010 – enamel, diamond, silver, gold

ALL IMAGES, PHOTOGRAPHY BY FERNANDO RAMAJO

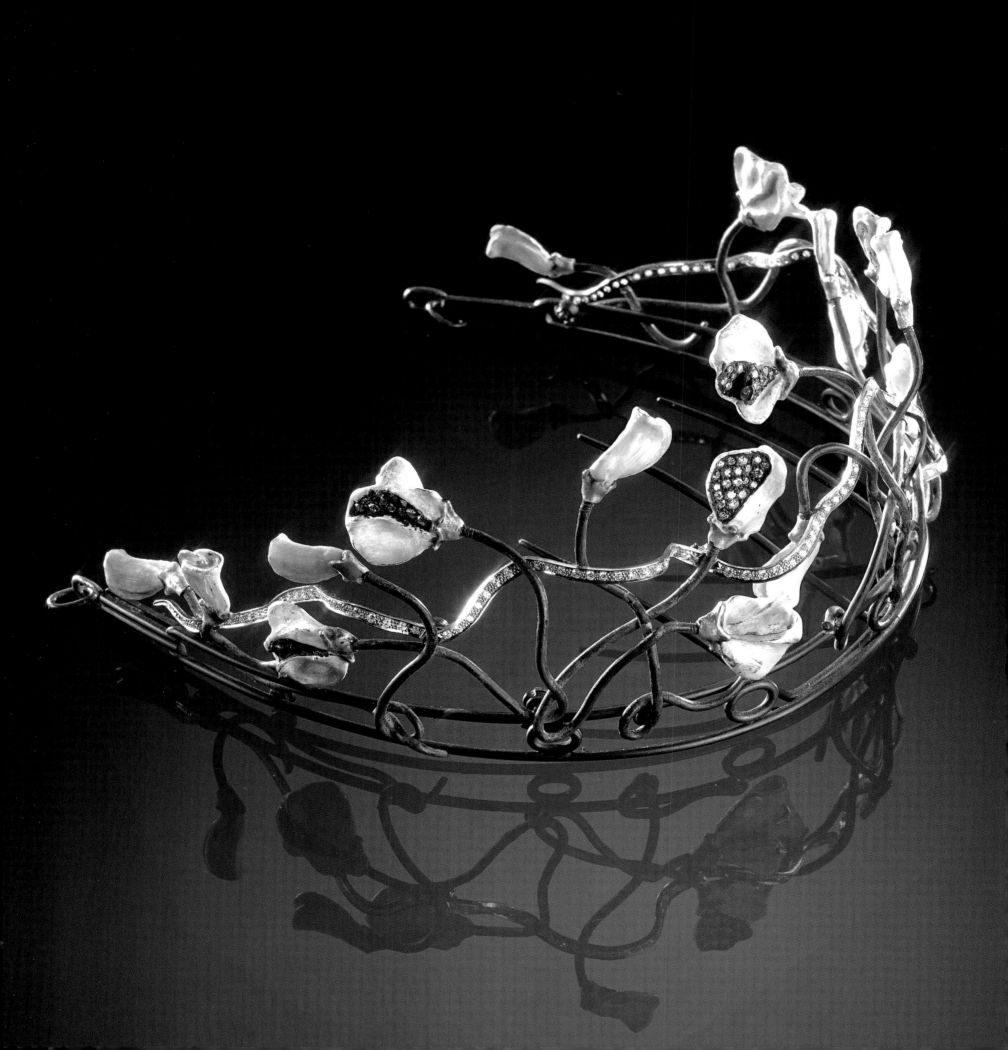

ABOVE AND BELOW: Butterfly brooch & design sketch, 2006 – Iodolite quartz, diamond, yellow gold

OPPOSITE PAGE: Bird brooch, 2000 – baroque pearl, ruby, amethyst, sapphire, diamond, silver, gold

ALL IMAGES, PHOTOGRAPHY BY FERNANDO RAMAJO

Suggestion is a great force in Camino's design, her delightful Butterfly brooch is set with wings of Iodolite quartz and the butterfly's veins are implied by the clever use of the quartz's inclusions. The simple outlines of the round pear-shaped diamond, also infers the body of the butterfly.

The atypical shapes of baroque pearls can suggest the wings of a bird. She blends cabochon rubies with a cabochon sapphire creating the bird's body, and its trailing tail feathers are a profusion of briolette amethysts, ruby drops and minute diamonds set in oxidised silver. The whole brooch has a wonderful feeling of weightlessness.

From unusual and rare gemstones and minerals she has created an extraordinary array of intimate and special one-of-a-kind jewels, which will still be admired for generations to come.

"It's about freedom, he was so free, he didn't care about anything, that is the most amazing and the greatest thing an artist can achieve. You can feel his emotion and THAT is what I want to include in my pieces." Cindy Chao talking about Van Gogh

CINDY CHAO
The Art Jeweller

A Family Heritage

Cindy Chao's childhood was spent in an artistic household with her grandfather, Zinan Hsieh, a well-known architect of temples in Taiwan. Memories of her grandfather have a great influence on Chao as an artist. He would sit at a long desk for ten hours a day and when Chao ventured into his study, her grandfather would give her a piece of paper and tell her to draw.

"At the time, I believed that I was drawing like my grandfather."

When her grandfather had finished sketching, he would ask Chao to explain what she saw. If she said, for example, that it was a front door, he would ask, why the *front* door? *"Don't forget that your front could be someone else's back door or side door"*. Slowly, she learnt to describe in a more three-dimensional way and not to state the obvious. The result is that when Chao designs a piece of jewellery, she immediately expresses and crafts her ideas in three dimensions, creating a model rather than a drawing or a design.

"I know what it should look like already, front, back and the side. I think that it was my family heritage which made the difference."

Her other great mentor was her father, a sculptor who instilled in her the necessity of always communicating through her work and making people understand and feel what she is feeling as she creates:

"You have to make people capture the message and the memento you are trying to present. It has to come alive."

Background

Chao studied for a short period at the FIT (Fashion Institute of Technology) and then she trained at the GIA in New York before returning to Taiwan in 2004 to set up as a jewellery artist. The first two years were difficult; having had to sell most of her possessions in order to keep going, she set about creating six beautiful pieces for her Four Seasons Collection. The challenge was not only financial, but also for someone who had no contacts within the jewellery business, finding the correct workshops and people who would follow instructions from a young 'nobody'. Then to sell: how was she going to sell her masterpieces? Contacting Christie's from Taiwan, she was accorded a 20-minute meeting with the jewellery director Rahul Kadakia.

ABOVE: Four Seasons Collection, Emerald ring, 2006 – cabochon emerald, pearl, yellow diamond, white diamond, white gold, yellow gold

OPPOSITE PAGE: Black Label Masterpiece Collection no.XVI, Phoenix Feather brooch, 2016 – fancy yellow diamond of varying colour tones, one fancy vivid orange-yellow diamond, one chameleon diamond, titanium
Dimensions: 18cm. The barbs are mobile.
(Provenance: Biennale des Antiquaires, Paris, 2016.)

Kadakia chose two pieces from her Four Seasons Collection for his 2007 end-of-year auction in New York. Though Christie's estimates were well below what it had cost Chao to make them, not to mention the years of work she had invested in their creation, she decided to take the risk. Her gamble paid off; they sold for over twice their estimates.

Chao was on her way, but things were still difficult. In 2009, following the sale of her first two pieces, she managed to set up a meeting with the buyers at Bergdorf Goodman; she was accorded twenty minutes to show her jewels. Chao showed her jewels to an initially dubious buyer. On seeing the small collection, Abby Huhtanen quickly made some calls and Chao found herself at the *W* magazine building, her jewels being photographed for an article, entitled 'The Chao Factor'. It was an extraordinary time for Chao, she returned to Taiwan to find hundreds of e-mails and texts waiting for her. Her beautiful 2009 butterfly brooch, the Royal Butterfly had made the front cover of the *WWD* magazine – it was the first time in the magazine's history that the editorial team had placed a jewel on its front cover.

The Smithsonian Butterfly Brooch

Among all the e-mails was a message from a collector wanting to buy the butterfly. Chao, however, wasn't sure that she wanted to sell it. The collector eventually came back to her explaining that he had sent a photograph of her butterfly to the Smithsonian Institution in Washington DC and the verdict had been extremely positive. The result was a permanent home for Chao's Butterfly brooch at the Smithsonian Institution, gifted by the collector who had finally bought it. The curator of the Smithsonian Institution, Jeffrey E. Post, stated that they wanted to show living contemporary jewellery which would "... *preserve the future of vintage, we want to show that here in the 21st century we already have this type of creation, craftsmanship to represent this generation.*"

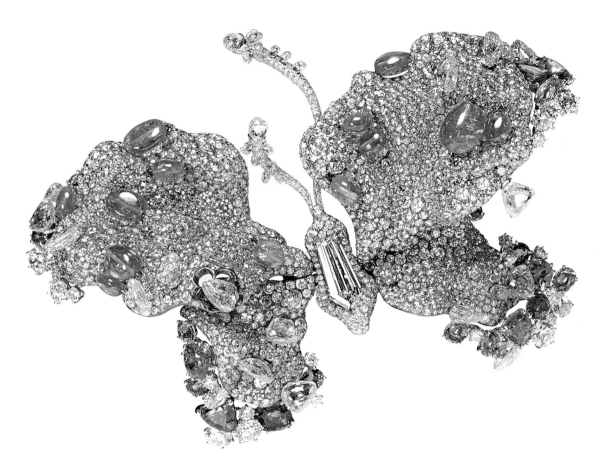

Butterflies

Chao's first butterfly was completed in 2008. It was at a time when Chao was still struggling to break through as a jewellery designer. She remembers thinking that this could be the very last jewel that she ever made, and so it took on an altogether more serious meaning for her:

> "It became my life symbol, my metamorphosis, my life spirit as well as my creation. So as I worked on the butterfly, I didn't treat it as a butterfly, I treated it more like a piece of me."

Now, Chao creates one Butterfly brooch a year. Each is different and has a different tale or collaboration to tell.

> "I really insist that I make only one butterfly a year, to symbolise my growing and myself."

Perhaps one of her most revealing collaborations was with actress Sarah Jessica Parker (SJP) in 2014. Parker has been a close friend for many years, and a stalwart supporter of Chao's talent, even before she had become better known. Parker always helped where she could, by assisting and turning up to Chao's events and they decided to collaborate on a butterfly jewel. The idea for the ballet dancer theme came to Chao on a visit to the Palais Garnier in Paris: the décor of the small room in which the ballerinas warmed up before going out to perform, was engraved in butterflies… Parker had attended the School of American Ballet in New York, the fit was perfect. The three pink conch pearls symbolise Parker's three children. The ethereal quality of the brooch is such that you can imagine a ballerina ready to take her position before performing. Note the setting of the brown diamond slices and the almost disguised setting of the cushion-cut fancy brown diamond.

In 2012, one of her iconic Butterfly brooches was sold in a Geneva jewellery auction for just under a million US dollars, nearly fives times its estimate.

ABOVE: Transcendence Butterfly brooch, 2012 — sapphire, cabochon sapphire, pink sapphire, diamond, white gold *(Provenance: Christie's Geneva — November 2012.)*

BELOW: Black Label Masterpiece Collection no. 1, Ruby Butterfly brooch, 2015/2016 — ruby (from Myanmar), rose-cut diamond, briolette diamond, oxidised silver, yellow gold

Jewellery style

Chao's jewellery has a sculptural style that gives her jewels a certain fragility and a sense of delicate elusive beauty to be shared for a precious moment in time, before disappearing like a mirage to another faraway place. Her raggedy insects and butterflies have stories to tell, to cherish before they move on, through storms to destinations unknown.

Rose-cut diamonds intermingle with diamond slices, briolette cuts, and cushion cuts as well as brilliant-cut diamonds; they all serve to create contradiction and contrast. The claw settings make for a rugged terrain, giving a continuity and link between her sculpted forms and the gemstones she so admires. The deliberate use of large, rose-cut diamonds over her smaller pavé-set gemstones creates an extra tension in her beguiling work. Chao's Tipsy brooch, for example, invites the eye to look at the deliberate placing of flat, rose-cut diamonds and the yellow diamonds on the stem, which are set to create small shadows giving an illusion of knarled bark. It is a very subtle method of suggestion.

Chao's jewels in the early years used a 3-dimensional textured gold, which allowed for fewer diamonds. The emerald ring from her Four Seasons Collection (2006) is a masterful lesson in design and economy of gemstones; the eye is drawn to the sprinkling of pearls with the emerald becoming part of the design rather than standing out. In the same collection, the necklace and bracelet use black diamond textured branches set with marquise white diamond leaves, resulting in a poetic rendition of winter.

Black and White

In 2009, Chao introduced her two lines: Black Label, unique masterpieces made by her workshops in Switzerland and France; and White Label collections, which are increasingly being made in Europe, with less complicated designs being made in Hong Kong.

From an artistic background influenced by both her father and her grandfather, and a Western education and Eastern heritage, Chao has emerged with her own, intoxicatingly individual concept for sculptural design and elegance.

ABOVE: White Label Collection, Donut rings, 2011 — diamond, brown diamond, fancy-coloured diamond, tsavorite garnet, sapphire, pink sapphire, yellow diamond, diamond, white gold, rose gold, yellow gold

RIGHT: Black Label Masterpiece Collection No. 7, Tipsy Brooch, 2009 — heart-shaped blue sapphire, multi-coloured sapphires, fancy-coloured diamonds, diamond, yellow gold

OPPOSITE PAGE: Four Seasons Collection, Winter bangle, 2007 — diamond, black rhodium-plated gold
(*Provenance: Christie's NY, 11 December 2007.*)

"Sculptures that breathe with you and are a part of your body."

AIDA BERGSEN
Nature's Sculptress

Aida Bergsen was brought up in Turkish Cyprus before moving to Istanbul in 1986, after her marriage. She studied 'Langues et Lettres' at Stendahl University in Grenoble. A sculptor at heart, Bergsen left the studios of Irfan Korkmazlar and Ümit Öztürk to participate in some workshops at the famous Saint Martin's College of Art and Design, London, which helped to broaden her vision and introduced her to smaller dimensions. The move to working on a smaller scale was almost accidental; she felt an instinctual need to express the relationship between sculpture and the human body, which in turn led to the ornamentation of the body. Bergsen used bronze as her medium for her large-scale sculptures and then to explore its possibilities as a jewel, which in itself created a bridge between the body and the ornament. Her jewels have an unmistakable sculptural aura.

Having graduated, Bergsen went on to an apprenticeship with the jewellery design studio, Mehmet Kabas in Istanbul. This pragmatic move allowed her to study ancient techniques, which she still incorporates in her jewellery today. The traditional workmanship of the Grand Bazaar is introduced to the immediacy of the contemporary needs of today.

For her Ottoman Embroidery rings, for example, Bergsen has created intricate trelliswork, highlighted by individual diamonds, the result is a patchwork of light.

LEFT: Ottoman Embroidery three-finger ring (on sculpted clay hand) – diamond, silver, rose gold
This ring takes its inspiration from the Topkapi Harem architectural details.

OPPOSITE PAGE: Ottoman Embroidery double ring – rose-cut diamond, silver, rose gold
Bergsen's inspiration is antique lace for this ring, which can either be worn chained across two fingers, or above and below the knuckle of the same finger.

Flora and Fauna

The cycle of life and death in the natural world provides Bergsen with great inspiration. It is about rebirth and the power of self renewal, she is interested in a holistic approach to nature where life returns to the earth in a never-ending cycle.

Diamond swallows with outspread wings and diamond-encrusted, enamel-winged grasshoppers and lizards recall the jewels of the late nineteenth century and the garland period of the turn of the twentieth century. Hers is a natural world, in its authentic regalia.

Her floral jewels have their origins in her childhood memories and they symbolise the legends of antiquity, of people transformed into trees to save them from certain death, only to return as flowers and live in a different form. Not for Bergsen the obvious beauty of roses or lilies; she takes troublesome bindweed and thistles and shows nature in its essence.

For her Flora brooch, she cleverly uses palladium, alongside silver and rose gold for its colour and lighter weight. A locust perches amidst the leaves, which are set *en tremblant*. The ivy ring, evoking her memories of Cyprus, employs traditional Turkish methods to set the rose-cut diamonds that decorate the leaves; she uses rose gold, oxidised and blackened silver for this ring, which covers the finger, in the same way that ivy might cover the trunk of a tree or wall.

FROM TOP TO BOTTOM:

Lizard brooch – opal, diamond, silver, rose gold

Ivy Finger ring – rose-cut diamond, diamond, oxidised blackened silver, rose gold
Bergsen uses traditional Turkish methods to set the diamonds in the silver ivy leaves. The ivy covers the finger as ivy might cover a tree trunk.

Swallows ring – diamond, silver, rose gold

OPPOSITE PAGE: Flora brooch – ruby, citrine, rose-cut diamond, diamond, oxidised silver with palladium, rose gold

The Darkside

Her Darkside Collection uses the theme of the vanities, an awareness of death as the natural way of life. She is seeking a spiritual, symbolic solution to her designs to create icons that challenge the wearer, she uses contrasting metals and shadows to help create this world. The serpent is a theme that runs through many of the jewels; big, fanged and terrifyingly present, set with diamonds and red ruby eyes, they create their own menace.

Magnifying glass pendants

Other than Bergsen's thematic collections and headpieces, she is particularly known for her distinctive loupes or magnifying glasses. Decorated with serpents or swallows these small works of art are both decorative and functional. The frames have all been delicately set, with pink gold sculpted wings on diamond-bodied swallows, or weaving vines of translucent green enamel leaves coiling delicately around the transparent void of the loupe.

Bergsen uses the sculpted gold and silver of her jewels to contrast with the colours of her gemstones and her enamelwork; she is quick to remark that this is unconscious, as what she is truly interested in are the shadows and their resulting impact on the jewel, rather than the more classic light and colour combinations to be found in fine jewellery.

Aida Bergsen's jewels cross over from the purely theatrical and artistic to jewellery that has an eternal presence, set with small gemstones that enhance the beauty of each of her sculptural pieces. Her inspirations from the past have been reinterpreted, making them both classical and subversive in equal measure.

TOP LEFT: Serpent earrings — diamond, silver, yellow gold leaf

BOTTOM LEFT: Serpentine Dance Medusa cuff — rose-cut diamond, oval-cut diamond, diamond, oxidised silver, yellow gold

ABOVE: Serpentine Dance Medusa ring (side and front views) — ruby, rose-cut diamond, oxidised silver, yellow gold

OPPOSITE PAGE: Flora Birds Nesting loupe/pendant — ruby, tsavorite garnet, enamel, rose-cut diamond, yellow diamond, cognac diamond, white diamond, silver, yellow gold

"Each gemstone is a different note. If it's a small group of stones, it's like chamber music; if it's a large group of stones, it's like a symphony."

ANNA HU
Composer of Gems

Destined for a great musical career, child prodigy Anna Hu won a prestigious competition in Taiwan playing her beloved cello. Having moved to the United States to continue her training, her dream was shattered by a shoulder injury. It was a difficult and emotional time; after all the years of practising, suddenly there was nothing to fill the endless hours, just emptiness. Then Hu remembered how as a little girl she had held a handful of gemstones and how they had entranced her. It was a moment of clarity for her; her parents were well-known gemstone dealers in Taiwan and in Hu's 'no nonsense' fashion, she decided that she would become a jewellery designer, or as Hu describes it: *"a composer of gems"*.

A New Path
Study started in earnest: first a course in Art History from Parsons School of Design and then a Master's Degree in Arts Administration from Columbia University. An internship at Christie's in New York led on to working at Harry Winston, the famous 5th Avenue jewellers of Hope Diamond fame. Here she came into contact with Maurice Galli, who not only inspired her but also encouraged her.

> *"I learned about designing from watching him as he worked, (he) shaped my creative vision."*

In 2007, a 30-year-old Hu founded her company, Anna Hu Haute Joaillerie. It took Hu a year to find a small prestigious location and to create enough jewellery to show. Her first piece, The Gnossienne brooch/necklace, depicts a crane in full flight above *ruyi* (cloud-like motifs, popular in Chinese lore). The piece was inspired by an ancient Chinese painting *Auspicious Cranes* by the Song dynasty artist and Emperor Huizong (1082 -1135). In Chinese folklore, cranes symbolise longevity and good luck, and immortals ride atop cranes to ascend to the celestial realm.

For Hu, this piece was the beginning, the bringing together of her Chinese culture and its symbolism with the exacting workmanship of the famous jewellery houses in the West and their contemporary and perhaps less complicated designs.

> *"The Gnossienne is the embodiment of everything that I am: a Chinese artist trained in Western craftsmanship, and a musician with a deep understanding of the melodic harmony of gems."*

Modern Art Deco bracelet – ruby, emerald-cut diamond, baguette-cut diamond, tapered baguette diamond, diamond, platinum

OPPOSITE PAGE: Gnossienne necklace, 2008 – baroque pearl, keshi pearl, jade, cabochon ruby, white diamond, white gold
Gnossienne is the term created by the composer Erik Satie to describe a new form of music composition. Hu uses it as a symbol for her new departure in jewellery design after leaving her cello career behind.

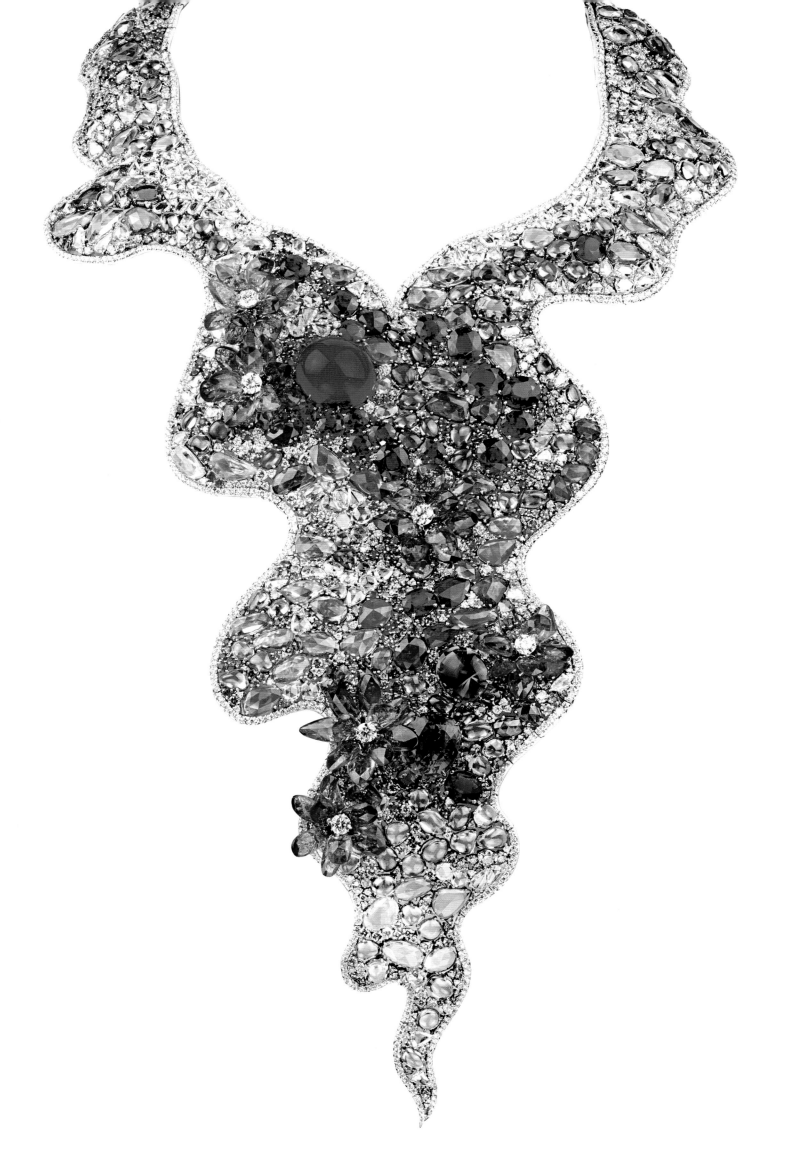

Art of the West

Each year she brings an important necklace to life; perhaps her most ambitious project to date has been her Monet's Water Lilies necklace, in 2011. It started with her father handing her a large selection of white rose-cut diamonds, which he thought would be enough to create a number of beautiful rings. Hu had other ideas. After visiting Monet's garden at Giverny, she was left with an indelible image of the sinuous bends of the lake and the play of shadows on the water's surface as the sun peeped through the trees and the thick vegetation bordering the lake. She set the rose-cut diamonds in open claw settings, imitating the shadows with pink tourmalines, morganites and purple and pink sapphires. She emphasised the gentle light from these cabochons and rose-cut diamonds with the brilliant adamantine lustre of smaller grey, pink and white diamonds, accompanied by sparkles of turquoise blue Paraiba tourmalines; the 'waterlilies' were set upright to give the whole bib a sculptural, three-dimensional quality. The large blue cabochon tanzanite, a drop of blue, shimmers with purple reflections flickering across the water's surface to the nearby pink tourmaline waterlilies.

From Giverny and Monet, Hu continued with another great impressionist artist's work – Vincent van Gogh's *Irises*. She spent over two hours studying the painting at the J. Paul Getty Museum in Los Angeles and working out how she could represent van Gogh's abrupt, thick brushstrokes. Her interpretation is a bangle with coloured gem-set lines of short *cloisonné* shapes representing the broad long leaves of the irises, and the iris petals are set with sapphires of varying shades to create shadow and perspective. The backdrop of yellow coloured diamonds and spessartite garnets serve as a contrast. Garnet has the lovely bright adamantine lustre of diamond; singly refractive, like diamond, it creates an evenness in the lustre of the background which subconsciously allows the other coloured gemstones to appear with more vitality. A stunning pear-shaped diamond is set as a single white iris growing amongst a sea of purple and yellow irises.

Symbolism of the East

If the Monet necklace represents the West, then her Celestial Lotus necklace created in 2009 symbolises the East. It was derived from a visit to Bhutan and its festival to the Buddhist master Guru Padmasambhava, who was born in a lotus flower. The necklace shows a lotus bud that encircles the neckline of the wearer to meet a lotus blossom in full bloom. Its petals seem to have been dipped into red ink, with the wash of resulting colour set with pink sapphires and rubies, animating an otherwise motionless flower. The beautiful lotus flower leaf, a radiating series of emeralds, demantoid garnets and tsavorite garnets, gives the piece a sense of movement with its realistic tear. Hu studied many paintings of the lotus flower as well as real blossoms, before attempting to create her own interpretation.

The lotus is revered in the Far East, representing purity and rebirth as it grows through the mud to produce a full beautiful pure flower contrasting with the muddy bed it lives in. The red lotus symbolises love, compassion and everything to do with the heart.

The Winter Plum is one of the Four Gentlemen depicted in Chinese painting throughout the ages, its accompanying 'Gentlemen' are orchid, bamboo and chrysanthemum. The plant blossoms in the middle of winter and is a symbol for resilience and perseverance. On her bangle, the gnarled onyx and black diamond branches are covered in ruby red blossoms against a snowy background of white diamond.

OPPOSITE PAGE: Monet's Water Lilies necklace, 2011 – cabochon tanzanite, blue sapphire, purple sapphire, pink sapphire, tsavorite garnet, tourmaline, Paraiba tourmaline, morganite, alexandrite, pink diamond, grey diamond, white diamond, white gold

RIGHT: Celestial Lotus necklace, 2009 – ruby, emerald, demantoid garnet, tsavorite garnet, pink sapphire (of varying intensity), yellow diamond, grey diamond, white diamond, titanium
In the Far East, the lotus represents purity and rebirth.

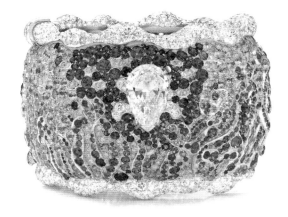

ABOVE:

Van Gogh Iris bangle, 2011 – demantoid garnet, emerald, blue sapphire, purple sapphire, spessartite garnet, D flawless pear-cut diamond (6.35ct); yellow diamond, white diamond, yellow gold

Four Seasons Collection, Winter Plum bangle, 2011 – ruby, onyx, black diamond, grey diamond, white diamond, white gold

TOP: Turandot Lily necklace, 2011 – natural Panjshir emerald beads (from Afghanistan), vivid yellow diamond, pink diamond, orange diamond, diamond, titanium
The necklace is inspired by Puccini's opera Turandot, *in which much of the story is based on a popular Chinese folk song, 'Mo li hua'.*

ABOVE LEFT: Persimmon Love ring – mandarin garnet, green sapphire, white diamond, white gold

ABOVE CENTRE: K solitaire ring – D flawless white diamond (10.10ct), rose-cut diamond, brilliant-cut diamond, baguette-cut diamond, white gold

BELOW: Jardin de Printemps ring – Colombian emerald (17.16ct), green garnet, tsavorite garnet, moonstone, fancy-coloured diamond, rose-cut diamond, marquise-cut diamond, brilliant-cut diamond, white gold

Musicality

Gemstones occupy a large place in Hu's works of art. Luckier than most jewellery designers in that she can depend on a steady stream of top-quality rare gemstones through her family, she has made the most of this chance to find new ways of expressing her musical soul. Her jewels, through their colours, all represent musical notes and it is in this way that Hu composes, by seeing the music in her mind. From the beginning, she was creating pieces which were inspired by the music of Beethoven and Rachmaninoff, passing by Stravinsky and Ravel. If the colours of her designs do not fit the colours in her mind, she will create a model to show what she wants, placing and repositioning the gemstones until she is satisfied. Time is not a hindrance, she will take whatever time it takes.

Many of her jewels have titles: special secret allusions to music, or private moments of inspiration that have touched Hu, such as her Ellington bangle and her Turandot Lily necklace.

Depth and Detail

Using the tradition of Chinese carving, in which not only the surface is sculpted but also deep into the stone, Hu creates jewels, especially rings, that have a layered effect so that when one looks at the surface, the wearer can see another bejewelled layer below and then another. This also defines Hu's attention to detail and the idea that even if the gemstone can't be seen immediately, it will add to the overall look of the ring. She is always conscious of the need to tend to the detail, the hidden detail.

Hu's Garden

The natural world has had a special influence on Hu since childhood. With the same zeal that she gives to her music, she creates jewelled ephemeral butterflies and sculpted flowers, which are as much a statement as they are a witness to her origins and her own artistic talents.

Achievements

Christie's first sold an Anna Hu jewel, the Beethoven Moonlight bangle set with moonstones and diamonds, in their Dubai jewellery auction in October 2009. In April, 2011, they sold her Golden Seahorse ring, confirming Hu's position as one of the most talented jewellery designers of her time. This was reaffirmed in 2013, when in May, Christie's Hong Kong sold her Orpheus ring – set with a stunning cabochon jade – for more than $2 million. In the November that same year her Côte d'Azur brooch sold in Geneva for over $4.5 million.

Further to these great achievements, Hu has received countless awards. The China Institute's award for 'Artistic Vision' in 2011 in New York, was yet another landmark for Hu; it was also the first time that a jewellery designer had been honoured with this prestigious accolade. This was followed in 2012 by being named International Jewellery Designer of the Year by Elle China and in 2013, Jewellery Designer of the Year by Elle Taiwan.

Within a short period, she has gone from realistic renditions to light and feminine jewels that are stylistically poetic and whimsical, bringing special meaning to the wearer. There can be no doubting of Anna Hu's place in jewellery design history.

ABOVE: Elixir of Youth brooch, 2011 – cabochon jade, purple sapphire, pink sapphire, sapphire, pear-shaped diamond, briolette diamond, diamond, titanium
The brooch represents Ganoderma, a form of mushroom used in traditional Eastern medicine. The pear-shaped and briolette diamonds represent holy water.

BELOW: Dragon Flower ring, 2011 – cabochon ruby (from Myanmar), sapphire, pink sapphire, green sapphire, purple sapphire, yellow diamond, diamond, white gold, yellow gold

THE PAST IS THE FUTURE

The granulation of ancient times has inspired the work of Elisabeth Treskow, Cornelia Roethel and Barbara Heinrich, whilst the filigree work of so much Southeast Asian and Indian peasant jewellery and 19th century jewellery in Europe has been the starting point for Cynthia Bach. Each has brought back a dying art to give it a new and more optimistic future.

The work of these artists must be applauded for the way that they have incorporated these age old techniques and given them new lives. Lydia Courteille started by taking old cameos and glyptics and transforming them from forgotten unfashionable brooches into huge statement rings. Artisans working in enamel have been given new hope through the designs of such artists as Luz Camino and again Lydia Courteille. The ancient techniques of lacquer work from China and Japan were revived through the highly original Lien (link) necklaces conceived by Suzanne Belperron and again in the 1970s with Elsa Peretti's bangles; more recently, lacquer work has been given a very modern interpretation by Victoire de Castellane for Dior Fine Jewelry and for her own collections, using daringly bright, acid, candyfloss colours.

Jacqueline Cullen has revived the use of Whitby jet, which until recently was synonymous with Victorian mourning jewellery. She has created matt compositions that play with light and contrast. Rooted in the past, her jewels are uncompromisingly futuristic.

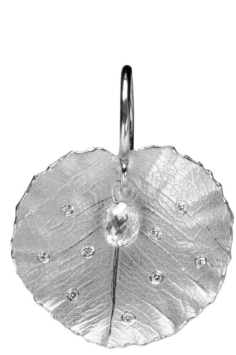

ABOVE: Cynthia Bach: Filigree Gitan Latin Cross pendant – diamond, rhodium-plated black gold

RIGHT: Barbara Heinrich: Briolette Diamond Leaf earrings – diamond, yellow gold

OPPOSITE PAGE: Jacqueline Cullen: Jet bracelet – jet, diamond, yellow gold leaf

"I would like my jewels to be connected to history. The past informs the present, we need to be aware of the styles that have gone before us, without repeating them."

BARBARA HEINRICH
The Midas Touch

Barbara Heinrich, master jeweller, designer and dreamer; her works are all based on her very close relationship with gold and its many properties. A symphony of textures and shapes in relief, small details with burnished edges highlight her work, a gentle mix to lull the senses. She tries to include four elements into each of her jewels: a personal expression, a contemporary component, an historic technique, and an eternal element that honours the principles of balance and proportion.

One technique from the past is granulation, which she uses to great effect. The individual granulations are used to outline or shadow the form of her intended jewel. Her close friends – the pumice, wire brushes and hand burnisher – all help her achieve the goal of an understated look. Heinrich hand burnishes everything so that she can get a varied finish and can control exactly where it goes.

"The textures are always four or five processes layered on top of each other to get the look I want."

Training
Heinrich was trained in the German tradition, working as a goldsmith's apprentice for three years before going on to study for her Masters in jewellery and hollowware design at the Pforzheim Academy. She was taught using Rudolph Steiner's philosophy that the flow of communication between the designer, the jewel and the silence is constant, so that the jeweller is completely at one with the job in hand.

"To this day, when I design I often don't know how I'll build it. I let the piece tell me."

On winning a scholarship to train at the Rochester Institute of Technology in New York, Heinrich was encouraged to use her own story and experiences and to put them into her work. These two styles of training have given Heinrich an advantage, she can use both an intellectual and an emotional approach to her designs.

"When I design, I visualise and I am completely absorbed; I can take a concept and run a thousand variations of that concept through my mind and then I draw the final result. I don't need to go through the drawing process to develop the work because I draw what I finally see and it will be to scale; I see things in three dimensions and I can draw to the tenth of a mm."

ABOVE: Zinnia ring, 2011 – natural silver blister pearl, yellow gold *Winner of the 2011-2012 International Pearl Design Competition Fashion Award.* PHOTOGRAPH BY TIM CALLAHAN

OPPOSITE PAGE: Sanctuary of Innocence pendant, 2006 – natural pearl, rabbit fur, yellow gold PHOTOGRAPH BY BARRY BLAU

A Closer Look

A perfect example of this is her complex linkage and interlocking system that she devised for a series of necklaces and bracelets. It started out as an assignment at college to create a necklace using the same links but in a three-dimensional manner. It took several years for Heinrich to figure out how to make her 'bestseller to be'. Her inspiration came from looking at the four points of a compass. At first glance, the necklace is deceptively simple, it is only on a closer look that one realises its true complexity.

In 2006 Heinrich combined rabbit fur with pearls to create a highly original pendant for her Secret Treasure project for the American Jewelry Design Council. Taking a closer look, the pendant pod has been created using a myriad of short, narrow gold rods creating a textural contrast to the fur. The smooth lustre of the scattered pearls adds a further contrast.

A Sense of Weightlessness

Barbara Heinrich's inspiration has its roots in simple organic pieces. With the increase in gold prices, Heinrich was looking for designs that could be used to create lighter, more affordable jewels for her galleries. Taking leaves and their delicate structure as the starting point, she used roller-printed imprints of the leaves and enhanced the gold foils by the detailed burnishing of the leaves' veins and edges. They have an ethereal quality, which in turn creates a lightness to the form. Staying with the leaf as her inspiration, she created an openwork necklace that defines only the leaves' veins and edges, dressed with diamond raindrops; the piece was the winner of the Gold Category at the 2009 Couture Design Awards.

ABOVE: Hammered Gold Leaf cuff, 2008 – diamond, yellow gold
PHOTOGRAPH BY HAP SAKWA

BELOW: Interlocking Link necklace, 2003 – yellow gold
Shown at the American Jewelry Design Council's travelling exhibition, 'Variations on a Theme: 25 years of Designs from the AJDC'.
PHOTOGRAPH BY BARBARA HEINRICH STUDIO

OPPOSITE PAGE: Leaf Outline necklace, 2009 – diamond, yellow gold
Note that the links all move.
Winner of the 2009 Couture Design Award – Gold category.

From her quest for lighter elements, another theme emerged, that of a simple blade of grass. Wrapping the grass around her finger brought back childhood memories of flowers in the hair; daisy chains around the neck and wrist and coming full circle back to her blade of grass. The matt finish of her gold is contrasted with her signature burnished edges. This theme then evolved into her Spiral Collection. The use of negative space to suggest shapes has created some of her most important jewels to date.

Another piece that explores the concept of negative space is her coral and gold necklace; the coral pit marks are echoed in the openwork gold 'bead'. It is a work of weightlessness and contrasting heavy opacity.

Heinrich's popular collections are exhibited in galleries throughout the United States. Heinrich adapts to what her galleries and clients want, without compromising on style. In the 1980s she designed heavier pieces of jewellery, but in today's economic climate, her jewels are light and make a greater use of the gemstone's natural outline.

ABOVE: Coral and Gold Openframe necklace, 2009 – Mediterranean 'decay' coral, yellow gold

BELOW: Selection of Wrap 'Grass Blade' rings, 2014 – yellow gold with tourmaline; chalcedony, tanzanite, ruby, sapphire, emerald, trillium and diamond accents
PHOTOGRAPH BY TIM CALLAHAN

OPPOSITE PAGE: Spiral 'Grass Blade' necklace – diamond, yellow gold

"When you look at a smooth pure shape, there has to be a broken edge, a fissure or a crevasse. I have a photo of a broken pavement which I took in Whitby – it's perfect. It's smooth and then you come to the edge and you see all the jumbled textures and shapes..."

JACQUELINE CULLEN
A New Twist to an Old Material

Jacqueline Cullen employs constraint in how she uses colour or, perhaps, it would be more accurate to talk about the absence of colour. She creates a sharp and instantly recognisable style using matt and bright surfaces in her Whitby jet jewellery. Inspired by all things volcanic, her underlying design ethos is contrast; there should be two different states, which, through their divergence, create a dramatic dynamic.

Background
Cullen came to jewellery after a career in sculpture and performing art; after three years at Saint Martin's College of Art, she launched herself into the jewellery world. She readily admits that as a student, her creations were more conceptual and sculptural, they were *"quite unwearable, even if they were deep and meaningful!"*

Interested in different materials and what messages those materials could bring to her jewels, Cullen's first contact with Whitby was from a bauble she had collected along with other bits and pieces. She felt an instinctual attraction to the Whitby jet:

> *"It suited my way of doing things and it fitted well with my aesthetics."*

The process used to shape jet attracted her; it is worked by grinding against lapidary wheels, removing material to create a form just as in sculpture. The conchoidal fractures that can be seen in jet are used to tremendous effect to underline the tension and clashes that Cullen seeks in her jewels. Each fissure and crevasse has been shaped by Cullen. The jet arrives in her workshop as a block, with no natural shapes as a guide, and just as a sculptor will chisel out a shape from marble, so Jacqueline Cullen reveals a shape from the jet.

The history of Whitby jet and gold granulation is not lost on Cullen; however, in bringing them together for her jewels, she is firmly focused on the present. Cullen's palette is restricted and more about light than actual colour. Eschewing the high gloss finishes seen on 19th-century jet mourning jewellery, Cullen opts for a matt finish on the jet, which has a softer appearance and is more tactile and sensual.

> *"I don't do it to a pattern, it's about non-planned 'deliberacy'; I'm not planning it but I know what I am doing; these granules need to bunch together in this area and then they need some space and then there needs to be a fissure..."*

The gold is electroformed, meaning that the metal is 'grown' over the surface and the small granules are then manually placed one by one, a labour of love.

ABOVE: Illustration by Richard Wilkinson showing Cullen's Black diamond feather collar
ILLUSTRATION BY RICHARD WILKINSON; PHOTOGRAPH BY COLIN CRISFORD; IMAGE COURTESY OF INTELLIGENT LIFE MAGAZINE (NOW 1843 MAGAZINE)

OPPOSITE PAGE: Black diamond feather collar, 2013 – jet, black diamond, yellow gold wire

ABOVE: Cuff – jet, champagne-coloured diamond, electroform yellow gold

TOP RIGHT: Electroform Gold Leaf ear pendants – jet, yellow gold leaf

RIGHT: Jet Disc Hoop earrings – jet, black diamond, yellow gold

BELOW: Black Diamond Disc cocktail ring – jet, black diamond, white diamond, yellow gold

OPPOSITE PAGE: Faceted Jet bangle – jet, black diamond

Over time, Cullen has gone on to create pieces with a higher value and moved away from the artisan market to that of luxury fine jewellery. Accordingly, in 2011 Cullen started to add diamonds to her collections. She plays with the dramatic contrast between the matt finish of the jet and the bright adamantine lustre of the black diamonds. Having experimented with different sizes of diamond, she has opted for tiny 1mm black diamonds, which have become integral to her design and give a sprinkle of light over the surface of the jet.

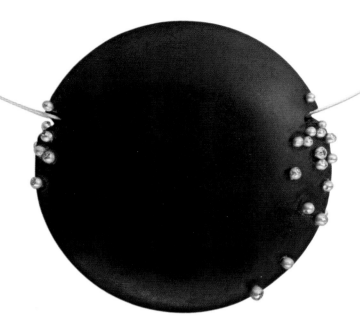

In the same way Cullen uses champagne-coloured diamonds, which are close in colour to 18ct yellow gold, to add glamour to her jewels. She sets many of her champagne- and sherry-coloured diamonds directly into her gold granules, which she then attaches to the jet.

Moving from the electroforming of her gold designs she has created a collection using jet spheres dotted with black diamonds, which can be worn separately as cocktail rings or stacked together to create a statement of unusual organic forms, similar perhaps to the Olgas (Kata Tjuta) in central Australia.

Since 2013, she has been part of Rock Vault, a group of British jewellery designers selected by a board to promote British jewellery design globally.

Recently, inspired by Modernist architecture, Cullen has been introducing a more geometric pyramidal form to her work. She is a designer to watch. With an original style, she breathes new life into old traditions, whilst creating jewels that are both intriguing and contemporary.

TOP: Jet pendant – jet, champagne-coloured diamond, electroform yellow gold

TOP LEFT: Jet Disc hoop earrings – jet, champagne-coloured diamond, yellow gold

BOTTOM LEFT: Jet Sphere cocktail rings – jet, black diamond, yellow gold

OPPOSITE PAGE: Pyramidal Form earrings – jet, black diamond, yellow gold

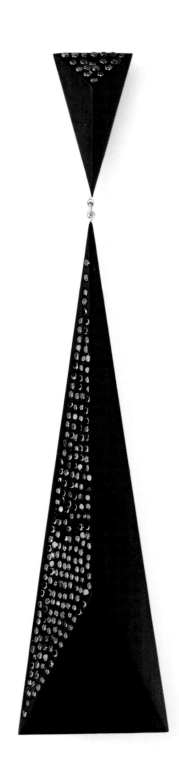

"When I developed the Crown Collection in 1991, one of my first signature textures was sumptious brocade fabric, resembling lace over gold."

CYNTHIA BACH
The Filigree Queen

Ebullient, with a larger-than-life personality, Cynthia Bach is a passionate jewellery designer who transforms old ideas into whimsical and dramatic jewels for today. Bach was always destined to become a jeweller. As a child, she took gemstones out of her mother's jewels to place into the gold treasure chest brought home by her roving US Air Force officer father. At college she experimented with sand casting (a method used in ancient times), using copper, plaster and wax moulds as well as coffee cans; and she persuaded her arts tutor, Bob Howell, to set up a jewellery course. Wanting to learn everything there was to know about the art of jewellery making, she apprenticed to master jeweller Jim Matthews for three years. On graduating from McMurray University in 1982, she and Jim Matthews married and have continued working together ever since.

The Telephone Call
1989 was the year that shaped Bach's destiny. After receiving a mysterious telephone call enquiring whether she and her husband would be interested in working for "a jewellery brand", negotiations revealed that it was Van Cleef & Arpels. Adventure and opportunity to design even more interesting pieces lured the couple to Los Angeles where they thrived, designing and working with the best. When the collaboration ended three years later, Cynthia Bach took her original collection to Neiman Marcus. The 'Crown Lady' talked her way in with her distinctive collection of gold and gem-set crown pins and rings.

Inspiration
Bach continues to be inspired by the past. She has built up an impressive collection of 15th-century crowns and relics from old churches, which include chalices, crosses and monstrances. From these ornately decorated artefacts spring new ideas and new ways of wearing a traditional concept. Crowns become rings and bracelets, and bracelets in turn become tiaras.

LEFT: Queen Lenore Crown brooch, 1988 – emerald, ruby, diamond, yellow gold

OPPOSITE PAGE: Peacock brooch, 2012 – carved labradorite, coral, tanzanite, Paraiba tourmaline, multi-coloured diamond, platinum, yellow gold.
Honourable mention at the AGTA Awards, 2013.

The Fine Art of Filigree

Bach is particularly well known for her work in filigree, a peasant tradition still popular in India and in other Asian cultures, dating back to Mesopotamia in 3,000BC and to ancient Egypt. Threads of silver and gold are twisted into lace-like outlines and sometimes combined with small granules of the same metal to create more elaborate ornamentation. Filigree was used in Italian and French metalwork from the 17th century to the late 19th century and Bach's inspiration comes from the great Italian jewellery master of the 19th century, Fortunato Pio Castellani.

Bach has combined various techniques to create her signature Gitan filigree, brocade and granulation work, having made her own tools in order to carve and sculpt the extremely delicate and intricate filigree in wax before it is cast.

TOP AND OPPOSITE PAGE: Odalesque du Soleil brooch (front and back) – diamond, yellow gold filigree work

ABOVE: Charm bracelet – gold filigree work

Rock Crystal

Bach's use of rock crystal is recent and takes its inspiration from the 1920s and '30s, when rock crystal became fashionable due to the extraordinary work of a few forward-looking designers, such as Boivin, Fouquet and Cartier. Bach combines her 'Gitan' metalwork with the transparency of rock crystal, creating a contemporary and lively effect.

> "I love the transparency and 'floatiness' of rock crystal against the solid rich permanence of metal."

Red Carpet Flair

For the 2004 Oscars, Cate Blanchett asked Bach to come up with some ideas; she particularly loved Bach's collection inspired by the jewels of the Indian Mughal period. Playing with the jewels, they piled on bracelet after bracelet, and a gold necklace was slung seductively down the bare back of Blanchett's Jean Paul Gaultier gown. The effect was instant, from the front, Blanchett looked like a thoroughly modern minimalist young woman, but from the back she was transformed into an Indian Princess.

Worn by Hollywood A listers, Cynthia Bach's jewels are firmly rooted in the now, with whispers of the past.

TOP: Collection of Crown rings – diamond, platinum

LEFT: Gitan ring – cabochon pink tourmaline, diamond, gold filigree work

OPPOSITE PAGE: Rock Crystal Maltese Cross pendant – rock crystal, diamond, platinum filigree work
Winner of the Couture Design Awards 2014 – Platinum category.

Alma Pihl

Coco Chanel
**Photograph by Man Ray, 1937. Courtesy of Chanel, Paris;
© Man Ray Trust / ADAGP Paris, 2012**

PART I

ALMA PIHL (1888-1976)
Further Reading: *Jewels from Imperial Saint Petersburg* by Ulla Tillander-Godenhielm (Unicorn Press Ltd., 2014)
Website: www.wartski.com

COCO CHANEL (1883-1971)
Exhibition: 1932: Bijoux de Diamants.
Further Reading: *L'Irrégulière L'itinéraire de Coco Chanel* by Edmonde Charles-Roux (Grasset & Fasquelle, 1974)
Website: www.chanel.com

SUZANNE BELPERRON (1900-1983)
Further Reading: *Jewelry by Suzanne Belperron* by Patricia Corbett, Ward Landrigan, Nico Landrigan, and Karl Lagerfeld (Thames & Hudson, 2015). *Suzanne Belperron* by Olivier Baroin and Sylvie Raulet (Antique Collectors' Club, 2011)
Website: www.belperron.com

JULIETTE MOUTARD
Further Reading: *René Boivin, Joaillier* by Françoise Cailles (Les Editions de L'Amateur, 1994)

OLGA TRITT
Exhibitions: 1929: Arts Club of Chicago; 1939: World's Fair New York
Accolades: February and May 1938, April and August 1939, May 1940: Featured on the cover of *Vogue*

ELISABETH TRESKOW (1898-1992)
Accolades: 1933, 1935, 1936: First prize of the German Society for Goldsmiths; 1937: Gold medal Paris World's Fair; 1938: Golden ring of honour from the German Society for Goldsmiths. Accolades came from Bavaria, the North Rhine-Westphalia and the City of Cologne
Further Reading: *Elisabeth Treskow: Goldschmiedekunst des 20 Jahrhunderts* (Museum für Angewandte Kunst, 1990)

MARGARET DE PATTA (1903-1964)
Exhibitions: 2012: 'Space-Light-Structure: The Jewelry of Margaret De Patta' retrospective at the Oakland Museum of California and the Museum of Arts and Design, New York

JEANNE TOUSSAINT (1887-1976)
Further Reading: *Cartier Jewelers Extraordinary* by Hans Nadelhoffer (Thames & Hudson, 1984). *Cartier – Style and History* (Réunion des Musées Nationaux – Grand Palais, 2013). *Cartier – The Legend* by Gilberte Gautier (Arlington Books, London)
Website: www.cartier.com

Suzanne Belperron
Courtesy of Belperron, New York

Elisabeth Treskow
ullstein bild / ullstein bild via Getty Images

Margaret de Patta
Photograph by Georg Strauss, 1948. Courtesy of the Archives of American Art, Smithsonian Institution

Jeanne Toussaint
Photograph by Nick Welsh, 1960s. Courtesy of the Cartier Archives, Paris

PART 2

Line Vautrin
Courtesy of Marie-Laure Bonnaud

Margret Craver
Courtesy of Silver Salon Forums

Vivianna Torun Bülow-Hübe
Courtesy of the Archive department at Georg Jensen

Nanna Ditzel
Courtesy of the Archive department at Georg Jensen

LINE VAUTRIN (1913-1997)
Exhibition: 1937: Paris World's Fair
Further Reading: *Line Vautrin – Bijoux et Objets* by Line Vautrin and Patrick Mauriès (Thames & Hudson, 1999)
Website: www.line-vautrin.fr

MARGRET CRAVER (1907-2010)
Exhibition: Museum of Fine Arts, Boston – Permanent collection
Accolades: 1985: American Craft Council's Gold Medal
Further Reading: *Making Hand Wrought Sterling Silver Jewellery* by Margret Craver (Handy & Harman, 1945)

VIVIANNA TORUN BÜLOW-HÜBE (1927-2004)
Exhibitions: 1961: 'The International Exhibition of Modern Jewellery 1890-1961', Worshipful Company of Goldsmiths; 1992: Musée des Arts décoratifs, Paris – Retrospective of 45 years of her work
Accolades: 1960: Lunning Prize for design; 1960: Gold medal at the Milan Triennale; London; 1992: Prince Eugen medal for outstanding artistic achievement
Further Reading: *Conversation with Vivianna Torun Bülow-Hübe* by Ann Westin (Carlssons, 1993)
Website: www.georgjensen.com

NANNA DITZEL (1923-2005)
Exhibitions: Numerous retrospectives for her designs in furniture and textiles as well as jewellery
Accolades: 1951, 1954, 1957: Silver medal – Milan Triennale; 1956 Lunning Prize for design; 1960: Gold medal at Milan Triennale
Further Reading: *Motion and Beauty – The Book of Nanna Ditzel* by Henrik Sten Moller; Rhodos International Science and Art Publishers (1998)
Website: www.georgjensen.com

MARIANNE OSTIER (1902-1976)
Exhibition: 1966: Finch College Museum of Art
Accolades: 1954, 1955, 1956: Diamond USA Award; 1960: First person to become a member of the International Diamond Academy after becoming a laureate 5 times (1955-1960)
Further Reading: *Jewels and the Woman – The Romance, Magic and Art of Feminine Adornment* by Marianne Ostier (New York, Horizon Press, 1958)

BARBARA ANTON (1926-2007)
Exhibitions: 1964: New York World's Fair; Museum of Fine Arts, Boston – Permanent collection
Accolades: 23 awards including the International Diamond Award and from the Cultured Pearl Associations of America and Japan

GERDA FLÖCKINGER CBE
Exhibitions: Numerous exhibitions and works in many museums' permanent collections including: Bristol City Museum and Art Gallery, Bristol, UK; Crafts Council, UK; Museum of Fine Arts Boston; Pompidou Centre, Paris; Schmuckmuseum, Pforzheim, Germany; Victoria & Albert Museum, UK; Worshipful Company of Goldsmiths, UK
Website: www.gerdaflockinger.net

ASTRID FOG (1911-1993)
Further Reading: *Georg Jensen – Silver & Design* by Thomas C. and Birgitte de Roepstorff Thulstrup (Gads Forlag, 2004)
Website: www.georgjensen.com

CORNELIA ROETHEL
Exhibition: 2015: Caroline van Hoek Gallery, Brussels

Astrid Fog
Courtesy of the Archive department at
Georg Jensen

Marianne Ostier

Barbara Anton
Courtesy of Kimberly Klosterman

Gerda Flöckinger
1955, Courtesy of the photographer Corry Bevington
Archive

Cornelia Roethel
Courtesy of Cornelia Roethel

PART 2 continued

Catherine Noll
Keystone Pictures USA/Alamy Stock Photo

Angela Cummings
Courtesy of Angela Cummings

Elsa Peretti
Courtesy of Tiffany & Co.

Wendy Ramshaw
Courtesy of Wendy Ramshaw

CATHERINE NOLL (1945-1994)
Further Reading: *Catherine Noll* by Chantal Bizot (Éditions du Regard, 2001)

ANGELA CUMMINGS
Website: www.assael.com

ELSA PERETTI
Further Reading: *Fifteen of my Fifty with Tiffany* (Fashion Institute of Technology, New York, 1990)
Website: www.tiffany.com

WENDY RAMSHAW CBE
Exhibitions: 1993: 'Art In Architecture', Royal Society Of Arts (UK). Numerous works in permanent collections: Australian National Gallery, Canberra (Australia); Birmingham City Art Gallery, Birmingham (UK); Cooper-Hewitt National Design Museum, Smithsonian Institution, New York (USA); The Crafts Council, London (UK); Kundstindustrimuseet, Oslo (Norway); Musée Des Arts Décoratifs, Paris (France); Museum of Modern Art, Kyoto (Japan); Museum Für Kunst und Gewerbe, Hamburg (Germany); National Gallery of Victoria (Australia); National Museum of Wales, Cardiff (UK); Nordenfjeldske Kunstindustrimuseet, Trondheim (Norway); Philadelphia Museum Of Art, Philadelphia (USA); Royal Scottish Museum, Edinburgh (UK); Schmuckmuseum, Pforzheim (Germany); Science Museum, London (UK); Stedelijk Museum, Amsterdam (Holland); Victoria & Albert Museum, London (UK); Worshipful Company Of Goldsmiths, London (UK)
Accolades: 1972: Council of Industrial Design Award; 1975: De Beers Diamond International Award
Further Reading: *Jewellery Studies Volume 4* by Jack Ogden and Johanna Awdry (1990); *Room of Dreams* by Wendy Ramshaw (The Harley Gallery & Ruthin Craft Centre, 2012); *Picasso's Ladies – Jewellery by Wendy Ramshaw* by Anna Beatriz Chadour-Sampson (Arnoldsche Art Publishers, 1998)

MARINA B
Further Reading: *Marina B – The Art of Jewelry Design* by Viviane Jutheau de Witt (Skira, 2003)
Website: marinab.com

MARIE-CAROLINE DE BROSSES
Accolades: 2016: International Women's Day talk held at the NMWA Museum

MARILYN COOPERMAN
Website: marilynfcooperman.com

PALOMA PICASSO
Website: www.tiffany.com

Marina B
Courtesy of Giorgio Bulgari, Marina B

Marie-Caroline de Brosses
Courtesy of Marie-Caroline de Brosses

Marilyn Cooperman
Courtesy of Franz Snieders

Paloma Picasso
Courtesy of Tiffany & Co.

PART 3

Victoire de Castellane
Courtesy of Dior Fine Jewelry

Alexandra Mor
Courtesy of Alexandra Mor

Ornella Iannuzzi
Courtesy of Ornella Iannuzzi

Neha Dani
Courtesy of Neha Dani

VICTOIRE DE CASTELLANE
Recent Accolades: Exhibitions: 2011: Gagosian Gallery, Fleur d'excès; 2014: Animalvegetablemineral; 2007: awarded the Légion d'Honneur; 2015: Visionaries Award from the Museum of Arts and Design of New York
Further Reading: *Dior Joaillerie – The Beauty and Craftsmanship of Dior Fine Jewelry,* by Michele Heuze; Rizzoli (2012)
Website: www.dior.com

ALEXANDRA MOR
Website: www.alexandramor.com

ORNELLA IANNUZZI
Recent Accolades: 2016: Gold Award. Goldsmith's Craft & Design Council Awards, UK – Jeweller category; 2015: UK Jewellery Awards – Jewellery Designer of the Year category; 2015: The Goldsmiths' Company Premier Award – Goldsmith's Craft & Design Council, UK; 2015: Gold Award, Fine Jewellery – IJL Precious Jewellery category – Goldsmith's Craft & Design Council, UK; 2014: – Lauréate du Prix D'Excellence – TTF Awards – France/China
Website: ornella-iannuzzi.com

NEHA DANI
Recent Accolades: 2014: Rising Star award – JCK Las Vegas
Website: www.nehadani.com

PAULA CREVOSHAY
Recent Accolades: Exhibitions: 2002: Carnegie Museum; GIA Museum; Lizzadro Museum – Voices of the Earth; 2009: Headley – Whitney Museum – Beyond Color; Smithsonian Institution – Conchita brooch, permanent collection; 2013: Carnegie Museum – Garden of Light; 2016: Musée de Minéralogie, Ecole des Mines, Paris – Illuminations, From Earth to Jewel.
Website: www.crevoshay.com

NATHALIE CASTRO
Recent Accolades: 2005: Laureat Comté Colbert; Exhibition: 2006: 'Joailliers Créateurs Exhibition, Paris

CLAIRE CHOISNE
Website: www.boucheron.com

BINA GOENKA
Website: binagoenka.com

Paula Crevoshay
Courtesy of Paula Crevoshay

Nathalie Castro
Courtesy of Nathalie Castro

Claire Choisne
Courtesy of Boucheron, Paris

Bina Goenka
Courtesy of Bina Goenka

Carla Amorim
Courtesy of Carla Amorim

Monique Péan
Courtesy of Monique Péan

Michelle Ong
Courtesy of Michelle Ong

Kara Ross
Courtesy of Kara Ross

CARLA AMORIM
Website: carlaamorim.com.br

MONIQUE PÉAN
Recent Accolades: 2015: First runner up Editor's Choice – Couture, Las Vegas
Website: moniquepean.com

MICHELLE ONG
Recent Exhibitions: 2006: Burrell Collection, Glasgow – Exquisite Jewels; 2011: Retrospective – Asia House, London
Further Reading: *21st-Century Jewellery Designers – An Inspired Style* by Juliet Weir-de La Rochefoucauld (Antique Collectors' Club, 2013)
Website: www.carnetjewellery.com

KARA ROSS
Recent Exhibitions: 2013: 'Aluminati: Students to Stars', GIA Museum; 2014: Museum of Art & Design, New York; 2015 & 2016: Masterpiece, London
Recent Accolades: 2008: Rising Star Accessories Award – Fashion Group International; 2012: Design Award – Women's Jewelry Association;

LYDIA COURTEILLE
Recent Accolades: 2012; 2013: nominated for the category 'audace et rareté', Talents d'or du Centre du Luxe et la Creation, Paris; 2012: Couture, Las Vegas – Award Best coloured gemstone jewel above 20,000$ US; 2013: Aesthetic Champion of the Champions HKTDC Hong Kong; 2014: Aesthetic Award – AGTA Spectrum Awards
Further Reading: *Lydia Courteille – Extraordinary Jewellery of Imagination and Dreams* by Juliet Weir-de La Rochefoucauld (ACC Art Books, 2016); *21st-Century Jewellery Designers – An Inspired Style* by Juliet Weir-de La Rochefoucauld (Antique Collectors' Club, 2013)
Website: www.lydiacourteille.com

SUZANNE SYZ
Further Reading: *Suzanne Syz – Art Jewels* by Suzanne Syz (Assouline, 2013); *21st-Century Jewellery Designers – An Inspired Style* by Juliet Weir-de La Rochefoucauld (Antique Collectors' Club, 2013)
Website: www.suzannesyz.ch

SYLVIE CORBELIN
Website: sylvie-corbelin.com

KAORU KAY AKIHARA
Recent Accolades: 2017: Matsuzakaya Art Museum, Nagoya – Retrospective – Four Seasons of Gimel –Tracing of Beauty – God is in the detail
Further Reading: *21st-Century Jewellery Designers – An Inspired Style* by Juliet Weir-de La Rochefoucauld (Antique Collectors' Club, 2013)
Website: www.gimel.co.jp

KATEY BRUNINI
Recent Exhibitions: 2017: San Diego Museum of Art – Art Alive
Recent Accolades: 2014: Most Fashion Forward/Editor's Choice, AGTA Awards Spectrum Awards
Website: kbrunini.com

LUZ CAMINO
Recent Exhibitions: 2016 & 2017: TEFAF Maastricht
Further Reading: *21st-Century Jewellery Designers – An Inspired Style* by Juliet Weir-de La Rochefoucauld (Antique Collectors' Club, 2013)

CINDY CHAO
Exhibition: Royal Butterfly brooch in Smithsonian Institution permanent collection since 2009; 2016: Biennale des Antiquaires, Paris
Website: www.cindychao.com

Lydia Courteille
Courtesy of Lydia Courteille

Suzanne Syz
Courtesy of Suzanne Syz

Sylvie Corbelin
Courtesy of Sylvie Corbelin

Kaoru Kay Akihara
Courtesy of Kaoru Kay Akihara

PART 3 continued

Katey Brunini
Courtesy of Katey Brunini

Luz Camino
Courtesy of Luz Camino

Cindy Chao
Courtesy of Cindy Chao

Aida Bergsen
Courtesy of Aida Bergsen

AIDA BERGSEN
Further Reading: *Fine Jewelry Couture: Contemporary Heirlooms* by Olivier Dupon (Thames & Hudson, 2016)
Website: www.aidabergsen.com

ANNA HU
Further Reading: *Anna Hu: Symphony of Jewels – Opus 1* by Janet Zapata, Carol Woolton, David Warren and David Behl (The Vendome Press, New York, 2012). *21st Century Jewellery Designers – An Inspired Style* by Juliet Weir-de La Rochefoucauld (Antique Collectors' Club, 2013)
Website: www.anna-hu.com

BARBARA HEINRICH
Recent Accolades: 2009: Couture Las Vegas – Best of Gold; 2011: Gold distinction award – MJSA Vision Awards; 2011: Lustre Award and Fashion Award – International Pearl Design Competition Cultured Pearl Association
Website: www.barbaraheinrichstudio.com

JACQUELINE CULLEN
Website: www.jacquelinecullen.com

CYNTHIA BACH
Recent Accolades: 2013: Honourable Mention – AGTA Spectrum Awards; 2014: 1st Prize Platinum – Couture, Las Vegas
Website: www.cynthiabach.com

FURTHER READING

ARTS & CRAFTS
International Arts & Crafts by Karen Livingstone; V&A Publications (2013)

Maker & Muse – Women and Early Twentieth Century Art Jewelry by Elyse Zom Karlin; The Richard H. Driehaus Museum (2015)

GENERAL
30 ans de Dîners en Ville by Gabriel-Louis Pringué; Editions Lacurne (2012)

Paris 1937 – Worlds on Exhibition by James D. Herbert; Cornell University Press (1998)

Beaux-Arts Exposition Coloniale Internationale de Paris 1931

The Journals of Jean Cocteau; Criterion Press, New York (1956)

Artists' Jewellery – Pre-Raphaelite to Arts and Crafts by Charlotte Gere and Geoffrey C. Munn; Antique Collectors' Club

American Jewelry – Glamour and Tradition by Penny Proddow and Debra Healy; Rizzoli (1987)

Georg Jensen – Reflections; Rizzoli (2014)

Beyond Extravagance – A Royal Collection of Gems and Jewels by Amin Jaffer; Assouline (2013)

Paul Iribe by Raymond Bachollet; Denoël (1982)

Les Bijoux de Chanel by Patrick Mauriès; Editions de La Martnière (2012)

L'Histoire des Van Cleef et Des Arpels by Jean Jacques Richard; Books on Demand (2010)

Art Deco Jewelry by Laurence Mouillefarine and Evelyne Possémé; Thames & Hudson (2009)

Pioneers of Modern Craft by Margot Goatts; Manchester University Press (1997)

Fabergé and the Russian Jewellers by Geoffrey C. Munn and Katherine Purcell; Wartski, London (2006)

No Stone Unturned by Claudine Seroussi Bretagne; Ernst Färber, Lucas Rarities, London (2012)

Bejewelled by Tiffany 1837-1987, edited by Clare Phillips; Yale University Press (2006)

Tiffany Style – 170 Years of Design by John Loring; Abrams (2008)

Van Cleef & Arpels – Treasures and Legends by Vincent Meylan; Antique Collectors' Club (2014)

Anna Hu
Courtesy of Anna Hu

Barbara Heinrich
Courtesy of Barbara Heinrich

Jacqueline Cullen
Courtesy of Jacqueline Cullen

Cynthia Bach
Courtesy of Cynthia Bach

APPENDIX 2: TOUSSAINT

Louis Cartier overlooked celebrated designer Charles Jacqueau for the role of Creative Designer in favour of Jeanne Toussaint. He wrote to his son-in-law, René Revillon to inform him of his decision. Below is the translation, see the original letter on p.76.

My Dear René,

I am handing you these designs for your opinion. As much as I believe that they should be made in rock crystal and diamonds I would like to see something which is more original or new. However if you find them to your liking and you think that they would sell then make them, we will learn from experience if they sell or not.*

I have no false pride and I would be delighted if someone was capable to take over from me to create the stock. As Jeanne Toussaint has excellent taste and is universally appreciated I am ready to leave designs for stock on her signature and under her responsibility.

It is in the obvious interest of the company to give her the artistic direction in my absence, even though I am afraid that it will be another new responsibility for her. I hope to be in Paris soon and would be happy to see you again as well as Anne-Marie. I hope that you are all well.

with my sincerest respect

Louis Cartier
Inform Collin of this decision.

* Could these be the bracelets made for stock in 1930 and sold to Gloria Swanson in 1932?

ABOVE: A jeweller working on the Bib necklace, ordered from Cartier, Paris by The Duchess of Windsor in 1947.
IMAGE COURTESY OF CARTIER, PARIS

OPPOSITE PAGE: Cartier: Bib necklace, 1947 – 1 heart-shaped amethyst, 27 emerald-cut amethysts, 1 oval-cut amethyst, turquoise cabochons, brilliant and baguette-cut diamonds, platinum, twisted 18kt and 20kt yellow gold
The Duke of Windsor supplied the amethysts for this special order for The Duchess of Windsor. The parure, which also included a brooch, earrings, bracelet and a ring "went on to form the focus of an order placed by The Duchess with Dior for a gown designed to go with the parure for a ball held in the Orangerie at the Château de Versailles in June 1953." (exhibition catalogue for 'Cartier Style and History' at the Grand Palais, Paris, 2013/2014).
PHOTOGRAPH BY VINCENT WULVERYCK; IMAGE COURTESY OF CARTIER, PARIS

4 nov. I932

Affaire CHANEL

Nous apprenons par un article tendancieux et très maladroit paru dans l'Intransigeant du 25 octobre I932 que la maison Chanel fait exécuter des bijoux en joaillerie et qu'elle organise une exposition pour le 5 nov.

La Chambre syndicale étant avertie, le président écrit à Mme Chanel et à l'Intransigeant.

Nous apprenons que les bijoux auraient été faits par Lemeunier et Rudhart qui ont employé plus de I5 ouvriers chacun pendant plusieurs mois.

3 novembre

Réunion à la Chambre syndicale: M.M. Chaumet, Cartier, Van Cleef Mellerio, Mauboussin, Radius

M. Paul Iribe, dessinateur, représentant de la maison Chanel expose la situation.

Mme Chanel n'a aucunement l'idée de faire concurrence aux joailliers; les négociants en diamant de Londres (Diamond Corporation Limited) auraient choisi Mme Chanel pour faire une propagande en faveur du diamant et surtout avec l'idée de supplanter le bijou faux. Les pierres sont donc confiées, tous les frais de monture, publicité, etc... pé de la fabrication. Mr Iribe a exécuté les dessins et s'est occu-

L'exposition est faite au profit d'oeuvres charitables présidées par la Princesse de Poix, Mme Paul Dupuy, Maurice Donnay. Il y aura ensuite une exposition à Londres Patronnée par la marquise de Londonderry et une à Rome, sous le patronage de la Princesse Colonna.

Après discussion nous remettons à M. Iribe une note demandant que les bijoux ne soient pas vendus, qu'ils soient démontés après les expositions sous le contrôle de la Chambre syndicale et que l'on indique aux visiteurs que les modèles peuvent être exécutés par leurs joailliers attitrés. Dans ce cas une redevance pourrait être accordée à M. Iribe, représentant de la D.C.L.

Nous demandons également une participation au produit de l'exposition, au profit des oeuvres de la Chambre syndicale.

La Diamond Corporation Limited est l'ex De Beers Syndicate

brut/-

4 novembre

On nous prévient que Mme Chanel n'accepte pas nos propositions; elle parait très irritée d'un article paru dans Candide d'hier auquel la Chambre syndicale est étrangère.

5 novembre

Mlle Chanel devait faire les honneurs de son exposition au Pt de la Ch. Synd. accompagné de M.M. Langérock & Radius V.Pdts ces M.M. sont reçus par M. Iribe, Mlle Chanel s'excusant à cause de son état de santé.

9 novembre

Rendez-vous avec le Pt de la Ch. Synd. Mr Radius & M. Iribe. Aucun fait nouveau. M. Iribe prétend que plusieurs pièces auraient été achetées par certains de nos confrères (?) Il prépare une exposition à New York et parait décidé à passer outre aux demandes des joailliers

12 novembre

Réunion à la Ch. Synd., rapport de M. Georges Fouquet qui est adopté. Mr Arpels proteste contre l'assertion de Mlle Chanel selon laquelle plusieurs de ses bijoux auraient été achetés par W.C. ce qui est absolument faux. A l'étude une série d'articles faits par des critiques d'art

I6 novembre

Visite à M. Baschet de M.M. Fouquet-Lapar, Georges Fouquet, Chaumet Mellerio et Radius. Les joailliers reconnaissent en principe que la propagande en faveur du bijou est intéressante pour eux mais regrettent:

I°) la façon dont l'article de l'Illustration a présenté l'Exposition Chanel et en particulier le titre "Rénovation du bijou" cette rénovation se traduisant par la création de modèles surannés n'apportant aucune idée nouvelle

2°) la fausse affirmation que la femme élégante portait du bijou faux

3°) l'importance exagérée que la couturière se donne dans cette affaire. L'Illustration a donc servi de paravent pour la publicité d'une maison de couture.

M. Jacques Baschet a été au courant de l'émotion suscitée par cet article dont il regrette l'importance et dont il critique la rédaction. Ils ont été sollicités par des présidents d'oeuvres charitables à qui ils n'ont pu refuser leur concours, mais les rédacteurs ont dépassé les instructions données.

25 novembre

M. Lemeunier, fabricant joaillier, a reçu 7 millions de brillants de la Diamond Corporation a charge par lui de faire les fonds pour un prix convenu de 600.000 frs. Lemeunier a payé la taxe à l'importation de 4 % soit 280.000 frs sans avoir fait vérifier les brillants par un des experts désignés par l'administration des douanes (M.M. Langérock & Radius) Or au moment de faire la réexpédition des bijoux qui doivent se trouver à Londres pour une exposition vers le 80 novembre, M. Lemeunier a été avisé par l'administration qu'il ne pourrait pas obtenir le remboursement des 280.000 frs. Le syndicat prétend que la faute incombe à M. Lemeunier qui doit seul en supporter les conséquences.

What was all the fuss about? The beginning of the 1930s was a time of massive economic decline and recession that affected all social classes. The crash of the New York stock exchange in 1929, and the consequences worldwide, led to a great lull in diamond sales, which was only exacerbated by a saturation of the diamond market after the discovery of deposits at Lichtenburg and Namaqualand. The public, aware of these new stocks, were losing confidence in the stability of diamond prices. The International Diamond Corporation, led by Ernest Oppenheimer, needed to bring diamonds back into favour and to the fore of high jewellery. They chose Coco Chanel, already a household name with a reputation for contemporary chic.

The Jewellery Houses in the Place Vendôme were up in arms about the idea that a mere dressmaker had the audacity to design diamond jewellery, which, to add insult to injury, was very forward thinking and really looked nothing like traditional high jewellery. They held several meetings about what to do with the upstart Coco Chanel... and refused to allow the jewels to be sold, insisting that they be broken up after the exhibition.

These offical documents detail the extraordinary negotiations:

4th November, 1932
We learn from a clumsy and mendacious article which appeared in the *Intransigeant* on October 1932 that the House of Chanel is making jewellery with precious gemstones and that they are organising an exhibition for the 5th November.

The 'Chambre syndicale' have been notified, the president is writing to Mme Chanel and to the *Intransigeant*. We learn that the jewellery has been made by Lemeunier and Rudhart who have each employed more than 15 workmen for several months.

3rd November
Meeting at the 'Chambre syndicale': Messrs. Chaumet, Cartier, Van Cleef, Mellerio, Mauboussin, Radius

Mr. Paul Iribe, designer, representing the House of Chanel exposes the situation.

Mme Chanel has no intentention of competing with the jewellers; the diamond dealers in London (Diamond Corporation Limited) had chosen Mme Chanel in order to create a favourable message for the diamond and certainly with the intention of displacing costume jewellery. The gemstones were thus assigned, with the costs of their setting, advertising, etc...at the D.C.L.'s expense. Mr. Iribe carried out the drawings and oversaw their creation.

The exhibition is in aid of charitable works presided over by the Princess de Poix, Mme Paul Dupuy, Maurice Donnay. There will then be an exhibition in London under the patronage of the Marchioness of Londonderry and one in Rome, under patronage of the Princess of Colonna.

After discussion, we wrote to Mr. Paul Iribe asking that the jewellery should not be sold, that they should be broken up after the exhibitions under the control of the 'Chambre syndicale' and that it should be indicated to the visitors that the models could be executed by their own jewellers. In this case a license fee could be accorded to Mr. Iribe, representing the D.C.L.

We also ask for a share of the profits from the exhibition to profit the works of the 'Chambre syndicale'.

The Diamond Corporation Limited is the ex De Beers Syndicate.

4th November
We are told that Mme Chanel does not accept our propositions; she seems very irritated by an article which appeared in the *Candide* yesterday of which the 'Chambre syndicale' has no knowledge.

5th November
Mlle Chanel should have honoured the President of the 'Chambre syndicale' accompanied by Messrs. Langerock & Radius, Vice presidents, at her exhibition. They were received by Mr. Iribe, Mlle. Chanel being excused due to her state of health.

9th November
Meeting with the President of the 'Chambre Syndicale' Mr. Radius and Mr. Iribe.

Nothing new. Mr. Iribe pretends that several pieces have already been bought by certain colleagues (?) He is preparing an exhibition in New York and seems decided to ignore the jewellers' demands.

12th November
Meeting at the 'Chambre syndicale', report by Mr. Georges Fouquet is adopted. Mr. Arpels protests against the assertion by Mlle. Chanel that several of her jewels were bought by W.C., which is absolutely not true. A series of articles written by some art critics are being studied.

16th November
Visit to Mr. Baschet of Messrs. Fouquet-Lapar, Georges Fouquet, Chaumet, Mellerio and Radius. The jewellers recognise in principle that the propaganda in favour of the jewel is interesting but they regret:

1) the way in which the article in *L'Illustration* presented the Chanel Exhibition and in particular the title 'The Jewel's Renewal', this renewal translated into the creation of outmoded models which introduced nothing new

2) the false affirmation that the elegant woman is wearing costume jewellery

3) the exaggerated importance that this dress-maker gives to the affair. *L'Illustration* thus served as a front for the advertising of a couture house.

Mr. Jacques Baschet knew of the emotion that this article incited and he regrets its importance and he criticises the editor. They had been asked by the presidents of the charities to whom they could not refuse to help, but the writers went beyond their instructions.

25th November
M. Lemeunier, jewellery artisan, received 7 million brilliants from the Diamond Corporation charged by him to make up the basis for an agreed price of 600,000francs. Lemeunier paid a tax of 4 % [sic; 46⅔ %] on their importation that is 280,000francs without having the brilliants verified by a designated expert by the customs administration (Messrs. Langerock & Radius). Thus at the moment when the jewellery was to be re-expedited to London for an exhibition around the 30th November, M. Lemeunier was advised by the administration that he would not be able to be reimbursed for the 280,000francs. The Syndicate claims that the fault is incumbent on M. Lemeunier who must alone support the consequences.

ACKNOWLEDGEMENTS

BELOW: Lydia Courteille: Sahara collection, Dung Beetle ring, 2017 – azurite, hauynite, topazolite, hessonite garnet, brown diamond, white diamond, yellow gold

OPPOSITE: Line Vautrin: Ramses necklace – turquoise enamel, bronze
PHOTOGRAPH BY JEAN-CLAUDE MARLAUD; IMAGE COURTESY MARIE LAURE BONNAUD VAUTRIN

OVERLEAF: Kaoru Kay Akihara for Gimel: Stick Man pin – black rough diamond, diamond, platinum

A book such as this is the product of the efforts and generosity of so many different people, many who went the extra mile to find a text, photo or an introduction. I would especially like to thank Olivier Baroin who always found a way for me to move forward when I found myself up against a wall.

I owe much to the many gallery owners, archivists and auction houses, who have been so enthusiastic and generous with their time, knowledge and numerous images. It goes without saying that the individual jewellery designers in Parts Two and Three have been of great support – without them there would be no book!

I should like to thank: Kaoru Kay Akihara; Carla Amorim; Kelly Amorim; Lamia Icame, Artcurial; Assael; Cynthia Bach; Véronique Bamps of Véronique Bamps, Monaco; Terri Barbero; Ward Landrigan, Nico Landrigan and Caroline Stetson Perkowski at Belperron LLC and Verdura; Aida Bergsen; Graeme Thompson, Susan Abeles and Jean Ghika at Bonham's; Marie-Laure Bonnaud-Vautrin; Caroline Boom; Jennifer Riley, Museum of Fine Arts, Boston; Nathalie de Place and Claudine Sablier, Boucheron; Claudine Seroussi Bretagne; Marie-Caroline de Brosses; Jean-Pierre Brun; Katey Brunini; Giorgio Bulgari; Marina Bulgari; Françoise Cailles; Luz Camino; Peita Carnavale; Sandrine Carrière; Alain Cartier; Michel Aliaga of Cartier; Victoire de Castellane; Nathalie Castro; Cécile Goddet-Dirles and Philippe Mougenot, Chanel; Cindy Chao; Chris Chavez; Claire Choisne; Vanessa Cron at Christie's; David Chu; Shawn Waldron and Pamela Griffiths at Condé Nast Archives; Marilyn F. Cooperman; Sylvie Corbelin; Lydia Courteille; Paula Crevoshay; Jacqueline Cullen; Angela Cummings; Neha Dani; Chris Davies; Jérôme Gautier of Dior Fine Jewelry; Dennie Nanna Ditzel; William Drucker, Drucker Antiques; Emma Farnworth; Fiona Druckenmiller and Thomas Tolan of the FD Gallery, New York; Avanti Goenka; Bina Goenka; Tomoko Hara; Hilary Heard; Barbara Heinrich; Hiro - Yasuhiro Wakabayashi; Daniel Morris, Historical Design Inc.; Stephanie des Horts; Adriane Houdmont; Melodie Wade, Houston Museum of Natural Science; Anna Hu; Ornella Iannuzzi; Gregory Scott Pepin and Ida Heiberg Bøttiger at Georg Jensen; Michael Kanner, Kanners; Susan Kaplan; Kimberly Klosterman of KKlosterman Jewels, Cincinnati; The Lakeland Arts Trust; Cécile Laurent; Corinne de Longuemar; Christopher Lopez-O'Ferrall; Sam Loxton, Lucas Rarities; Bernard Cohen, Macklowe Gallery, New York; Carineh Martin; Max McCormack; Isaac Pineus, Modernity Sweden; Alexandra Mor; Lone Neilson; Nancy Norton; Harry Fane, Obsidian Gallery; Michelle Ong; Stefano Palumbo; Matthew Senff Patterson; Monique Péan; Elsa Peretti; Audrey Friedman of the Primavera Gallery, New York; Wendy Ramshaw; Véronique Mamelli at Réunion des Musées Nationaux; Rheinisches Bildarchiv, Cologne; Phyllis Roback London; Cornelia Roethel; Kara Ross; Stefan Richter, RPB Jewels, Miami; Pat Saling of Pat Saling, New York; Franz Schnieders; Lee Siegelson and Sarah Davis of Siegelson, New York; Catherine Weber at Skinner's Auction House; Marisa Bourgoin, Archives of American Art, Smithsonian Institution; Mary Higonnet, Claire de Truchis-Lauriston, Madeline Firestone and Sarah Sutherland at Sotheby's; Martin Travis of Symbolic & Chase, London; Suzanne Syz; David & Sonya Newell-Smith of the Tadema Gallery, London; Fernando Tapia; Jen McGuire, Tiffany & Co; Catherine Cariou, Van Cleef & Arpels; Thomas Holman and Geoffrey Munn of Wartski's, London; David Watkins; Ann Westin; Georgia Powell, The Worshipful Company of Goldsmiths; Ben Ziegler; Emma Zilber.

Finally, I should like to thank my publisher ACC for their continued support and encouragement, in particular James Smith, Susannah Hecht and Lynn Taylor.

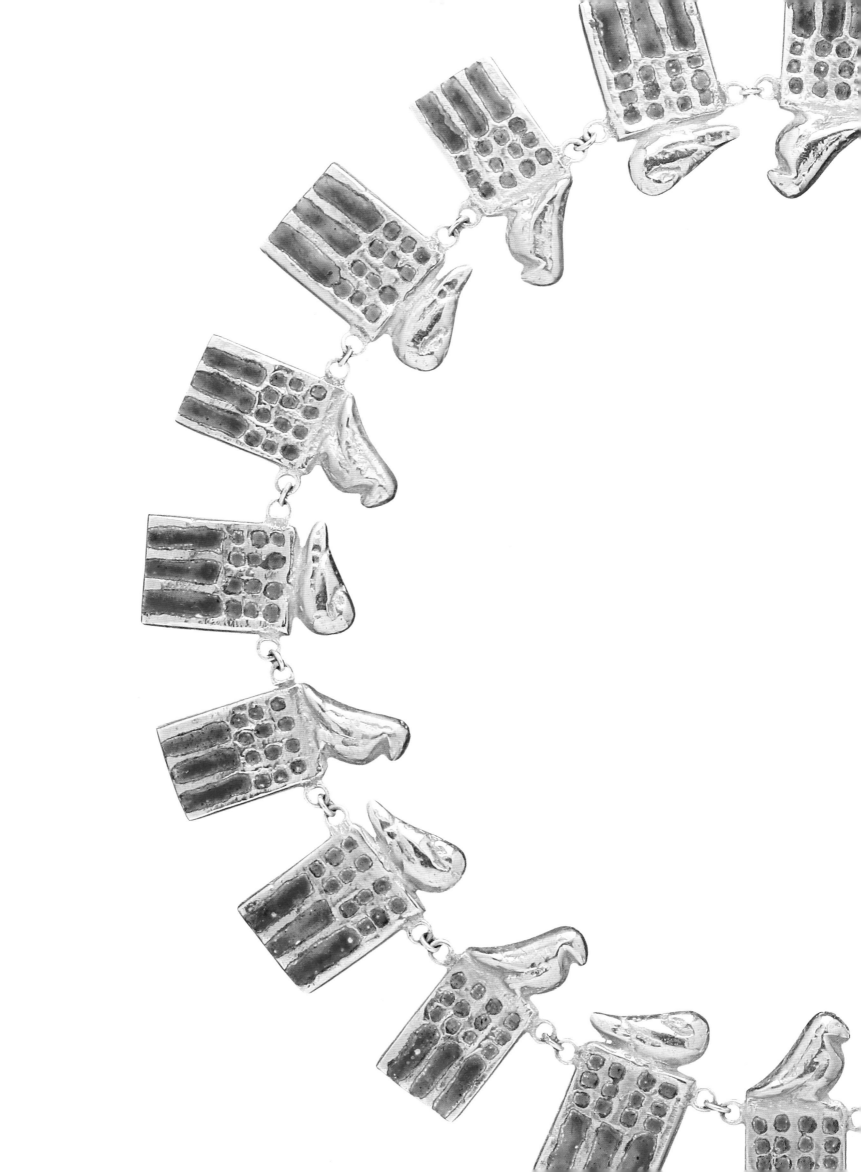